FAITH AND FICTION

FAITH
AND
FICTION

CREATIVE PROCESS IN
GREENE AND MAURIAC

BY

PHILIP STRATFORD

1964

UNIVERSITY OF NOTRE DAME PRESS

Publication of this book was aided
by a grant from the Ford Foundation
Copyright © 1964 by the
University of Notre Dame Press
Notre Dame, Indiana
Library of Congress Catalog Card Number 64-17065
Manufactured in the United States

TO

KYLIE

WITH MY LOVE

CONTENTS

Introduction   ix

1 A Comparative Preface   1

2 Lost Childhoods: Prison and Escape   32

3 Mauriac: Poet into Novelist   65

4 Greene: Romance to Realism   87

5 Greene and Melodrama   111

6 Mauriac and *Le Roman Noir*   140

7 Catholic Themes: The Divers Movements of Nature and Grace   163

8 The Catholic Novelist and Creation   201

9 The Novelist as Playwright   243

10 The Novelist and Commitment   283

Bibliographical Notes   333

Index   343

A Visit to Morin," one of the four short stories in Graham Greene's recent collection, *A Sense of Reality,* concerns an aging Catholic novelist, now "on the point of abandonment by his public," whose former impact is described in these terms:

He had offended the orthodox Catholics in his own country and pleased the liberal Catholics abroad; he had pleased, too, the Protestants who believed in God with the same intensity that he seemed to show, and he used to find enthusiastic readers among non-Christians who, when once they had accepted imaginatively his premises, perhaps detected in his work the freedom of speculation which put his fellow Catholics on their guard.[1]

Morin is French and one immediately thinks of Mauriac, of his career-long skirmishes with *bienpensant* factions at home, of his international reputation, of the strain of Jansenism in his work which within the French Catholic fold is often considered a species of Protestant error, and of the imaginative daring of his novels which makes them of doubtful value to the orthodox moralist and educator. But the same general description could apply equally well to Greene. He, too, has constantly drawn the fire of conservative elements in his own country, of Evelyn Waugh, for example, who once hinted that *The Heart of the Matter* was "mad blasphemy."[2] Greene has also enjoyed enormous popularity abroad, particularly in France, among common readers and liberal Catholic critics alike. It has become almost a cliché to speak of the individualistic, Protestant flavor of his Catholicism, and his influence has reached far beyond Catholic, or for that matter, Christian circles.

Morin, of course, is neither Greene nor Mauriac; he is the self-substantial hero of this story, a character and not a key. But let that pass. He does serve to point up some of the interesting similarities between these two writers whose names have so often been linked in summary critical parallels. It is my intention to pursue the comparison in detail, to define common traits, to isolate distinguishing characteristics, and, reading each in the light of the other, to display what is mutually illuminating in their theory and practice of the art of the novel.

Despite its comparative nature, this is not a study of influence. A case might be made for Greene's debt to Mauriac. He first discovered Mauriac at an impressionable age when establishing his own novelist's point of view. He read *Thérèse* in 1930,[3] *The Knot of Vipers* in 1933, *God and Mammon* in 1936, and *The Life of Jesus* in 1937,[4] all in English translation. These might well be considered germinal books for Greene if one were to take off on a chase after literary echoes. But during the same period Greene also came under the influence of Webster, James, Ford, Aiken and Eliot. And although he once suggested that his "attempt to deal with Catholic themes . . . is owed to a reading of Mauriac,"[5] he later qualified this confession by calling it "the sort of thing that one says under pressure."[6] With such mixed evidence it is perhaps better to leave the question of early influence nebulous, saying only, as Greene does, that one is influenced by everything one reads, and accepting his statement that, if there was any influence, "it was an unconscious one."[7]

The influence-seeker would undoubtedly want to make

something of the fact that just after the war Graham Greene was responsible for initiating the Collected Edition of Mauriac's novels in Gerard Hopkins' translation, and that, as director for Eyre and Spottiswoode, he saw the first half-dozen volumes of the edition through the press. But by this time Greene was secure in his own novel, and though he saluted Mauriac as "the greatest living novelist,"[8] he had now reached the age of autonomy. The question of direct influence does not seriously arise, then, any more than in the reverse direction where Mauriac, reading Greene late in life, has enthusiastically acknowledged the genius of a kindred spirit, while pointing out what he judges to be some essential differences between them.

The fact remains that, although there has been no clearly identifiable cross-fertilization, Mauriac's and Greene's careers have followed a roughly parallel course. Despite differences in style and tradition, they have confronted many of the same creative problems, and their solutions often complement one another. And, as Catholic novelists, they have both been absorbed in the debate between artistic aims and religious beliefs. That complex interplay of faith and fiction makes up the core of this study, for it is the tension which results from this unresolved conflict that gives singularity and distinction to their creative work.

In analyzing the artistic development and growth of religious sensibility in the two, I follow a simple chronological pattern, with one exception. My first chapter circumscribes the subject, outlines the main themes to be treated, and introduces the comparative method to be used. Thereafter, I trace the progress of the two novelists from childhood and adolescence, through literary apprenticeship to artistic maturity, concentrating on those elements, technical and personal, which shape creative vision. An important part of the book deals with the influence of Catholicism on the novelist, both as it provides him with themes and subjects, and as it conditions his imagination. Although the focus is on fiction, the last chapters investigate experiments in other genres as interest in the novel wanes with age, achievement, and new and conflicting obligations.

Throughout my study I have tried to avoid criticizing the critics. Greene and Mauriac have both written widely and perceptively on the problems which arise from their novels, and I have preferred to let them speak for themselves when this was possible. My job has been to collect and collate their statements about the practice of their art and test them against their accomplishment. As with any study of contemporaries where the evidence is not all in, one's judgment must be tentative, and while one may be suggestive, literary speculation of the flamboyant kind must be constantly checked against what evidence there is. With this limitation in mind, the following remarks by Mauriac fairly represent my own critical standard:

A good critic, in my view, is one who, rather than expect a writer to be something other than he is, will try to discover in his works whether he has been faithful to the laws of his own universe, whether he has relied only on his own natural gifts, whether he has avoided falling back on certain formulas and certain fads. ... A good critic can only wish that a writer should exhaust his own possibilities, not try to surpass them. No universal rule exists which permits the critic to condemn a writer by its standards. The good critic will look for no touchstone outside the author that he is studying.[9]

Many people have helped me at various stages with this book. I would like to single out for special thanks my professors, Charles Dédéyan of L'Institut de Littératures Modernes Comparées at the Sorbonne and Geoffrey Bullough of King's College, London, who started me on the subject; Murdo MacKinnon, my department head at the University of Western Ontario, for his constant encouragement; and my colleagues, Ross Woodman and John Graham, for their clear criticism. I am also indebted to the Nuffield Foundation and the British Council for research grants which made study in England possible.

INTRODUCTION

I am particularly grateful to François Mauriac for having granted me a valuable interview, and to Graham Greene for his generous and friendly help on several occasions and for having carefully read over the manuscript.

Parts of this book have been rewritten from articles which originally appeared in *The Tamarack Review, Wisconsin Studies in Contemporary Literature, The Kenyon Review* and *The University of Toronto Quarterly,* and any unchanged passages reappear with permission of the editors. Quotations from other sources are acknowledged in the footnotes.

NOTES TO INTRODUCTION

N. B. No page references will be given for quotations from the fictional works of either author. The texts used are Heinemann's *Uniform Edition* of Greene's works, and Gerard Hopkins' translation of Mauriac's *Collected Novels,* published by Eyre & Spottiswoode. Most other quotations from Mauriac are from his *Oeuvres Complètes,* Bibliothèque Grasset, Paris. Where titles are given in French, the translation is my own. I am grateful to Mr. Greene, Messrs. William Heinemann Ltd., and The Viking Press, Inc., for permission to quote from Greene's works, also to Eyre & Spottiswoode Ltd., and Farrar, Strauss and Company, Inc., for permission to quote from *Mémoires Intérieurs* and Mauriac's *Collected Novels* in Gerard Hopkins' translation; and to Éditions Bernard Grasset for permission to quote from Mauriac's *Oeuvres Complètes.*

1. "A Visit to Morin," *A Sense of Reality* (New York, 1963), p. 65.
2. Evelyn Waugh, "Felix Culpa?" *Commonweal,* XLVIII (July 16, 1948), 323.
3. "The Art of Fiction," *The Paris Review,* No. 3 (Autumn, 1953), p. 33.
4. *The Lawless Roads* (London, 1955), p. 114.
5. Kenneth and Miriam Allott, *The Art of Graham Greene* (London, 1951), p. 25.
6. "The Art of Fiction," *The Paris Review,* No. 3 (Autumn, 1953), p. 33.
7. *Ibid.*
8. "La Civilization chrétienne est-elle en péril?" *Essais Catholiques* (Paris, 1953), p. 17.
9. "Journal II," *Oeuvres Complètes,* XI, 156.

"Creative art seems to remain a function of the religious mind. . . ."
Graham Greene

"Dans le péché et dans la grâce, je n'ai, au fond, jamais parlé que du Christ."

François Mauriac

1

A COMPARATIVE PREFACE

When challenged with the idea of a comparison of his work with Mauriac's, Graham Greene's immediate reaction was to ask, guardedly: "Isn't it rather like comparing chalk and cheese?"[1] That is a valid question. And though a basic premise of this study is that there *are* significant underlying similarities between the two novelists, one must at least allow for the antithetical view; for many critics and readers, though not with such good cause, may share Greene's skepticism. I do not propose to pursue his analogy directly, but to give him the benefit of his doubt I have chosen for introductory examination two novels which are provocatively different. *A Kiss for the Leper* (1922) was Mauriac's first successful novel. "It is the first of my books," he writes, "which I do not blush to acknowledge."[2] *A Burnt-Out Case* (1961) is the cornice-stone of Greene's career, and he has recently intimated that it may well be his last major work of fiction.[3] At first glance there may seem to be little more to bridge the gap of forty years' very different experience which separates these two novels than the freakish fact that leprosy is referred to in both their titles.

Of course, they are not quite so distant. Each, early and late, is characteristic of the author's best work—*A Kiss for the Leper* prophetic of what was to come, *A Burnt-Out Case* developing from past fiction as much as from new experience. As representative novels they pursue an artistic purpose which has been common to the two novelists in most of their fiction. Greene describes it, prosaically, in the preface to this book as "an attempt to give dramatic expression to various types of belief, half-belief and non-belief." Both writers have, at times, vigorously protested against being classified as "Catholic" novelists, and they have both asserted, as Greene puts it, the right of the artist to be "disloyal"[4] to any institution, political or religious. Since much of their work, on the authority of this artistic license, has dealt broadly and sympathetically with various types of half-belief and non-belief, it has always been a source of scandal and irritation to the rigidly orthodox. But however anti-institutional their novels have been, they have always been dominated by a strong religious concern; and even when they have apparently had little to do with problems of faith, they bear the imprint of a creative attitude which is indelibly Christian.

These shared characteristics are accentuated in comparing the two authors' appraisals of one another. Greene believes Mauriac's major accomplishment to lie in his creation of character. Unlike the heroes of Virginia Woolf or E.M. Forster, Mauriac's characters, writes Greene, "have the solidity and importance of men with souls to save or lose." They "exist with extraordinary physical completeness . . . but their particular acts are less important than the force, whether God or Devil, that compels them." His importance to the English reader, Greene maintains, is that he reaffirms the religious sense in the novel and the sense of the supernatural importance of the human act. "If Pascal had been a novelist," he writes, "we feel that this is the method and the tone he would have used."[5]

For his part, Mauriac praises Greene's gift for detecting "the hidden presence of God in an atheistic world" and his skill in tracing the subtle, subterranean movements of Grace operating outside the orbit of the temporal Church. The importance of Greene to the generation of Sartre and Camus, writes Mauriac, is that to the existentialist claim of universal absurdity he opposes the mystery of an Infinite Love. And for the smug and complacent Catholic, as for the overscrupulous, Mauriac suggests that Greene echoes the message of St. John of the Cross—that on the last day it is on our love that we will be judged.[6]

The general moral outlook and purpose of the two novelists is so close that their assessment of each other is reflexive and equally well describes what they set out to do in their own novels. Mauriac has likened the presence of Grace in his own bleak work to those underground streams which flow beneath the sandy soil of Les Landes, that desolate, pine-forested region south of his native Bordeaux. He has the same message for narrow-minded Catholics, for those, as he describes them, "who by their mediocrity, avarice and injustice . . . create a vacuum around the Son of Man who came to seek out and save that which was lost."[7] And Greene, perhaps encouraged by Mauriac's example, set out in 1938 to give his characters a supernatural dimension and to do what he could himself to restore the lost religious sense to the English novel. "Murder, if you are going to treat it seriously at all," he wrote at that time, "is a religious subject."[8]

But when one turns to individual works, and in particular to the novels in question, the differences between the two authors may seem more striking than their similarities. To clearly define these differences, I would like to examine each novel briefly under the headings of setting, atmosphere, and character. Greene has an uncanny knack of choosing newsworthy settings for his novels. *Our Man in Havana,* which was treated as an amusing secret-service fantasy when it first appeared (Greene himself called it a fairy-story),[9] turned out to be in many details a true fore-shadowing of the kind of political activity which was to reach the front page with Castro's coup six months later. *The Quiet American,* set in Indo-China, came off the press only a few months after the French defeat at Dien Bien Phu. And many earlier novels had the same kind of political actuality. So it was not surprising to find that he had again stolen a march on the march of time with *A Burnt-Out Case.* Like his own Doctor Colin, whose expert fingers could de-tect the first thickening of the skin which is the sign of in-cipient leprosy, Greene had once again correctly diagnosed the inflammation point of a new world crisis and set *A Burnt-Out Case* in the heart of the Congo. The strange, the distant, the dangerous, and often the uncivilized and the subtropical have always exerted a strong influence on Greene. He began to explore the backwaters of the modern world with his first thriller, *Stamboul Train* (1932), and eight of the fifteen novels since then have been set outside England. Even among those set in England, the majority describe an underworld of gangsterdom and of the hunted spy, a world as distant from ordinary experience as geo-graphically remote Mexico, Vietnam or the African interior.

How different are the settings of all Mauriac's fiction. From Greene's international scope we focus down to the mi-crocosm of provincial France. Most of Mauriac's novels are situated within a fifty-mile radius of Bordeaux. The root of his inspiration is so deeply sunk in his native soil that, despite the fact that he has lived mainly in Paris since 1906, his occasional descriptions of the capital ring false, like those of a countryman uneasy and suspicious in the metrop-olis. The settings to which he returns in novel after novel are those of his provincial youth, the vine country on either side of the Garonne River, the marsh and forest of Les Landes, and the ugly familiar streets of Bordeaux. "It is as if a door closed within me at twenty," he writes, "on what was to be the subject of my work."[10]

Both novelists achieve many of their best effects by the creation of atmosphere based on these settings, and each has created an atmosphere distinctively his own:

Jean Péloueyre lay stretched upon his bed. He opened his eyes. The scraping of cicadas sounded from all round the house. Sunlight oozed between the slats of the Venetian blind like molten metal. . . . The whole house was frozen into immobility. Not a door was allowed to be open or shut, not a word or a sneeze must break the overwhelming silence.

These are the opening lines of *A Kiss for the Leper*. Nature is a dominant symbol in Mauriac's work. Not hostile to man, though oppressive, it represents the elemental passions which sweep through his characters. Jean Péloueyre is a miserable figure (described as a cricket, a larva, a worm), yet the ferocious sun stands for his ugly body's consuming passion for Noémie Artiailh, the thick, pretty, country girl (described always as a flower), who is condemned to become his bride. Standing against the natural vigor of sun and passion is the damp, silent, closely-shuttered house which encloses the cold constraints of family and society. The church, too, represents forces of resignation and mortality, and in this novel Mauriac speaks of "that earthly chill as of a newly-dug grave which envelops the living when they go down the steps into old churches which are slowly settling beneath the heavy hand of time."

Atmosphere works like this all through the novel, associated not only with theme but with plot and character. On the face of it, the marriage of Jean and Noémie is one of the most crippling kind. Nothing is bred of it but disgust on her part and self-loathing on his, until the day that Jean falls ill of tuberculosis and Noémie finds that she can at last give herself wholly to him without resentment in untiring efforts to nurse him back to health. Her devotion acts like Grace on Jean's misery and self-contempt. He formerly thought of his life as a stagnant swamp pool, "but under that sleeping surface had stirred a life-giving freshet, and now, having passed through life like a corpse, he was, on his death-bed, as a man reborn."

Jean dies, and Noémie is left with nothing but her loyalty to the dead to arm her against the lascivious attentions of a young doctor (associated with a threatening storm). She is strongly drawn to him, and her whole body rebels against the aridity of widowhood symbolized in the parched, pine-forested estate she has inherited from her husband. But when a chance comes, during a walk on a lonely country road, to meet the doctor again, she turns and flees into the bracken:

Across the dry heath she ran, until, at last, worn out, her shoes filled with sand, she flung her arms about a stunted oak whose brown leaves were still unshed, and quivered in the hot breeze— a black oak which had about it something of the look of Jean Péloueyre.

These are the closing lines of this novel by a writer who refers to himself as "a novelist of atmosphere,"[11] and that they are characteristic of his whole work can be seen by this quotation from an article written thirty years later:

It has been my special province to create analogies between land-scape and character, between nature and the passions, between storms of the heart and storms of the heavens; to show the souls of my characters and the branches of the pines tormented by the same gales; to render the ardour and torpidity of Les Landes and the force of those fires which devour the earth like a passion, and of the hail that stones the crucified vines.[12]

Greene, too, is a novelist of atmosphere, and wherever his setting may be, it is stamped with the unmistakable character of what the critics have come to call "Greene-land." This is the world of the seedy, the tawdry, a world of failure and of acute little discomforts. Usually it is asso-ciated with the waste and ugly by-products of civilization, but in *A Burnt-Out Case* Greene manages to invest even the heart of the primitive Congo with these qualities. The small,

6

battered paddle-steamer with its peeling paint that takes Greene's hero up the river carries seediness into the jungle: the cramped quarters, "the engulfing heat," "the green jungle wall, brown at the top like stale cauliflowers," the captain sitting in the saloon with a box of beads manufacturing cheap rosaries (the boat is owned by a mission and its captain is a priest), "the engine, somewhere below the altar and the Holy Family, groaning like an exhausted animal," the vampire-bats creaking over the forest, the cockroaches lurking in the cupboard, the mosquitoes and the tsetse flies. . . .

The captain read his breviary with a fly-whisk in his hand, and whenever he made a kill he held up a tiny corpse for the passenger's inspection, saying "tsetse"—it was nearly the limit of their communication for neither spoke the other's language with ease or accuracy. . . .

This is typical Greeneland: nature inert or decomposing, yet still impressive enough in its sluggish way to show up the forces of civilization as degenerate, makeshift and ugly; and in this lethargic struggle between insufficient man and indifferent nature, the only active life, that of the insects, small predators and disease.

Those who remember Greene's travel books on Mexico and Liberia, or the novels drawn from these books, *The Power and the Glory* and *The Heart of the Matter,* will find the atmosphere of this latest novel to be entirely familiar. And in novels where nature plays no great part, Greene evokes even more strongly, with the wasteland of modern society as his basic material, this atmosphere of seediness, degeneracy, disease and corruption. Yes, Greene is also a novelist of atmosphere, although apparently his Greeneland is very different from Mauriac's Les Landes.

Their treatment of character varies as widely. To begin with a minor point, Mauriac always uses a much smaller cast than Greene. In *A Kiss for the Leper* there are two main characters, two secondary ones, and half a dozen others lightly brushed in. In *A Burnt-Out Case* Greene surrounds his hero, Querry, the passenger on the paddle-steamer, with seven figures of major importance to the plot, and the background is crowded with minor characters, like the riverboat captain in his white soutane.

Querry, like many of Greene's heroes—the whiskey priest, secret agent D., the killer Raven, and unlike all of Mauriac's—is an ambiguous, almost allegorical figure. When the novel was coming into shape, Greene thought of him as "X."[13] And though he finally assumed a surname, Querry still suggests a question mark. *A Burnt-Out Case* is history, but until far into the action his origin, his profession, and his purpose in the Congo remain a mystery, and he fulfills an unusually passive role in the rest of the novel. In relation to other characters he does not act but is acted upon; he is the still center of the action, a sounding board for the curiosity of others, and a mirror for their self-questioning. Here is a description of him as he is first seen by Doctor Colin of the leper hospital:

A man was walking up the avenue towards him. He raised his hat, a man of his own age, in the late fifties with a grizzled morning stubble, wearing a crumpled tropical suit. "My name is Querry," he introduced himself, speaking in an accent which Colin could not place as French or Flemish any more than he could immediately identify the nationality of the name.

And that ambiguous sketch is the only physical description that Greene gives of Querry anywhere in the novel.

Of course this anonymity and inertness is rendered dramatically. Querry has his reasons for wishing to remain incognito and for refusing to commit himself to action. Successful in his profession and successful in love, he has reached the saturation point in both, and he has come to this leper village "at the end of the line" to bury himself from the world and the flesh. But Rycker, a Belgian *colon,* and Parkinson, a syndicated journalist, recognize him, run him to ground, and resurrect his international fame as an ecclesiastical architect. And Marie, Rycker's young wife, for her own purposes revives the myth of his prowess as a lover. Besides being firmly resolved to remain ex-architect and ex-lover, Querry is a confirmed ex-Catholic. But he can no more resist the combined efforts of Rycker, Parkinson and Father Thomas, a pathologically pious priest at the mission, to turn him into a non-conformist saint than he can halt the contagious spread of his worldly reputation. In the end these forces crush his passive resistance and destroy him, and we are never sure whether the enigmatic Querry is another Schweitzer, as Parkinson paints him in his Sunday-pictorial prose; a saintly man, as Father Thomas believes, going through a dark night of the soul; still *The Querry*, as Rycker sees him, insufferably vain under a veneer of mock-modesty; or really a burnt-out case, as the agnostic Doctor Colin diagnoses it—a man mutilated by success like a leper by his leprosy, but in whom, after mutilation, the progress of the disease has finally been arrested. "He was an ambiguous man," says one of the Fathers at the end of the book, and Greene purposely leaves the final interpretation of Querry's character in question.

Mauriac, on the contrary, does interpret. He asserts what Greene has called, writing of *A Woman of the Pharisees,* the traditional right of the novelist to speak in his own person.[14] Moreover, his characters are never Querrys in the sense that they all exist, as Greene says, "with extraordinary physical completeness." On his own admission, Mauriac models them on people he has known.[15] Their names are not ciphers but typical family names of the southwest. His characters take up residence in his imagination like real people and go on living there from novel to novel. He speaks of them as existing with such compelling reality that they often dictate the shape of his work. He writes of having to struggle against them, and claims that without this struggle the creative act is purely mechanical.[16] Emphasizing the importance of character in Mauriac's work, Greene points out that events are used "not to change character (how little in truth we are changed by events . . .) but to reveal characters—reveal them gradually with an incomparable subtlety." "One is never tempted to consider in detail M. Mauriac's plots," he says in the same essay. "One remembers the simple outlines of *Le Baiser au Lépreux*, but the less simple the events of the novel the more they disappear from the mind, leaving in our memory only characters whom we have known so intimately that the events at one period of their lives chosen by the novelist can be forgotten without forgetting them."[17]

Greene's characters, although all are by no means as intentionally vague as Querry, do not exist with this same immediacy. They are never rooted in a landscape or in a well-defined society or class like Mauriac's characters who take on substance and solidity from their dependence on tradition and environment. Greene's novels are nearly always populated with aliens, and *A Burnt-Out Case* is a case in point. None of the characters in that novel is at home in the Congo. Even Querry's mutilated native boy, Deo Gratias, comes from a distant tribe and yearns dumbly to return to a barely remembered place called Pendélé. The rest are white aliens who are denied even the pleasures of nostalgia. It is a strange fact that the image which Greene uses most frequently in his novels to convey a sense of belonging (and it is used again here) is the unhappy memory of a boarding school, already an impersonal and public place. "The Congo is a region of the mind," Greene states in the preface to his novel, and his homeless characters, who do not find a secure habitation there, or anywhere else for that matter, are less psychological studies of real beings imprisoned in a world of fact than metaphysical types existing in a limbo outside time and place.

Furthermore, Greene's character types tend to be repeti-

10

tive in a manner different from Mauriac's. In his collected novels Mauriac has created a family of characters, not necessarily in the *roman fleuve* tradition, though individual characters frequently reappear in later novels, but linked together, as it were, by common hereditary traits. Yet beneath the family likeness each member exists as an individual. Greene's characters differ widely on the superficial level as to the background and circumstances of their lives, but they are more likely to be successive reincarnations of a few basic ideas. To compare Greene's other African novel, *The Heart of the Matter,* with this one—Helen Rolt, the schoolgirl shipwreck victim who becomes Scobie's mistress in that novel, appears as Marie Rycker who almost becomes Querry's here; Mrs. Scobie's self-conscious orthodoxy is only slightly exaggerated to produce Rycker's religious bigotry; Father Clay in the earlier novel resembles Father Thomas in this one, while Father Rank is the same type as some of the more enlightened priests at the leper village; Scobie's boy, Ali, becomes Querry's boy, Deo Gratias, and Yusef and the journalist Parkinson are the same greasy and obese incarnation of corruption. Writing to explain that none of the characters of *A Burnt-Out Case* is drawn from life, Greene describes them in his preface as "formed from the flotsam of thirty years as a novelist." Indeed, these basic types, appearing sometimes with various submarine accretions, and sometimes weathered smooth to the prototype, have kept bobbing up in all of Greene's fiction. Despite the geographical variety of his settings he can accurately be described as a novelist who is continually rewriting the same novel.

Now to draw these observations on setting, atmosphere and character into a focus, I would like to relate them to the different traditions out of which the two novelists write. To begin with, they have this in common, that each has taken a sub-species of contemporary fiction and adapted it to his own purpose. Greene is indebted to the modern spy story or crime thriller in much the same way that Mauriac is to the *roman noir* of the French pulps for providing a well-established popular tradition which handles the sensational aspects of current problems in a speedy narrative style. And it is interesting to see both novelists making use in their novels of devices of wide current interest such as Freudian and film techniques.

But as soon as one leaves the popular contemporary models and begins to look for deeper traditional roots, a gulf begins to open between the two authors. Mauriac's literary heritage stems on one side from the lyric poetry of Francis Jammes and Maurice de Guérin, on the other from the middle-class psychological novel of the nineteenth century. In this connection it is worth noting that Mauriac repudiates the influence of the great figures—Balzac, Flaubert and Zola—and aligns himself with a tradition of minor novelists; praises Constant's *Adolphe* and Fromentin's *Dominique,* is familiar with Abel Hermant and Georges Ohnet, and acknowledges Paul Bourget as master.[18] This is partly due to the fact that Mauriac has always remained thoroughly bourgeois himself, and partly because his main interest has always been psychological realism rather than social realism or naturalism. And this last point is driven home if one traces his literary lineage back a step further to the classical dramatist Jean Racine.

Mauriac has written frequently about Racine, biographical essays and criticism, and the acuteness of his analysis is due to his close identification with his subject. To stress their affinity I would like to quote an excerpt from the recent *Mémoires Intérieurs,* in which Mauriac describes the style of Racine's dramatic verse:

What is Racine's own is a rigorous continuity . . . of passion brooded on, expressed, clarified and sharply delineated by means of a small number of perfectly ordinary words which, together, compose a piece of music; music without either dissonances or studied harmonies—suggestive, certainly, but antipathetic to mere dreaming, being closely linked with a reality which, more often than not, is excruciating. There is no escaping from it, not a moment's respite. . . . We are locked in a cage, held captive behind the rigid lines of verse, all of them alike, face to face with naked passions turning their eyes in upon themselves, describing themselves, telling us about themselves with a lucidity which their fury neither limits nor debases.[19]

Just as Racine's definition of tragedy, *"des caractères, un catastrophe,"*[20] fits the narrow range of action and the emphasis on internal conflict in Mauriac's novels, so the passage quoted describes well the spareness and intensity of Mauriac's own prose style and that unflinching penetration with which he analyzes desire, disgust and renunciation in a novel such as *A Kiss for the Leper.*

While considering this classical influence, it is interesting to specify that Mauriac's novel owes something to one seventeenth-century drama in particular, Corneille's *Polyeucte.* Jean Péloueyre does not simply die but seeks out his own death like the hero of Corneille's tragedy. And Noémie's resolution to renounce the doctor's love and take the way of self-sacrifice and suffering parallels Pauline's conversion. Mauriac's realism, his reduction of theme and character to the bourgeois level, and his emphasis on the petty miseries of warped passions no doubt leave nothing but an ironic echo of Corneille's heroic passions and martyrdom. But the echo is intentional, for Mauriac makes Jean recall a verse from Corneille several times in the closing pages of the novel, and *"Mon Polyeucte touche à son heure dernière"* are the last words which disturb the surface of his fading consciousness. In terms of traditional sources one might describe *A Kiss for the Leper* as Corneillean in theme, Racinean in style, and provincial bourgeois in detail and setting, after the school of the late nineteenth-century realists.

Turning now to Graham Greene, if one were to name a source-book for *A Burnt-Out Case,* a logical choice would be Conrad's *Heart of Darkness*. Many critics have observed a strain of Conrad in Greene's work, particularly in his early novels. He had always shared Conrad's feeling for Africa as revealed in *Heart of Darkness*, wrote that it "impressed Africa as an imaginative symbol on the European mind,"[21] and, in fact, took the novel with him on his own trip up the Congo. It was the first time, Greene admits in his journal of this voyage, that he had read Conrad since 1932 when he had "abandoned him . . . because his influence on me was too great and too disastrous."[22] Even twenty years later it was still considerable. The battered, "tin-pot steamboat"[23] in *A Burnt-Out Case* is Conrad's. Descriptions of the oppressive, massive beauty of vegetation are similar. The same kind of mystery hangs about Querry and Kurtz—one the enigmatic traveller, the other the enigmatic goal of a quest—even to the several interpretations of their characters which are left open at the end of each novel. The Congo itself represents much the same thing to both authors—for Conrad, too, it is more "a region of the mind" than a geographical place, and sixty years before Greene he analyzed its character in terms that would be accepted sympathetically by the later novelist. Like Greene, Conrad was interested in recording "the mental changes of individuals on the spot."[24] He writes about the unreal air of plotting, backbiting and intrigue among the "faithless pilgrims"[25] of the river stations, which is reproduced as the dangerous gossip and distorted myths that grow up around Querry in Greene's novel. In *Heart of Darkness* Conrad relates how a Danish riverboat captain is murdered over a question of two black hens, and his only other Congo story, "An Outpost of Progress," tells how two Belgian traders meet their deaths in a dispute over some lump sugar. Like Rycker's wild revenge on Querry (convinced that he has been made a cuckold, he shoots the innocent and defenseless architect), this absurd violence is generated in the Congo of the mind, in a mind obsessed, to use

Conrad's words, "by a suggestion of things vague, uncontrollable, and repulsive, whose discomposing intrusion excites the imagination and tries the civilized nerves of the foolish and the wise alike."[26] To be sure, this state of mind develops with unnatural facility in a place like the Congo, but it is certain that Conrad considers it not a psychological, but a metaphysical ailment, and on the deepest level his novel, like Greene's, describes the universal fascination of the savage and the incomprehensible—"the fascination of the abomination."[27] There can be no doubt that Greene read this interpretation with fraternal feeling, just as he absorbed so much detail in creating his own narrative of what Conrad called "a weary pilgrimage amongst hints for nightmares."[28]

All this by way of introduction to the tradition out of which Greene writes which is different from Mauriac's in nearly every respect. Clearly it is the adventure novel that is in his blood, and Conrad and Stevenson are, at the least, his literary godparents. The exotic setting, the taste for the grotesque which borders sometimes on the absurd, the heightened coloring, the loose-ranging action, the high density of incident—all these are shared characteristics. Accentuating now one, now another of these qualities, one may trace the various feeders which nourish the root of his inspiration. On the one hand Greene himself has often drawn attention to the strong influence of his boyhood reading in a tradition of popular melodrama. It was Marjorie Bowen's *The Viper of Milan,* he says, that first gave him the urge to write, and he has frequently championed Rider Haggard, Percy Westerman, Anthony Hope, John Buchan, and other novelists of this type. Referring to a different but related aspect of Greene's work, T. S. Eliot once suggested[29] that he carries on a tradition of fantasy in the English novel stemming from Stevenson and continued by Chesterton and Waugh. But whereas Chesterton and Waugh excel in humorous and satirical fantasy, says Eliot, Greene has chosen the fantasy of nightmare. It is true that Greene is an obsessional writer, and interesting to remark that this is the quality which he stresses in his brilliant but rather idiosyncratic criticism of Henry James, the novelist to whom he owes most from the point of view of technique. And if one wished to find a parallel for Mauriac's affiliation with classical French tragedy, one could refer to Greene's close familiarity with seventeenth-century English literature, and especially to his interest in the violent Jacobean melodrama of Ford, Tourneur, and John Webster.

To recapitulate briefly, where now do Mauriac and Greene stand in this comparative assessment? Provincial setting vs. international; an atmosphere of passionate and tormented nature vs. one of inert and seedy degeneracy; clinical portraiture of character vs. ambiguous or type figures; and as for sustaining traditions, the psychological novel vs. the novel of adventures; the realistic vs. the fantastic, and classical French tragedy vs. Jacobean melodrama. Perhaps now the wedge between Mauriac and Greene has been driven far enough to make any possible rapprochement seem an interesting wager.

This discussion of the different traditions out of which the two novelists write has, however, actually been preparing their reunion. The comparative method that I wish to use is a simple one: mathematically speaking, I plan to divide each author by his tradition and compare the resulting quotients. But before applying this method to the examination of *A Kiss for the Leper* and *A Burnt-Out Case*, I would like to illustrate its operation in comparing the religious attitudes of Greene and Mauriac, and one must begin by a brief analysis of the divisors, that is, the religious traditions which have influenced them.

Both are Catholics, true, but traditional Catholicism in France and England differs as widely as the literary traditions we have just examined. As Greene has said, "Roman Catholicism takes on extraordinarily different forms in different countries."[30] Catholicism in England is a broken tradition, discontinued for a crucial three hundred years. When the hierarchy was legalized again in 1851, the Catholic Church found itself in a minority position both numerically and psychologically, and it set about swiftly and positively to regain something of its past importance. The character of intellectual English Catholicism in the last century has been, in consequence, vigorous, polemical, self-conscious, better represented by the Church militant than by the Church suffering, and in literature best characterized in the writing of Hilaire Belloc and G. K. Chesterton.

From the French point of view, from the point of view of an uninterrupted Catholic tradition of eleven centuries, the character of English Catholicism must often seem excessive, rather like the enthusiasm of the recent convert. In a country like France where Catholicism is in a secure and traditional majority, two phenomena can be observed. First, a great many religious assumptions can be made without explanation. The language of the Faith is universally spoken, and many abstract principles of dogma are used without ostentation as current vocabulary. A French writer, even a non-Christian, may take it for granted that his public, while it may not have a very sophisticated grasp of theology, has nevertheless assimilated a good deal of doctrine, much in the same way that English writers up to the present have been able to assume a widespread familiarity with the King James Bible. Second, where there is little or no competition from rival sects, there is a great deal of open, varied, and critical expression of religious opinion within the fold. In England—a country, as the French say, with thirty religions and only one sauce—the ranks of the Catholic minority are more serried. A rover in religious matters like Greene is pressed to standardize and publicize his religious affiliations; consequently, to ensure his artistic freedom, he feels obliged to disown the title of Catholic novelist and to make a sharp distinction between art and religion, treating the latter as a private concern. Mauriac, on the other hand, has made countless public professions of faith and has felt free to include in them the full expression of many shades of dissent, doubt and anxiety, and describes his faith as "flux and reflux around a central rock."[31] It may be too much to suggest that, compared to militant English Catholicism, the French Church represents the everyday Church suffering, but on the whole the character of Catholicism in France is one of passive endurance rather than one of active proselytism. At any rate, it is not at all unlikely that the English Catholic may view askance the range of opinion and the variety of observance which fall within the compass of French Catholicism.

This does not, of course, pretend to be a full analysis of the complex nature of either French or English Catholicism. It is, rather, a generalized picture of what one might call the climate of Catholicism in the two countries. Nor does the religious outlook of either Greene or Mauriac coincide exactly with the national image. In fact, each author in certain respects has reacted strongly against it. Yet each has been strongly conditioned by the national climate as the following textual evidence shows.

Greene has written with an undertone of envy of "the uninterrupted tradition of a Christian state of mind, thought and style"[32] in France, and, as mentioned earlier, much of his literary criticism dwells on the crippling effect to the English novel of the loss of a religious sense which he sees operating in the works of Mauriac. Yet despite his praise of Mauriac he confesses that he feels ill at ease among the abstractions of French religious thought. He shuns the public examination of conscience which is so typical of Mauriac and the French in general, and writes, "If my conscience were so acute as M. Mauriac's showed itself to be in his essay God and Mammon, I could not write a line."[33] And finally, although he admires Mauriac's subtlety in the creation of character, he finds that he is often too astringent in his handling of religious themes. "Mauriac's characters sin against God," he once explained, "whereas mine, try as they may, never quite manage to. . . ."[34]

On the reverse of the medal, Mauriac is impressed by the freshness of Greene's discovery of Catholicism. "The French Catholic is introduced to religion by the main door," Mauriac writes:

He is brought up on the official history of Catholicism, and has taken sides in all the great debates that have wracked the Gallican church over the centuries. . . . The work of an English Catholic novelist always gives me a sense of being lost. It takes me into a familiar country, into my own spiritual domain in fact . . . but by a secret door hidden in the wall, and as I follow the hero of the novel through the tangled branches, suddenly I recognize the main drive and the wide lawn where I played as a child. . . . Graham Greene has penetrated surreptitiously into an unknown kingdom, into the kingdom of nature and Grace. No preconceptions trouble his vision. No previous experience conditions his own explorations. . . . One would even say that he had no model of sanctity in mind, only corrupt nature and all-powerful Grace.[35]

Implicit in this description of Greene's work is a criticism that Mauriac makes explicit elsewhere:[36] that Greene's handling of Grace and nature is too strained; that Grace is introduced into the novels as a *deus ex machina,* and that Greene willfully entangles the thickets of corrupt nature; in short, that his treatment of religion is, from the French point of view, highly melodramatic. "He tries to make religion too difficult," was Mauriac's comment on Greene's treatment of Catholicism in the novel. And confronted with Greene's statement, "Mauriac's sinners sin against God. . . ," he merely remarked, "We all sin against God. Any sin is a sin against God. . . ."[37]

It is obvious from these remarks that to compare the religious views of Greene and Mauriac objectively, one should make allowance for the Frenchness of Mauriac's criticism of Greene, and vice versa. In other words, that one should divide the traditional influence in each case and, as suggested, compare the quotients. But having set up this sum, I would like to delay the solution until later and return to more literary matters. The same comparative procedure can now be applied to those three aspects—setting, atmosphere and character—under which we contrasted the two novels.

As for setting, although Mauriac restricts himself to one of the French provinces little known to the French themselves, this limitation is at once common and superficial. As Mauriac himself has written: "The whole of humanity lives in the most humble person we have known, and all the countries of the world exist within the familiar horizon of our childhood. The gift of the novelist lies precisely in his power to make evident the universality of that narrow world where we were born and where we have learned to love and suffer."[38] Even more interesting, if we consider the traditional limitation of the French novel to be its psychological bias, is the sense of discovery which runs through Mauriac's criticism and fiction. No matter how small his cast, how single his theme, how narrow his subject in physical terms, he is still an adventurer into the *terra incognita* of the mind. He enthusiastically cites the discoveries of Freud and the example of Proust as opening a way for the modern writer out of the impasse of the old style psychological novel, and aligns himself with those of his contemporaries who are, as he says, "obsessed and attracted by regions hitherto forbidden the novelist, as adventurers are by the ever-dwindling area of unexplored territory on the globe."[39] And *A Kiss for the Leper* in its bold but subtle treatment of sexual frustration does push back the forbidden frontier.

As for Greene, one may now ask, how important is the variety and sensationalism of his setting? Or more properly speaking, how is it important? Obviously it is profitable to be newsworthy, as Greene learned early in his career when he switched from historical romance to modern thriller with *Stamboul Train,* "because of the desperate need one had for the money."[40] Also, in his own tradition Greene breaks no new frontiers, but simply follows a well-established national genre of adventure stories written by itinerant Englishmen. But this does not touch the private reasons for his wanderings, and one must ask further what inner compulsion drives him to explore these out-of-the-way corners of the world. Is it a love of danger, or a desire for risk bred out of a sense of boredom? Greene's adolescent flirtations with death (he tells in a well-known essay how he experimented with poison and played Russian roulette half a dozen times as a schoolboy), seem to suggest this. But *A Burnt-Out Case* provides a more searching analysis of the question. Superficially, Querry's flight from civilization into the heart of the Congo *is* motivated by boredom and disgust. But what he seeks there is, on a deeper level, what Greene has sought in all his own explorations of the uncivilized, whether underworld or jungle. "When one sees to what unhappiness, to what peril of extinction centuries of cerebration have brought us," he writes in his travel book on Africa, *Journey Without Maps,* "one sometimes has a curiosity to discover if one can, from what we have come, to recall at what point we went astray."[41] And Greene finds in the Congo, as he found in Liberia, in Mexico, in Indo-China, or for that matter in the concrete jungles of Brighton and London, a primitive violence and a primitive simplicity in conflict and in motive for action which permit him to trace back the thread of human conduct to its mysterious origins.

Greene once likened the explorer and the writer, saying that they had the same "creative sickness" and were driven by the same need "to fill in the map as to fill in the character or features of a human being." Querry, described as one "who always wanted to go a bit further," is such a man. He also shares another trait common to writer and explorer which Greene defines as "the urge to surrender and self-destruction."[42] This abandonment to the unknown has a metaphysical counterpart, and Querry's voyage must also be described as a spiritual quest. In his preface Greene discounts the sensational value of setting his story in an African leproserie and describes it as "the kind of setting removed from world-politics and household preoccupations where [questions of belief] are felt acutely and find expression." In losing himself here, Querry makes discoveries in the *terra incognita* of the soul. *A Burnt-Out Case* is prefaced by a quotation from Dante, and one might see *Pilgrim's Progress* as the traditional prototype for this novel though, allegorically, Conrad's *Heart of Darkness* is quite adequate in this respect, for it does much more than just explore the physical heart of the dark continent. Writing about the adventure novel a few years after *A Kiss for the Leper*, Mauriac spoke of the genre as an Anglo-Saxon specialty, and praising the work of Conrad and Stevenson in particular said, "the important thing, if this type of novel is to exist as literature, is not the adventure, but the adventurer."[43] And certainly Greene would approve this judgment.

The novelist renders his discoveries in the unknown by his creation of atmosphere and character. Speaking before a Catholic congress in Brussels, Greene protested how ill at ease he was with the abstract language of theology which was quite familiar to his French audience. "The great abstractions of the Faith rattle emptily in my mind," he said. "I cannot grasp them until they have been given tangible human form," and he invoked the Apostle Thomas as patron saint of the English "because we must see the marks of the nails and put our hands into the wounds before we can understand."[44] Just so, Greene's task as a novelist has been to make tangible certain abstract principles and problems of faith, and his search for material which he could transform into the novelist's sharp vision of reality has taken him throughout the world. But the operative word is "transform" and Greene carries his own atmosphere with him into experience. In this regard his Congo no more resembles the real Congo than Mauriac's Bordeaux country resembles the south-west corner of France as seen by a more objective, or indeed, by any other observer.

And here one must dispel the artificial distinction made by Greene between the French and English style of expression, or at least make it more precise. The Apostle Thomas should be the patron saint of all novelists, not just of the English, for Mauriac no less than Greene is concerned with the task of making the abstract concrete. "The whole art of the writer of imagination," says Mauriac, "is to make visible, tangible, odiferous a world full of criminal tendencies, and of sanctity, too."[45] He speaks of himself as "a metaphysician working in the concrete." "Thanks to a certain gift for atmosphere," he continues, "I try to render the Catholic universe of evil in terms of sight, touch and smell. The sinner about whom the theologian gives us an abstract idea, I make incarnate."[46]

No, the two novelists do not differ in kind, but in degree. In their choice of imagery to create atmosphere, one might distinguish between them by stressing the broad and curious range of the English novelist, or the elemental intensity of the French one. The difference between them is the difference between an author who sees the whole of humanity in the humblest person he has known, and one who seeks the continuity of human behavior in the most diverse characters and circumstances. Mauriac has gone down in depth into a rather narrow experience to find his symbols; Greene has continuously extended the range of his experience in search of his. The difference between them is tuberculosis in Les Landes and leprosy in the Congo, but both in their own terms have made the same kind of diagnosis of diseased humanity.

Far more complex than the incarnation of abstract

thought in setting or atmosphere is its incarnation in character. As Mauriac suggested, it has been his special province
to embody the sinner in fiction. His novels are studies in
conscience of lepers, poisoners, vipers and dark angels.
There have been some doves, too, but he has always ap-
proached sanctity through what is "miserably human in human nature,"[47] and he speaks of "a certain sulphurous light"
peculiar to him which bathes even the most elevated of his
characters. "I do not defend it," he says, "it is simply
mine."[48] Greene's novelist's domain is the same. The heroes
he has chosen—gunmen, mobsters, spies, outlaws, adventurers in love and crime—represent evil in physical rather
than in moral terms, accentuate violence rather than cruelty.
But his basic material is the same and, stripped of Greene's
particular coloring, his essential hero is recognizable as
that sinner described by Péguy in the epigraph to *The Heart
of the Matter*: "The sinner is at the very heart of Christianity. . . . None is so competent in matters of Christianity.
None, if it is not the saint."

   With special reference to *A Burnt-Out Case,* we have already noted the ambiguity of Querry's character which
makes him an allegorical figure and suggests an association
with "query." Like most of Greene's heroes he is also a
"quarry," a hunted man, pursued by his deeds in the persons of the Ryckers, Parkinson and Father Thomas—in
short, a sinner pursued by conscience. Behind these two
associations is a third, carried in the cognate "quest." As
stated earlier, Querry's is a spiritual adventure, and, in this
larger symbolical frame of reference, Greene's hunted
heroes are all sinners launched on a quest for salvation,
like Bunyan's pilgrim. Because they are more realistically
conceived, Mauriac's heroes do not yield so conveniently
to allegorical interpretation, and when one does consider
them in this way, one must recognize that the two novelists
treat different types of sinners. Taking *A Kiss for the Leper*
as a representative example, one has to admit that Mauri-

ac's heroes are more prisoners than pilgrims. And one can also observe the same link between his characters, Racine's imprisoned heroes, and the traditionally hedged-in hero of French fiction, as between Greene's pilgrim and the picaresque hero of the typical English novel.

But the essential difference lies again in the national prototype, and there are marked similarities, general and particular, in the way that each author has handled his traditional hero. Both Querry and Jean Péloueyre are mere shadows of their seventeenth-century counterparts. Both are driven by disgust rather than motivated by grand passions or noble aspirations. Both inspire more antipathy than fear, pity or awe in the reader. And the intention of each author *vis à vis* his reader is that, denied the pleasure of heroic elevation or self-satisfying identification, he shall still identify, despite his dislike, and learn to understand and sympathize with the unlovable hero.

It is true that this degeneration of the hero is common to the whole of modern fiction. But when one examines the particular acts of the heroes of these two novels, there are more significant likenesses to be noted. In each case the spring of the reader's sympathy is released by an act of self-sacrifice on the part of the hero, by a kiss to the leper. Jean, although he is in an enfeebled state of health himself, secretly tends a friend who is dying of tuberculosis and thus contracts the fatal disease. Noémie's sacrifice is rendered in even more dramatic terms because of the subtle use of Christian symbolism as a backdrop for her action, a source of atmosphere which Mauriac incorporates in all his fiction and which gives poetic intensity to his work even more than his use of nature. When Noémie sees the doctor for the last time on the lonely country road but fights off her desire, turns, and runs headlong into the arid heath, her agony, like that of every true martyr, in an oblique but unmistakable fashion is reminiscent of the passion of Christ. Bracken rakes her face, brambles scratch her hands as she runs, stumbling and sweating, finally to fling her arms around the stunted oak "which had about it something of the look of Jean Péloueyre." This is her kiss to the leper, and she is as surely crucified on the stunted tree as she is crucified to Jean Péloueyre in a much less subtle image which Mauriac uses earlier to describe the agonies of the wedding night.

Greene's novel, too, contains its act of self-sacrifice, its kiss to the leper. The native boy, Deo Gratias, who has been assigned to Querry and who is a fingerless, toeless, burnt-out case, strays into the jungle (perhaps in search for Pendélé), and Querry, strangely stirred for the first time out of his sense of impotence and indifference, goes into the jungle at night after him. He follows the narrow path thinking it may well peter out in the undergrowth, that "it may well mark the furthest limit of human penetration." At last he finds the boy who has fallen into a shallow gully, broken his ankle, and, with his "hands like boxing gloves," cannot drag himself up the slippery bank again. Querry tries to lift him, but cannot, and starts off for help. But seeing him leave, "Deo Gratias howled, as a dog or a baby might howl. He raised a stump and howled, and Querry realized that he was crippled with fear. The fingerless hand fell on Querry's arm like a hammer and held him there."

Although it is placed about one-quarter way through the novel, this passage is central to the whole book. It marks the turning point from case to cure in Querry's career, from that state of emotional disgust at the opening in which he detests laughter "like a bad smell" to the point where, "his face twisted into the rictus of a laugh," he perpetrates his first joke. The passage which describes Querry's night in the jungle is dense with suggestive metaphor. I have hinted at a few of the implications; to state them baldly and out of context: at the furthest limit of human penetration is self-sacrifice and love, and Querry, nailed to Deo Gratias, learns enough of this mystery to start back from aridity and despair and, by a kiss to the leper, through sympathetically sharing his fate, begins his restoration to whole humanity after having been so long himself a burnt-out case. The visible sign of Querry's cure is his renewed ability to laugh. "I think I'm cured of pretty well everything," he tells Doctor Colin on the eve of his death, "even disgust. I've been happy here." And afterwards the doctor confirms his cure, saying: "He'd learned to serve other people, you see, and to laugh." It is the same restoration that Jean Péloueyre knows at the end when Noémie's devotion stirs under the stagnant surface of his existence like a life-giving freshet, "and now, having passed through life like a corpse, he was, on his death-bed, as a man reborn."

In their treatment of Grace operating in the lives of their characters there is really not much to choose between Greene and Mauriac. From the French point of view, Greene's handling may seem melodramatic, but Grace *is* gratuitous and melodramatic, and in accusing Greene of overemphasis Mauriac forgets that he himself has been accused of the same thing by French critics. As for the astringency which Greene senses in Mauriac's treatment of religious themes, here again it is a question of national perspective. How the novelist shall introduce the melodramatic action of Grace in his novel is an interesting technical problem which we will examine in detail in a later chapter. That he *does* introduce it is perhaps the important thing. Mauriac chooses the French way of psychological analysis, realism, and often abstract statement. His religious drama is played out in broad daylight on the open heath. Greene uses ambiguity, allegory, and the grotesque—traditional English devices—and his spiritual drama is set in the shadows of a jungle night. Yet the techniques of the two novelists have this in common: that they are both poetic in the sense designated by Ford Madox Ford when he describes "poetic" as "not the power melodiously to arrange words, but the power to suggest human values."[49] And both are designed to incarnate "the divers movements of nature and Grace"[50] with maximum complexity.

But finally, perhaps, as I have said, the important thing is that Grace is present. And it is present not only in theme and action in the two novels, but also operates through the authors' attitudes towards their characters. In briefly developing this theme, I would like to return to the question of leprosy which I dismissed as a fortuitous affinity at the start of the chapter but which, as it turns out, has never been very distant from the central subject. A preoccupation with the abnormal, the diseased and the monstrous is another trait common to both novelists. Mauriac quotes Baudelaire at the opening of *Thérèse Desqueyroux*:

Seigneur, ayez pitié, ayez pitié des fous et des folles! O Créateur! peut-il exister des monstres aux yeux de celui-là seul qui sait pourquoi ils existent, comment ils se sont faits, et comment ils auraient pu ne pas se faire . . .

And Mauriac answers in an essay contemporary with his famous novel: "There are no monsters," he writes in *Le Jeune homme*, "We are not so different from them."[51] Both he and Greene have used the same phrase from Bossuet: "One must go as far as horror to truly know oneself,"[52] and both believe that it is only in descending to this depth of understanding that the novelist truly fulfills his vocation. While Mauriac states that the only field of investigation for the novelist is what is "miserably human in human nature," Greene writes that his duty is "to roam experimentally through any human mind. The novelist's task," he says in *Why Do I Write*, "is to draw his own likeness to any human being. . . . Isn't our attitude to all characters more or less—there, and may God forgive me, goes myself."[53]

Greene has referred several times in his work to Father Damien, priest at the leper colony at Molokai whom R. L. Stevenson championed against the attack of the Reverend

Dr. Hyde of Honolulu, and at one time Greene seriously considered writing his biography. Father Damien was accused by Dr. Hyde of being vulgar, unclean, stubborn, sectarian, impure in his relations with women, and disobedient to the rules of The Board of Health. "The leprosy that killed him," wrote Dr. Hyde, "can be attributed to his vices and his negligence; others have done a great deal for lepers, our own Protestant pastors, government doctors and others, without following the Catholic goal of meriting eternal life."[54] This leper priest who, despite the failings so carefully catalogued by Dr. Hyde, was considered by many to be a saint, irresistibly drew Greene's sympathy. In fact, he became one of the primary sources for the persecuted whiskey-priest hero of *The Power and the Glory,* a novel in which Greene also castigates the attitude of self-righteous moral rectitude in the person of the pious Catholic woman.

Writing of Stevenson's defense of Father Damien, Greene says, "The novelist has this in common with the priest, that he studies mankind only after having plumbed the depths of his own soul and heart. If only to defend himself, he must defend others. He dare not oversimplify."[55] Both Mauriac and Greene describe with great subtlety in their novels the repercussions of a Christian, that is, of a Christ-like act—a kiss to the leper—on the lives of their characters. But beyond this choice of religious theme lies the Christian implication of the creative act itself, valid for all their novels whether they treat directly of leprosy and sacrifice, or not. In Father Damien's identification with the lepers, and in Stevenson's identification with Father Damien, lies that act of sympathy and charity which is basic to a priest's and creative writer's vocation alike. And in the compassionate identification of Greene and Mauriac with their characters lies the strongest bond between them as Catholic novelists. It permits Greene to state with conviction that "creative art seems to remain a function of the religious mind,"[56] and Mauriac to say without ostentation,

"In sin or in Grace I have, finally, never spoken of anyone but Christ."[57]

With the help of two specific novels we have opened the subject of the fundamental similarities between "chalk and cheese." The general configurations of the comparisons have been illustrated. The task is now to individualize this common creative attitude by tracing it back in each case to its origin, and by following it forward through its various expressions in the lives and works of these two novelists.

NOTES TO CHAPTER 1

1. Personal interview with Graham Greene, January 1, 1962.

2. "Préface," *Oeuvres Complètes,* I, i. (*Oeuvres Complètes* is hereafter cited as *O.C.*)

3. *In Search of a Character* (London, 1961), p. 8. But Greene is now at work on a new novel, *A Man of Extremes,* and a play, *Carving a Statue.*

4. *Why Do I Write?* (London, 1948), p. 31.

5. "François Mauriac," *The Lost Childhood* (London, 1951), pp. 70-73.

6. "Mes grands hommes," *O.C.,* VIII, 429-32.

7. "Préface," *O.C.,* IV, iv.

8. "Cinema," *The Spectator,* CIX (June 17, 1938), 1096.

9. "Preface," *Our Man in Havana* (London, 1958).

10. "Vue sur mes romans," *Le Figaro* (November 15, 1952), p. 1.

11. "François Mauriac," *Writers at Work* (New York, 1959), p. 44.

12. "Vue sur mes romans," *loc. cit.*

13. *In Search of a Character,* p. 74.

14. "François Mauriac," *The Lost Childhood,* p. 70.

15. "François Mauriac," *Writers at Work,* p. 43.

16. "Le Romancier et ses personnages," *O.C.,* VIII, 292-99.

17. "François Mauriac," *The Lost Childhood,* pp. 71-2.

18. "Le Roman," *O.C.,* VIII, 263-84.

19. *Mémoires Intérieurs* (London, 1960), p. 155.

20. Cited in "Préface," *O.C.,* V, i.

21. "Fiction," *The Spectator,* CL (February 10, 1933), 194.

22. *In Search of a Character,* p. 48.

23. Conrad, "Heart of Darkness," *Youth* [Nelson edition], p. 104.

24. *Ibid.,* p. 65.

25. *Ibid.*, p. 85.
26. "An Outpost of Progress," *Tales of Unrest* (London, 1909), p. 129.
27. *Youth*, p. 56.
28. *Ibid.*, p. 70.
29. Personal interview with T. S. Eliot, December, 1952.
30. "The Two Maritains," *New Statesman and Nation*, XXXI (January 26, 1946), p. 72.
31. "Préface à Trois Récits," *O.C.*, VI, 120.
32. "La civilization chrétienne . . . ," *Essais Catholiques*, p. 18.
33. *Why Do I Write?*, p. 31.
34. "The Art of Fiction," *Paris Review*, No. 3 (Autumn, 1953), p. 34.
35. "Mes grands hommes," *O.C.*, VIII, 429-30.
36. See *Bloc-Notes* (Paris, 1958), p. 181, or "Préface," V. de Pange, *Graham Greene* (Paris, 1955), p. 10.
37. Philip Stratford, "One Meeting with Mauriac," *The Kenyon Review*, XXI (Autumn, 1959), 618.
38. "Un Auteur et son oeuvre," *Paroles Catholiques* (Paris, 1954), p. 92.
39. "Le Roman," *O.C.*, VIII, 270.
40. *Journey Without Maps*, Uniform Edition (London, 1962), p. 19.
41. *Ibid.*, p. 10.
42. "Books in General," *New Statesman and Nation*, XLIII (June 21, 1952), 745.
43. "Le Roman," *O.C.*, VIII, 270.
44. "La civilization chrétienne . . . ," *Essais Catholiques*, pp. 19-20.
45. "Journal III," *O.C.*, XI, 262.
46. "Journal II," *O.C.*, XI, 154.
47. "Dieu et Mammon," *O.C.*, VII, 317.
48. "Journal II," *O.C.*, XI, 155.
49. Cited by Greene in "Cinema," *The Spectator*, CLVIII (February 26, 1937), 356.
50. "Préface," E. Rideau, *Comment lire François Mauriac* (Paris, 1945), p. 7.
51. "Le Jeune homme," *O.C.*, IV, 436.
52. Cited by Mauriac in "René Bazin," *O.C.*, VIII, 482; cited by Greene in "Message aux catholiques français," *Essais Catholiques*, p. 13.
53. *Why Do I Write?*, p. 47.
54. "Les paradoxes du christianisme," *Essais Catholiques*, p. 46.
55. *Ibid.*
56. "Mr. Maugham's Pattern," *The Spectator*, CLX (January 14, 1938), 59.
57. Pierre-Henri Simon, *Mauriac par lui-même* (Paris, 1953), p. 58.

2

LOST CHILDHOODS:
PRISON AND ESCAPE

$\mathbf{M}$auriac claims that a door closed within him at twenty on what was to be the subject of his work, and in his essay, "The Lost Childhood," Greene states that his vocation as a novelist was determined at fourteen. Like the romantics, both write of childhood as the most susceptible and decisive period in life; but in *Brighton Rock* Greene cynically twists Wordsworth's line, "Heaven lies about us in our infancy," into "Hell lay around them in their infancy," and in *Thérèse* Mauriac traces the criminal tendencies of his heroine back to her earliest years. "Our destiny, once we begin to isolate it," he writes in that novel, "is like those plants we can never dig up with all their roots intact. . . . Even our childhood is, in a sense, an end, a completion." On the other hand, the purity of childhood plays an important symbolic role in the novels of both writers, but that will have to be analyzed later. What I would like to examine now is the way that attitudes shaped in childhood have permanently influenced the mature creative outlook of each novelist.

This investigation is beset with difficulties and limitations. Biographical material is meager and often unreliable, and it will be some time before all the evidence is made public and can be meaningfully brought to bear on the novels. For the time being one must depend on a few autobiographical statements and on those instances when the author betrays himself into a revelation. But as both Mauriac and Greene in their own criticism have freely experimented in this kind of literary divination, one may take their example as a precedent and begin to survey the ground for future biographers.

Mauriac has given a much ampler and much gentler account of his childhood than Greene. In fact, from the first reading of an essay like *Commencements d'une vie,* or novels like *The Stuff of Youth* and *The Frontenac Mystery* which describe his childhood in guise of fiction, it seems highly improbable that such a secure, sheltered, and unadventurous youth should have prepared the anxiety, bitterness, and tragic gloom of the major novels. But these works fall into the category of public reminiscence and only occasionally reveal the novelist's private universe. As I shall have to denature them somewhat in order to draw that private world into sharper focus, it is only fair to state that I take up the dark clues and bypass much of the happiness in the extracts that follow.

One thing that even a superficial reading of *Commencements d'une vie* reveals is the extreme sensitivity of the young Mauriac: "A sad child, wounded by everything."[1] Even his most commonplace experiences were lived out with alarming intensity. Although he has written in a kindly way of the Marianist Fathers who educated him at l'École Grand-Lebrun on the outskirts of Bordeaux, in his case the boy's familiar resentment of school swelled to dreadful proportions. In the horse-drawn omnibus that took him to school, the rain-streaked windows seemed to be faces streaming with tears. The suburban streets on the way "took on a doleful, tragic character incomprehensible to anyone but me." At school he lived in terror of his masters, of not knowing his lessons, and of being called on in class; in the noisy recreation period the boy "who was punished because he would not play" saw the image of his future, saw himself "jostled, downtrodden, defeated." He would escape for an hour at a time to lock himself in the foul-smelling latrines "for the simple reason that here at least I could be alone." At last, "the fetters were loosed, the slab lifted from my tomb," and he was free to return home to his adored mother from whom he "could not bear to be separated even for a single day."

Mauriac's father died when he was just twenty months old and he writes that he never became reconciled to the misfortune of not having known him. This accounts for his almost feverish affection for his mother, and for the somewhat pathetic sense of family solidarity which clings to *The Frontenac Mystery.* With three older brothers and an older sister he was brought up in a woman-centered world. His mother, his maternal grandmother whose house the family shared, and her nun-companion coddled the child who was "weak and sickly looking" without really understanding him. And in the Bordeaux apartment and at his grandmother's country house just outside the city (called Château-Lange and known locally as *la maison des curés* because of the frequent visits of the clergy), he knew the stifling atmosphere of strict bourgeois piety which pervades *The Stuff of Youth.*

His mother's family had long been established in the old quarter of the city, and thanks to them he knew Bordeaux both past and present. But his father's side of the family was an even richer source of inspiration. Thirty miles to the south-east, up the Garonne River, lay properties which had belonged to the Mauriacs for generations. With a few exceptions all Mauriac's novels are set in his grandfather's vineyards at Malagar on the right bank of the river, or in

34

his grandmother's pine-forested estate near St. Symphorien, a few miles to the south. If it was a brief reprieve to escape from the terrors of school to the haven of home, the long summer holidays in this country were a total release. It was here that Mauriac learned that almost pagan love of nature and absorbed all those wild and sultry details of climate and landscape that he was later to turn into his own particular poetry.

Just as important to the future novelist were certain incidents in the family history which were bound to appeal to his dramatic sense. Death dominates Mauriac's memories of this branch of the family. His paternal grandmother died within a year of his father, and his grandfather when Mauriac was five. He writes of the sinister character of their town house at Langon (the setting for *Genetrix*) and of his fright when he was taken into the shuttered room and shown the curtained bed and the place the coffin stood. Jacques Mauriac had been strongly anti-clerical all his life (as was Mauriac's father), but on the day of his death he became reconciled to the faith, and it was generally accepted in the family that he had been miraculously touched by Grace. This probably accounts for the half-dozen death-bed conversions spotted throughout Mauriac's work. That is of incidental interest. Far more important is the durable effect this accent on death had on his young imagination whose morbid cast is given free play, for example, in the semi-fictionalized *Stuff of Youth*.

Jacques, the adolescent hero of this novel, whose birthday is celebrated in conjunction with *le jour des Morts,* is brought up by three old women in perpetual mourning, his aunt, his grandmother, and Soeur Marie-Henriette, a nursing sister. He has lost both parents in rather romantic circumstances. His mother had "died of a broken heart" when her artist-husband (a composite of Gauguin and Rimbaud) left to paint in the South Seas. His father is given out for dead in the family until his real death at Tahiti is announced in his son's fifteenth year. In imagination Jacques holds long and tearful colloquies with both dead parents. Near the end of the novel when Jacques is eighteen and has gone to Paris, he is saved from a promiscuous love affair by the death of his grandmother which calls him back to Bordeaux, and a little later we find him at the death-bed of his best friend. These four deaths have this in common: that they release a buried capacity for affection in the hero. It is only when he sees his grandmother lying dead, for example, that he fully realizes her qualities and her tenderness towards him, and the death of his friend allows Jacques to cherish him in memory as he never had in life.

The same is true, figuratively speaking, of his relationship with his cousin Camille. Their adolescent love, which takes up most of the novel, finally dies a natural death. But no sooner does the hero realize this than he begins to fall in love again with the Camille of his memory. "Scarcely aware of what I was doing, I began to invent a legend for the little girl now dead. When I was no longer close to her I should be able to create an image cut to the measure of my heart . . . ," is Jacques's reaction when he discovers Camille, not dead, but simply grown up. In part, this is in character and just romantic effusiveness, and betrays a budding artistic temperament, for even when Jacques was close to Camille as a child, "I was forever having to reshape her that she might more properly resemble the image I had in mind, and add my brush-stroke to God's handiwork." But it also reveals a lugubrious preoccupation with death, reinforced by this farewell meditation addressed to Camille which closes the novel: "O! dear lost child . . . day by day [we shall] draw closer until that moment when our hands, no longer touching in this life shall be at rest, crossed in the same gesture on our two hearts stilled in death. . . ."

"*La foi nous sauve* . . ." had been the last words of Mauriac's anti-clerical grandfather. For Mauriac himself the Catholic faith, pointed up by his mother's decidedly Spanish piety, was at once a refuge and a new source of anguish. Here he found a Father even more understanding than the one he had lost, but also more dreadful. Certain aspects of Catholic doctrine and liturgy filled him with joy and sensual pleasure, but others reinforced and dramatized his childhood fears. On the yearly visits to the family grave, while his mother recited the *De Profundis,* he imagined the door of the tomb to be the gateway to purgatory. Stirring the evening fire he redoubled the torments of the damned in the red coals and fancied the rising sparks to be liberated souls. Above all, the strict religious discipline in the austere household left its mark on his imagination. The children were put to bed in a mortuary posture, their arms folded in a cross, a rosary twined in their fingers. The scapular was never taken off, not even for the bath. Long prayers, long devotions, and long, fastidious examinations of conscience lead Mauriac to write of "the narrow Jansenist world of my devout, unhappy and introverted childhood."[2] And although he is describing Jacques, there is little doubt that the timid, pious child who tortured himself "with thoughts of death and eternity, brooding on the general confession and ill-defined sins of which I supposed myself guilty," is Mauriac himself.

"I was not free to sin like others," thinks the hero of *The Stuff of Youth.* "Against sin God had armed me with . . . timidity, disgust, and scruples which had as much to do with family as with religion. At the very moment of my threatened fall, all the dogmas of my faith, all God's commandments [were] promulgated in my heart by the voice of conscience." Mauriac writes that in his own childhood "the terror of 'wicked thoughts' betrayed itself by a kind of tic, a grimace, a shaking of the head from side to side as if to say 'no' to sin." Because of natural timidity, his sheltered life, and the rigor of his upbringing, he was spared exposure to sexual temptation until relatively late. "Though I was more imaginative and sensitive than any of my comrades," says Jacques in *The Stuff of Youth,* "a secret magic kept me firmly pent within the frontiers of the kingdom of purity."

Already in *Commencements d'une vie,* however, there are hints of a stirring of the flesh. "A child who has never seen the sea," writes Mauriac, "senses its presence and hears its subdued roar long before he actually reaches it; already he seeks out the taste of salt on his lips, already nothing grows in the burning sand. . . . In the same way evil makes itself known from afar." In Bordeaux where the docks crowded the heart of the city, the vulgarities of the street were an open secret. The first time Jacques finds himself alone in the city after dark (on the night of his fifteenth birthday), he is accosted by a prostitute and flees, overcome by excitement and terror. To Mauriac's puritan imagination, evil, sex, and popular pleasures were one. It was an old Bordeaux custom to herald in the Lenten season, not on Mardi Gras, but on Ash Wednesday with a carnival in Caudéran, a suburb famous for its snails. Mauriac remembers as one of his strongest childhood impressions the sight of the masked revelers: "On this day of penitence, every mask was to my eyes a man in a state of mortal sin. . . . I was fascinated by the spectacle of these creatures who had willed themselves an eternal death, and whose grotesque cardboard faces mocked heaven." In *The Stuff of Youth* Jacques speaks of "the contrapuntal themes" in the drama of his life, the one represented by the saintly Abbé Maysonnave, the other by a libertine uncle. At one point in the novel he sees the latter standing in violet pajamas at the balcony of a suburban villa, probably in Caudéran, with a woman of easy virtue. Maria Cross, the wayward heroine of *The Desert of Love,* has a villa in the same neighborhood, and the balcony scene is repeated in slightly altered circumstances and with much greater impact on an adolescent mind in *A Woman of the Pharisees,* when Jean de Mirbel sees his mother and her lover at the window of a village inn. Behind these reminiscences and their fictional counterparts stands an early experience of the same nature. In a filmed interview Mauriac speaks of having seen, through the curtained window of the school omnibus (Grand-Lebrun was situated in Caudéran), a man and a woman copulating. Perhaps this explains why the suburban streets took on "a tragic character incomprehensible to anyone but me," and the sharpness of an image in *The Stuff of Youth:* "The little suburban road, loud with the din of electric trams, stretched before me, as harsh and squalid as life."

Enough details have now been disengaged from this brief and selective survey of Mauriac's childhood to attempt an analysis of how these experiences and sensations helped to shape his emergent creative vision. One of the most striking things about all Mauriac's accounts of his childhood is the sustained note of regret that runs through them. Even though the semi-autobiographical novels have adolescent heroes and are cast as conventional fiction and not treated as memoirs, they are bathed in an aura of middle-aged melancholia. These and the autobiographical essays are alive with the sadness of an unfulfilled past: regret for the lost parent; regret that there seemed to be no means of evasion from the narrow circle of the family or the confinement of a provincial capital—"For years," writes Mauriac, "I turned in my city like a rat in a trap"; regret at his own sensitivity that singled him out from other boys and made him a stranger to their games, their company and their pleasures; regret, finally, that he was not free to turn prodigal, and that, like Jacques, he "had not, like other men, that freedom of action that would have let me be a sinner."

Yet when Mauriac's horizon did broaden and he escaped from adolescence in Bordeaux to young manhood in Paris, he experienced a livelier regret at what he had left behind than he had ever felt before. The nostalgia for lost youth, for lost innocence, for his lost childhood in short, haunted him, and he very soon realized that his vocation as a writer would be to return voluntarily to the narrow world of his childhood and relive its joys and miseries in varied fictional reincarnations.

This sense of loss and the consequent turning back into the past gives Proustian importance to the role of memory in Mauriac's creation. "The natural state of the writer is a kind of incurable sickness which obliges him to sacrifice present life to past memories," he writes in *Bordeaux ou l'adolescence*, "Or rather it obliges him to create new life from that which is already spent. . . . Everything I write that is prompted by present experience miscarries unless it finds a correspondent reality in the Bordeaux of my memory." And, more succinctly, he has written of his act of creation: "I do not invent, I rediscover."[3]

The natural bent for reminiscence dictates the confessional tone of much of Mauriac's criticism which is never objective and is usually shot through with autobiography, for example, *La Rencontre avec Barrès, Du Côté de Chez Proust,* or *La Mort d'André Gide.* It also leads him to excel in the short meditative essay which has become the earmark of his journalism and is illustrated in such works as his *Journal,* his *Bloc-Notes* or *Mémoires Intérieurs.* Furthermore, it has determined the form of several novels. Besides *The Stuff of Youth,* another early novel, *Questions of Precedence,* is written from the point of view of the first person narrator, and two of his best mature works, *The Knot of Vipers* and *A Woman of the Pharisees,* as well as several short stories and some of the most successful passages of third person novels, are cast in the form of the reflective interior monologue or personal journal.

So much for the evidence. Now for the intriguing question, what is the impulse behind this creation through evocation of the past? Is it a flight from reality? Not in the ordinary sense. As Mauriac relates it, his childhood was more fraught with anxieties than his adult life, and yet he willingly went back to it for inspiration. Is it, on the contrary, a return to exorcise childhood fears and obsessions from the vantage point of maturity, a desire to manipulate in fiction those things that he was manipulated by in reality? This is a nearer guess. One remembers the strange relief brought to Jacques in *The Stuff of Youth* by the death of family, friends, and love. At the time of adolescence, he explains in the novel, "there is so rich a ferment in our hearts that the immediate past is forgotten, and with it, all those joys and sorrows, which only yesterday made up the substance of our lives. I have used the word forgotten, but forgetfulness is not the reason for the change in us. Rather it is the need to lay in a store of memories for future winters." This describes rather than explains the phenomenon. What is important to retain is the idea that there is never a clean break with the past. One may fail in one's relationships with others, love may cool, friendship may never come to fruition, but as long as they can subsist in memory, one has not lost hope of redeeming them. That, I think, is closer to a true explanation.

By the same token, Mauriac's return to his childhood is an effort to justify its sadness and its mute, incomprehensible suffering without simply recriminating the persons and external circumstances that formed it. It is a continued and generous effort to understand the mysterious springs of childhood and adolescent sensibility which no simple psychological explanation can satisfy. So it is that so many of Mauriac's heroes have lost one or both parents, that the mother figure is so predominant in his work, that death is such a preoccupation. And it is in an effort, neither to exorcise nor explain away, but to understand that he has so often reassumed his own boyhood anguish in the creation of adolescent heroes, who are persecuted by timidity at school and self-persecuted in puberty by the struggle between awakening sensuality and inbred religious scruples.

It is tempting to fix on Mauriac's fascination with adolescence as the basis for a literary psychoanalysis of the author. In a later chapter I will have occasion to refer to

Claude-Edmonde Magny's criticism of the possessive paternalism which Mauriac exercises over his characters. For the time I would simply like to point out the limitations of too mechanistic a view of this adolescent-fixation. In a brief but clever study, Françoise Mallet-Joris maintains that Mauriac's female characters fall into two principal types, both predetermined by an adolescent's conception of womanhood: the mother and the young girl. She notes that Mauriac never represents a mature woman who has found self-fulfillment in marriage, and further, that the unhappiness of his heroines seems to stem from regret that they are no longer virgins, compounded by the fact that they have been frustrated of the joys of normal motherhood.[4]

More by omission than by intention, this criticism leads one to consider an aspect of adolescence which is constantly emphasized in Mauriac's work: its strong idealism. On this bridge Mauriac links the poet and the child. "A poet is a man who has never wholly ceased to be a child," he writes, "a child who has survived the passage of time . . . a child without a rail to keep him from falling, a prey to all the passions of the heart and flesh, to all the secret frenzies of the blood." And the poetic passion he describes as "the madness of the adult who remains a child." He attributes his own transition from poetry to the novel to a hereditary conservatism passed down from his canny bourgeois ancestors which forbade him to abandon himself to the poetic madness, and he questions whether his bitterness in the characterization of this class in his novels is not a kind of revenge by the frustrated poet in him against these bourgeois guardians.[5] On the positive side, however, Mauriac has retained much of the poet in his novels, and even part of that intransigence, that refusal of the world which for him characterizes poet and child alike. That he should wish to see woman, then, principally as mother and virgin is not at all out of keeping with that adolescent and poetic idealism which he has never completely abandoned, and which finds its mature expression in his religious belief.

In this sense one can add considerably to Françoise Mallet-Joris's analysis and say that while Mauriac's view of woman may be adolescent in its perspective, it reaches beyond this naïvete to take on an important spiritual dimension. It clearly asserts that woman has a calling beyond that of happy sexual adjustment, and treats the abnormality of the heroine not simply as psychological frustration, but as the woman's share of the "madness" of child and poet. This madness might now be described, in a phrase that Mauriac is fond of quoting, as "the folly of the cross,"[6] which is nothing less in the strictest terms than the sign of a vocation to sanctity. And indeed, as will be seen, if Mauriac's heroines are frustrated of physical happiness in love, it is because they are obscurely but passionately drawn by a sense of this higher vocation.

This discussion leads one to consider, from a slightly different angle, another kind of frustration as one of the generating forces behind Mauriac's creation. In an essay entitled *La Province* (1926), he gives a rather paradoxical justification of a narrow and barren childhood as a rich background for the novelist. It is worth quoting at some length:

The greatest good fortune that can befall a man born to write novels is to have had a provincial youth. . . . This author, son of a provincial line, raised in a Catholic and provincial family, need not set out to search for characters. Characters crowd in upon him ready to accomplish everything that his destiny has denied him. Every temptation resisted, every adventure in love rejected by this solitary and Jansenistic child is a character in embryo that slowly takes form until it finally forces its way into the light and utters its own cry. Where the father has never had access, the child of his imagination will pass unimpeded. . . .

Above all, the study of the human heart benefits from a frustrated adolescence checked by the thousand and one obstacles that the piety of a provincial family can set in the path of his awakening sensibility. In this time of desire and refusal he is trained to struggle against himself, and thanks to a continual examination of conscience he is initiated into the art of tracking down the most secret of his motives, of unmasking the lie of his acts. He learns to strip them of their façade of respectability and to lay bare their true meaning.

And what better means of knowing others than this method which permitted him to know himself. In his chaste and introverted childhood he has understood the basic nature of all men and women. He can penetrate their hearts all the more surely because he has despaired of knowing them in reality. He ignores nothing of the woman he knows he will never possess in body. The only way of possessing her is in the mind, but he observes her as ardently as if he held her in his arms, and she becomes totally his in imagination to the point that later he can draw her out of his own substance and give her life.

Living characters in fiction are never those one has possessed in reality. A hopeless passion is lucid. . . . Bodily possession creates only a mirage; desire and repletion in turn transform and deform the creature one loves. . . .

To have studied the ways of the world serves only to control and confirm one's own interior discoveries. The single necessity is not to have lived in Paris, but to have lived, struggled, and suffered for many years in the secret solitude of one of our provinces. . . . The delicious and criminal experience of the world that Pascal speaks of engenders fewer great works than the bitter privation of worldly pleasures, than experience suffered in the sickroom, or in one of those dead old houses buried in the French countryside.[7]

Whatever one thinks of the general validity of Mauriac's theory, one thing is certain: the novelist in question is himself, and that this analysis, while it may seem specious if applied to another, reinforces the significance of the sense of regret and frustration which stamped his own childhood.

The necessity of inhibition is a curious creative premise, but it relates closely to Mauriac's Jansenistic upbringing and is a partial apology for it. Beyond this, it postulates the field for the novelist's exploration as that forbidden territory to which, as a child, Mauriac was denied or denied himself access. But his adult and imaginative freedom to explore this territory still operates under certain reserves, since the world which he describes is not usually the adult world of "free" experience, but the world of frustrated childhood. Mauriac enjoys the excitement of revealing some of the then unknown sources of adolescent anguish, but he docs not destroy the excitement by explaining them all, and the reality of the mysterious sadness of his childhood acts as an absolute check on any rationalization of the causes of his misery. Memory, not documentation or fancy, is the medium which allows a certain liberty but also imposes its own discipline, and that is why Mauriac works best in the genre of imaginative reminiscence.

The underlying tension implicit in this type of creation is well revealed in the passage quoted from *La Province*. Its odd mixture of bitterness and pugnacity, of regret at missed opportunity and pride in unworldliness, also throws light on another important aspect of Mauriac's creative vision established in adolescence. In her essay, Françoise Mallet-Joris accurately describes Mauriac's fictional world as "a universe conceived at that fascinating time of life when, to the horror and delight of the adolescent, everything around him lives ardently, takes sides, is engaged everywhere in a universal struggle. Here is the source of violence in Mauriac's work; of that strange colouring he gives to the passions; of those symbols . . . which slightly distort reality, which bespeak an existence lived on two different levels and that kind of second sight without which there is no durable art."[8]

This duality which runs through Mauriac's adolescence is evident in most of the novels, particularly the early ones. Broadly speaking, it is expressed as a struggle between the flesh and the spirit, between the passions and conscience, between a pagan sensuality and a Christian sensibility. The battle is not always ranged in two distinct camps as the adolescent is inclined to see it, but in one novel, *Lines of Life*, Mauriac simplified the conflict and opposed two young men, the devout and scrupulous Pierre Gornac and the passionate and sensual Bob Lagave. Writing of this characterization in 1950, Mauriac said: "I see in these two to-day as I did then, the incarnation of my own profound contradiction. I recognize myself in the one as in the other, as in enemy sons yet born of the same flesh."[9] More often than not, these two characters are fused into one in Mauriac's fiction. At times the character of Pierre Gornac dominates the hero or heroine, at times that of Bob Lagave. But the ascendant side of the character always attracts its opposite, and the internal conflict which results embodies Mauriac's own "profound contradiction." This dramatic tension, the play of these "contrapuntal themes," which take their origin in Mauriac's adolescence, provide not only a subject, but also that creative stress which gives vitality, uniqueness and necessity to all his work, and "that element of disquiet without which," Mauriac writes, "there could be no art."[10]

We have almost finished this tour of the closed circuit of Mauriac's inspiration. The pattern that recurs in his childhood is one of confinement and frustrated desire for evasion. At school he dreamed of home. More subtly, but just as surely, home represented another kind of imprisonment, and he suffered from the lack of privacy and lack of personal attention, inevitable in a large family; the "over-strict family discipline"[11] and close moral supervision; and the indifference or hostility of other members of his Bordeaux family to his poetic vocation. The summers in the country seemed to promise a complete release, but the state of pure pleasure was insupportable. After the first week, the shadow of the end of the holidays began to hover over his joys and give them a pathetic heightening,[12] and later his passionate love of nature was seriously checked and challenged by religious scruples. Finally, the torments of childhood and adolescence seemed over, and Paris and independence offered escape from provincial imprisonment. But it was too late. From behind "the bars of scruples, of the bans imposed by relations and sunken-eyed instructors who do not understand" the child beckoned, and in imagination Mauriac returned to become again "captive in an arid and a burned-up land."[13]

"To love one's prison, to prefer one's prison, is, in reality, to prefer oneself."[14] This image aptly describes the realism of Mauriac's introspection, for turning into his past was no refuge, but another sort of confinement. It was accepting the fact that one's character is one's destiny, and it was accepting in its fullest sense the obligation he felt "to be true to the child that I was."[15]

But to describe the prison of the self with the greatest possible lucidity, in all its beauty, horror, and singularity, was perhaps in the end a way of transcending it. And here it is not too fanciful to introduce a religious analogy and say that the prison represents *la condition humaine* and all its limitations, overshadowed by the absolute limitation of death. Mauriac has spoken of his bourgeois family's obsession with death and how, in their religious and sentimental life, the dread of death played a powerful role which, as we have seen, greatly influenced him as a child. He has pointed out how, on a practical level, the money and the property that his ancestors left as their heritage took on an enormous importance as a means of defeating death. "They might die," Mauriac explains, "but their property remained."[16] In a sense Mauriac's own investment in literature might be considered as being prompted by the same peasant instinct of self-preservation. His sense of perishability was extremely acute. "The race with death began for me at the age of eighteen," he has said, "from the time I left college. I began to die from that moment." And he has spoken of his work as a continued effort "to nourish and keep alive the poet who, in the words of Saint-Beuve, dies in every man at the age of twenty."

But there is another way of interpreting this instinct for self-preservation, this desire to save that which is destined to be lost. For the Christian, the possibility of defeating death becomes a reality when the prison of the self is drawn into the light of eternity. "Self-preservation is not the deepest instinct," writes Graham Greene; "we have learnt since childhood the Christian doctrine of the greater love."[17] It is perhaps the supreme test of this love not to know how to love one's enemy, or one's neighbor, but, in true humility, to know how to love oneself, and how to accept for oneself the Christian belief in the absolute value of an individual human destiny. This is a theme which both Mauriac and Greene have treated in their novels, and, in general, the projection of oneself into fictional characters is perhaps the best way of honoring individuality while at the same time remaining detached and observant, truthful and charitable, to one's character and, ultimately, to oneself.

It is not too much to suggest that Mauriac's lifelong effort to redeem his past may be seen in this light. Vanity has little to do with the deepest impulse behind his creation. Lucidity, he has written, is the first requirement of sanctity,[18] and the kind of lucid and exhaustive analysis on which his fiction is constructed is less an act of self-indulgence than one of self-sacrifice. "To write is to deliver oneself up,"[19] Mauriac feels, and in his sincere dedication to reveal through fiction the secret springs of his own nature one can describe his artistic vocation as the natural complement of his vocation as a Christian.

By way of autobiography Graham Greene has given only a few disconnected recollections in the prefaces to two travel books and in two short personal essays. Yet there can be no doubt that he believes as strongly as Mauriac in the formative influence of the novelist's early years. "The impressions of childhood are ineffaceable,"[20] Greene writes, and in an essay on Dickens he states: "The creative writer

perceives his world once and for all in childhood and adolescence, and his whole career is an effort to illustrate his
private world in terms of the great public world we all
share."[21]

Before attempting to generalize about the effect of childhood experiences on his creative outlook, one must first
simply record some of the ineffaceable early memories, as
disjointed and surrealistic as they are. "The first thing I
can remember at all," Greene writes in *Journey Without
Maps*, "was a dead dog at the bottom of my pram. . . . Another fact was the man who rushed out of a cottage near
the canal bridge with a knife in his hand; people ran after
him shouting; he wanted to kill himself."[22] Another early
memory is of seeing an airplane crash from the window of
the day nursery.[23] A little later, at the age of twelve or
thirteen, he tried his first experiments with death, and recalls "the disappointing morning in the dark room by the
linen cupboard on the eve of term when I had patiently
drunk a quantity of hypo under the impression that it was
poisonous."[24] This was followed, on various occasions, by
doses of hay fever lotion, deadly nightshade, and twenty
aspirins which he swallowed and then went swimming in
the empty out-of-term school baths.

With adolescence he began to reason about experience
and to follow up more systematically some of his impulses
and phobias. "Like a revelation, when I was fourteen I realized the pleasure of cruelty. . . . There was a girl lodging
close by I wanted to do things to; . . . I didn't do anything
about it, I wasn't old enough, but I was happy; I could think
about pain as something desirable and not as something to
be dreaded. It was as if I had discovered that the way to enjoy life was to appreciate pain."[25] At sixteen, in open rebellion, he ran away from school and home, and subse-
quently was sent to a London psychiatrist for several
months' treatment—"perhaps the happiest months of my
life."[26] In the early autumn of 1922 there were further flirta-

tions with suicide: "I was seventeen and terribly bored and in love with my sister's governess—one of those miserable, hopeless, romantic loves of adolescence that set in many minds the idea that love and despair are inextricable."[27] This mixed motive and the discovery of a small pistol among his elder brother's possessions led to half a dozen solitary games of Russian roulette spaced out over the next year and a half. Finally the excitement wore off, and he put the pistol back. "But the war against boredom had to go on,"[28] and so, at Easter in his nineteenth year, he lied to his parents that a friend had invited him to Paris, went there, saw Mistinguette, a Communist rally menaced by the police, and, from his hotel window, a man and a woman copulating: "They stood against each other under a street lamp like two people who are supporting and comforting each other in the pain of some sickness."[29] The next Easter, as editor of the university literary review, *The Oxford Outlook,* he wrote to the German Embassy in London, offering to investigate rumors of French repression in the occupied Rhineland, against an expense paid trip. His offer was accepted, and he reported his findings in the next issue of *The Outlook.*[30] Spurred on by the success of this exploit he wrote again, offering on his next holiday, in guise of an Oxford student on a walking tour, to act as courier and secret agent for the German government. This proposal was accepted, but, fortunately perhaps for Greene's future, the Treaty of London was signed, the French withdrew their support from the Separatists, and his services were no longer required. In one last attempt at espionage, Greene offered his walking tour disguise to the Irish Republic, but when they, too, refused, with a mixture of relief and chagrin he settled down to prepare his final university examinations. After graduating from Balliol he briefly considered service in the Nigerian navy and actually accepted a job with a tobacco company which promised travel to China. But these odd possibilities fell through, and, rather prosaically, he began his professional career as junior sub-editor on the *Nottingham Journal.*

These are some of the "primary symbols"[31] and outstanding experiences contained in Greene's piecemeal memoirs of his first twenty years. Immediately one notices the histrionic, not to say neurotic quality of many of them, and one wonders how much ought to be classified as artificial coloring, for, as Mauriac warns, in choosing and fixing certain elements of the past for an artistic purpose, almost inevitably the writer falsifies true experience.[32]

Although it is impossible to judge whether Greene has chosen representative details for his souvenirs, it is revealing that most of the events which he considers noteworthy lie outside the normal range of a boy's experience. One would hardly guess from them the unexceptional character of his youth: the averagely timid and retiring childhood; the large family (he was the fourth child of six); the comfortable middle-class background in a small provincial town, Berkhamsted, an hour by train north of London; the unpretentious schooling and the uneventful years at Oxford where he took a second in modern history. But behind this unexceptional record lies an intense private life, marked by the same kind of poetic sensitivity that fostered the artist in Mauriac in his own bourgeois milieu.

In Greene's case this sensitivity was thwarted and stimulated by the one really unusual feature of his life: the fact that his father was headmaster of the boy's school at Berkhamsted, and that ever since he could remember he had lived "on the frontier" between the public life of the school, where he and his brothers were enrolled, and the private life of home and family, the two separated only by "a green baize door in a passage by my father's study."[33] He hated the school, "the great square Victorian buildings of garish brick." He hated the school life, "the pitchpine partitions of the dormitories where everybody was never quiet at the same time; lavatories without locks; 'There, by reason of the great numbers of the damned, the prisoners are heaped together in their awful prison . . .'; walks in pairs up the suburban roads; no solitude anywhere at any time." He hated the stone stairs, the cracked disciplinary bells, "the smell of iodine from the matron's room, of damp towels from the changing rooms, of ink everywhere. . . ." He hated the sadistic masters and the school's repressive attitude towards sex which spread obscenity and smutty-mindedness among the boys. He hated school all the more because just on the other side of the green baize door, where he was forbidden to go except on holidays, was peace and privacy and the smell of "books and fruit and eau de cologne."

Because of the artificiality of this separation, Greene's hatred of school was even more intense than Mauriac's, and because his sentence of weekly imprisonment in alien territory was imposed and enforced from the friendly side of the border, he carried his resentment home with him. Although Mauriac, too, suffered from the terror of school, he resigned himself to it more readily because he could clearly draw up his allegiances between school and home, between term in Bordeaux and holidays in the country. But for Greene there was a constant confusion of values, a permanent sense of injustice, and betrayal at the heart.

Hell is the image that Greene most readily associates with his schooldays: "Hell lay around them in their infancy," and hatred is the dominant emotion: "For hate is quite as powerful a tie as love; it demands allegiance." His unhappy acts of revolt—his running away, his early attempts to poison himself—were undertaken in despair rather than in any firm hope of evasion. They were simply rebellious protestations, doomed almost beforehand to failure. It was necessary to react, to plan to escape, but the reality remained the prison. "For a long while it was only hell that one could picture with a certain intimacy. . . . One began to believe in heaven because one believed in hell."

In accommodating himself to a sense of failure and betrayal, Greene showed earlier maturity, perhaps, than Mauriac, in whom the struggle between heaven and hell, translated into various sets of symbols at different stages in childhood and adolescence, remained a constant in his experience. This permanent sense of conflict took on the significance of legend for Mauriac and became the necessary condition of his creative act. In much the same way, the sense of injustice, betrayal and failure are the obsessive themes rooted in childhood experience which underlie all Greene's mature work.

With Mauriac, as we have seen, it is the sense of regret which is operative in his imaginative return to his childhood. Greene's more precocious coming to terms with his prison resulted in what he calls the emotion of boredom. "It had always been a feature of childhood," he writes. "It would set in on the second day of the school holidays. The first day was all happiness, and, after the horrible confinement and publicity of school, seemed to consist of light, space and silence. But a prison conditions its inhabitants. I never wanted to return to it, but yet I was so conditioned that freedom bored me unutterably."[34] And he speaks of the several months he spent with the psychoanalyst in London as fixing him in his boredom "as hypo fixes the image on the negative."

Fixed in his boredom, his prison, his hell, what he sought outside it was excitement or pleasure fierce or sharp enough to counteract it. Moderate pleasure was not a strong enough antidote. But he discovered "the pleasure of cruelty," discovered "that the way to enjoy life was to appreciate pain." Similarly his excitements tended to be dangerous and extreme, and he discovered that "it was possible to enjoy again the visible world [after Russian roulette] by risking its total loss."[35] This seems to be almost the reverse of Mauriac's thin-skinned sensibility that felt conflicts everywhere, even in the most commonplace experience. One would hardly accuse Greene of being insensitive, but it is a curious twist to sensibility that makes him go to such lengths to keep it alive. In the end this leads to the same kind of adolescent overstatement that is implicit in Mauriac's vision of a divided world, but there are certain important differences: Mauriac's drama is interior, and the natural state is one of continual tension; for Greene the natural state is one of grim boredom, and external stimulus is needed to throw the drama into relief; he must actively resist his prison whereas Mauriac experiences conflict enough in the simple effort of submission to his. This difference explains the fact that Mauriac finds the strain between sexual desire and frustration an adequate symbol taken from "the great public world we all share" to embody his own private vision, while Greene needs all the shocks and perils of violent physical adventure. One might also remark that while both reacted to the idea of a struggle between good and evil with adolescent fervor, for Greene evil always came from the outside: in the person of the villain, the traitor, "Collifax, who practised torments with dividers; Mr. Cranden with three grim chins, a dusty gown, a kind of demoniac sensuality."[36] For Greene also, evil is more commonly related to nightmarish childhood fears than to ideas of temptation or impurity. In the title essay to *The Lost Childhood* he describes as remaining "a permanent part of the imagination," the witch who waited for him "in dreams every night in the passage by the linen cupboard by the nursery door."[37] And in an *Oxford Outlook* review he states that for the child "comfort is not a reality, nor even the common discomfort caused by an angry nurse. The real things are the terrible things. The stairs to bed, the empty cupboard on the landing, and the witch with the white puffed hands and the fleshy face, who waits always round the corner." Mauriac's sense of evil might have a more conventional moral and religious background, Greene's a literary and superstitious twist, but on the essential they were both agreed: that life was an imprisonment, and that the dream of evasion, although it might be necessary, was a chimera. "There are pleasant dreams of winter teas, of hot buttered toast and frizzled Dick, but reality finds its way even here, in the curtain that sluggishly stirs, though the window is closed."[38]

This analysis of the growth of Greene's sensitivity is constructed on the rather slim evidence of a few incidents from his childhood. It becomes more convincing when we see some of the patterns repeated in his adult life. Without yet going deeply into the question of his religious views, I think it is fair to say that he was temperamentally adjusted to Catholicism long before he joined the Church. On the one hand, Roman doctrine, and particularly the doctrine of Original Sin, took into account the reality of that "awful prison" that he perceived about him in his childhood. On the other, Roman discipline and dogma provided a strong antidote to mere apathetic pessimism in the presence of evil. In his preface to The Lawless Roads, Greene criticizes the tepid Anglicanism of his boyhood because it could not supply potent enough symbols either to describe or counteract reality as he had begun to know it. In a larger context he criticizes "the ugly indifference"[39] of European religious practice in comparison with the naïve but passionate faith of persecuted Catholics in Mexico. Tepidity, indifference, or boredom in the face of unpleasant reality, and the need to find some difficult, vital, not to say heroic alternative— here is the boyhood pattern repeated in mature religious experience.

It is also carried over into his creative life. After psychoanalysis, "for years, it seems to me," writes Greene, "I could take no aesthetic interest in anything visual at all," and it was the risk of total loss that made it possible "to enjoy again the visual world."[40] The danger of flagging sensitivity seems to have haunted Greene all his life. In his latest journal, In Search of a Character, he complains again of short memory and "very little visual imagination," and remarks that he had to make four separate trips to Indo-China to establish details for *The Quiet American*.[41] In a sense all his travels, which have been both adventuresome and extensive, are at least partly explained by his avowal that he had rather be frightened than bored.[42] Yet, and here is the interesting thing, even in the midst of new adventure, the dialectic between confinement and escape continues. How agreeable and necessary, he states in his Congo journal, to create a routine, however trivial, to stave off the oppressiveness of the strange and the unknown.[43] "The real delight of travel," he once wrote, "is not the strange but the familiar seen in incongruous surroundings."[44] And finally boredom strikes him down in the heart of the Congo, and he longs to return to civilization again, hoping, incidentally, to experience a reverse shock when he rediscovers the familiar.

This alternation between the familiar and the unknown in the external circumstances of his life corresponds to the interior tension in Mauriac's. But for Greene the physical pattern has a psychological equivalent, too. "How can life on the border be other than restless?"[45] he asks, referring to his odd, divided allegiances as a schoolboy, and he has described his particular predicament more fully in these words: "One didn't know where one stood, and that might be a good definition of nightmare. The world of nightmare is a world without defences because at any moment your defences may turn against you. What is the use of trying to see ahead, of preparing for attack when, suddenly, your best friend can turn into your worst enemy?"[46] Even in his adult life Greene has never been able to escape from an intermediary position, caught between two paradoxes, caught between horror and fascination with one side of the border, and love and impatience with the other. His favorite image for describing the human condition is that of a battlefield, and more specifically the no-man's land between warring trenches. The restlessness of the man condemned to inhabit that nightmarish no-man's land is as characteristic of Greene as that *inquiétude* sprung from a profound internal contradiction is of Mauriac.

But is the creative act itself, for Greene as it is for Mauriac, a liberation, even if only through the dramatization of one's confinement? Certainly the desire for evasion is a dominant theme in all Greene's fiction, and as such it will be studied in a later chapter. For the present it is sufficient to point out that there is no happy escape in his fiction, unless it is into death, and interpreting the different deaths of his characters one can only say that the happiest among them are those who die having most fully felt out and accepted the limits of their prison.

One must question more deeply, however—considering the number of suicides and attempted suicides in Greene's fiction and his own childhood experience—the significance of death as perhaps the true primary symbol of escape, in regard to which any coming to terms with one's prison is mere rationalization. In much of his early poetry Greene toyed romantically with the idea of the adventure of death, and at nineteen wrote, in the same vein, of Walter de la Mare's *Ding-Dong Bell:*

This book is all on the one subject, Death, for it is almost the last state left which keeps that bite of mystery that is essential for man. We have mapped out the world and the body, and so with a kind of timorous hesitancy, that is itself a delight, man creeps towards it. Columbus could lose himself in a new world; modern man can hope for the same relief only in this unknown.[47]

But though he continued to consider the risk of death a serious possibility in fact and in imagination, his speculations on the subject became much more searching and precise. Comparing the writer and the explorer, he recognized, for instance, the appeal of physical danger which answered a common "urge to surrender and self-destruction" more fully than the creative act: "You cannot surrender yourself so completely to a book or a picture as you can to the chances of death."[48] His desire for a life of action was particularly acute, and he writes sympathetically of "the tug between the claims of life and literature," in Stevenson's later years: "Endangering his life every day, he lived for no apparent purpose except perhaps a desperate desire to prove that he could be something other than a writer."[49] Greene undertook his own journeys of exploration for somewhat the same purpose.[50] Furthermore, stricken with sickness in the interior of Liberia, he found that the effect of coming close to death was a violent reaction: "I had made a discovery during the night which interested me. I had discovered in myself a passionate interest in living. I had always assumed before, as a matter of course, that death was desirable."[51] This did not mean, of course, that one could turn one's back on death. "Our awareness of life bears a direct relation to our awareness of its end," he wrote, and qualified as self-deceptive an attitude which allowed death to be "less important than a change in government."[52] Death, then, was no escape but an inescapable reality, one of the bars of his prison. Writing with great sympathy of "The Escapist," a renegade German exile and stowaway he met on the boat on his return from Mexico who faced imprisonment in Hamburg, Greene comments: "It was only one more thing to escape from, for escapists get accustomed to prison, hunger, sickness. Sometimes one wonders what it is they do—with so much hardship—escape."[53]

Here again is the pattern of alternance, expressed in terms of danger, physical sickness and death, but very like the central tension of Mauriac's creative drive. And for Greene, even as far back as childhood, both elements in the dialectic between life and death, prison and escape, had to be present. Prison was unbearable, but freedom was unutterably boring. Greene calls the months spent at the London psychiatrist's "probably the happiest months of my life."[54] The happiness resulted from the fact that he had escaped temporarily from the oppressive atmosphere of school, also because he found himself "the incontestable center" of this new experience. "I was expected to examine the most trivial of my thoughts with the utmost seriousness." He lived at the psychiatrist's house and spent part of every morning recording in a note book his dreams of the night before, a habit which he continued on his return to school.[55] (It is pertinent to note by contrast that at the same age Mauriac was accustomed to keeping a written record of his "examination of conscience.") But although he had escaped from his hatreds, and the treatment "cured me of my nightmares," he welcomed the fact that he was obliged to conform to a certain discipline. "It was not liberty," he says, "because I was not free to do what I wanted. But it is certain that real freedom would be a little terrifying for a child." He returned home, "correctly oriented, able to take a proper extrovert interest in my fellows (the jargon rises to the lips) but wrung dry."[56] As soon as he recovered a little of his vitality, he began to react against happy, normal, neutral stability. "I had discovered the perfect cure," he says, referring to the pistol he found in the corner cupboard. "I was going to escape in one way or another,"[57] and so began his adventure with Russian roulette on the Berkhamsted common.

In the end there was no real cure, and escape through adventure was fugitive, gratuitous, somehow unreal. But when he had made the attempt, when he had, so to speak, retold the story of his escape on his return to prison, in the cell of himself, then it became important; assimilated to total experience and personality it became potent to act against despair without violating the reality of the hell that lay around him, without destroying the paradox. "It is for the act of creation that one lives,"[58] Greene writes, and though the illusion of escape, in fact or in fiction, might be a necessary stimulus for that act, it is not, finally, a substitute for the more complex creative experience. John Russell gives some idea of that complexity in this passage from a review of Greene's volume of essays, *The Lost Childhood:* "He is the prisoner of his allegiances, but one who lives his captivity with such passion that it seems to many others, and perhaps even to himself, the image of an ideal freedom."[59]

In one of these essays, entitled "The Burden of Childhood," Greene compares three writers, Kipling, H. H. Munro, and Dickens, whose unhappy childhood decisively marked everything they wrote. "Life which turns its cruel side to most of us when we have begun to learn the arts of self-protection," states Greene, "took these writers by surprise during the defencelessness of early childhood," and he goes on to suggest that each of them developed a style and an attitude answerable to that unhappiness. Kipling and Munro, he says, created machine-like styles in self-defense. Kipling protected himself "with manliness, knowingness, imaginary adventures of soldiers and empire builders." Munro protected himself with sharp cynicism and brittle wit. Dickens, on the other hand, writes Greene, "learnt sympathy . . . developed a style so easy and so natural that it seems capable of including the whole human race in its understanding."[60] Greene's own style and attitude developed more like Dickens' than Kipling's or Saki's. His fiction is not designed as a means of self-protection, but as a way of self-understanding. And just as much as Mauriac's, his creative effort has been to remain true to his lost childhood. "We are all of us emigrants from a country we remember little of," he writes;

it haunts us and we try to reconstruct it, but all that is most important about it escapes us. We feel we have never been so happy since we left it, or so miserable, but we can't remember how happiness felt or the quality of the misery; we watch our children's eyes for hints: knowledge has altered the taste of every emotion . . . but just because we know so little we feel the heavy responsibility of not understanding.[61]

This note of regret harks back to Mauriac. And in some respects Greene feels the same nostalgia for childhood as he does. Greene quotes Herbert Read: "The only real experiences in life are those lived with a virgin sensibility—so that we only hear a tone once, only see a colour once, see, hear, touch, taste and smell everything but once, the first time." Noting that the creative spirit in Read "has remained tied to innocence," Greene suggests that "one of the differences between writers is this stock of innocence: the virgin sensibility in some cases lasts into middle age."[62] We have seen how concerned Greene himself was to maintain a certain purity and intensity of sensibility, and this is exactly what he sought and found on his first visit to the African interior: "This journey, if it had done nothing else," he writes in *Journey Without Maps*, "had reinforced a sense of disappointment with what man had made out of the primitive, what he had made out of childhood. Oh, one wanted to protest, one doesn't believe, of course, in 'the visionary gleam,' in the trailing glory, but there was something in that early terror, in the bareness of one's needs. . . . The sense of taste was finer, the sense of pleasure keener, the sense of terror deeper and purer."[63]

Yet there is an implicit distinction between Mauriac's sense of lost childhood and Greene's. For Mauriac the purity of childhood and of the child's world does exist; it is later sullied by experience, but in his fiction he tries to convey something of the conflict between experience and this lost innocence. For Greene it is the purity of sensibility that dulls, but the child's world is already a miniature replica of the adult one, perceived with an immediacy and a poetic clarity which he seeks to rediscover in his own creation. It is this view which leads him to emphasize in childhood the elements of "boredom, malice or nightmare,"[64] to write of the child's world as "the world of moral chaos, lies, brutality, complete inhumanity,"[65] or to say that "childhood is life under a dictatorship, a condition of perpetual ignominy, irresponsibility and injustice."[66] For Mauriac childhood is lost in the sense that its innocence is past before it is even realized. For Greene this sense of nostalgia may count too, but what makes his vision even more bitter is the thought that childhood is really lost in the sense that it is already fallen. "Hell lay around them in their infancy."[67] And, "In the lost childhood of Judas, Christ was betrayed."[68]

NOTES TO CHAPTER 2

1. This and following quotations, unless otherwise indicated, are taken from "Commencements d'une vie," *Oeuvres Complètes*, IV, 125-52 (*Oeuvres Complètes* is hereafter cited as O.C.), and its companion-piece "Bordeaux ou l'adolescence," O.C., IV, 153-76. My full translation of "Commencements d'une vie" appears in *The Tamarack Review*, No. 27 (Spring, 1962), pp. 3-19.

2. François Mauriac, *Writers at Work* (New York, 1959), p. 42.

3. "Vue sur mes romans," *Le Figaro* (November 15, 1952), p. 1.

4. Françoise Mallet-Joris, "Les personnages féminins dans l'oeuvre de François Mauriac," preface to *Le Desert de l'Amour*, Le meilleur livre du mois (Paris, 1959), pp. 35-7.

5. *Mémoires Intérieurs* (London, 1960), pp. 35-6.

6. "Souffrances et bonheur du chrétien," O.C., VII, 262.

7. "La Province," O.C., IV, 476-7.

8. Françoise Mallet-Joris, *op. cit.*, p. 36.

9. "Préface," O.C., I, iv.

10. *Mémoires Intérieurs*, p. 37.

11. *Ibid.*, p. 17.

12. *Ibid.*, p. 16.

13. *Ibid.*, p. 57.

14. "Bordeaux ou l'adolescence," O.C., IV, 174.

15. "Vue sur mes romans," *loc. cit.*

16. This and the following quotations from "Ma vie et mes personnages," 12 radio interviews with Mauriac by Jean Amrouche, broadcast on R.D.F. beginning March 16, 1952.

17. "A Lost Leader," *The Spectator*, CLXV (December 13, 1940), 646.

18. "René Bazin," O.C., VIII, 482.

19. "Dieu et Mammon," O.C., VII, 279.

20. *The Ministry of Fear*, Uniform Edition (London, 1950), p. 102.

21. "The Young Dickens," *The Lost Childhood* (London, 1951), p. 54.

22. *Journey Without Maps*, p. 31.

23. *Ibid.*, p. 279.

24. "The Revolver in the Corner Cupboard," *The Lost Childhood,* p. 175.

25. *Journey Without Maps,* p. 31.

26. "The Revolver in the Corner Cupboard," *The Lost Childhood,* p. 174.

27. *Ibid.*, p. 173.

28. *Ibid.*, p. 176.

29. *Journey Without Maps,* p. 31.

30. "The French Peace," *The Oxford Outlook,* VI (June, 1924), 212-16.

31. *The Lawless Roads,* Uniform Edition (London, 1955), p. 5.

32. "Commencements d'une vie," *O.C.,* IV, p. 128.

33. This and following quotations from "Prologue," *The Lawless Roads,* pp. 3-14.

34. "The Revolver in the Corner Cupboard," *The Lost Childhood,* p. 174.

35. *Ibid.*, p. 175.

36. *The Lawless Roads,* p. 4.

37. "The Lost Childhood," *The Lost Childhood,* p. 15.

38. "No. 2 Joy Street," *The Oxford Outlook,* VI (December, 1924), 359.

39. *The Lawless Roads,* p. 30.

40. "The Revolver in the Corner Cupboard," *The Lost Childhood,* pp. 174-5.

41. *In Search of a Character,* p. 9.

42. Jenny Nicholson, "Graham Greene, A 'Third Man' in Real Life," *Picture Post* (August 14, 1954), p. 19.

43. *In Search of a Character,* p. 27.

44. "The Unsentimental Journey," *The Spectator,* CXLVIII (June 11, 1932), 837.

45. *The Lawless Roads,* p. 4.

46. Ronald Matthews, *Mon ami Graham Greene* (Paris, 1957), pp. 49-50.

47. "Ding-Dong Bell," *The Oxford Outlook,* VI (June, 1924), 244.

48. "Books in General," *New Statesman and Nation,* XLIII (June 21, 1952), 745.

49. "Kensington to Samoa," *ibid.*, XXXVI (November 27, 1948), 469; cf. also "The Art of Fiction," *The Paris Review,* No. 3 (Autumn, 1953), p. 37.

50. "At Home," *The Lost Childhood,* pp. 189-90.

51. *Journey Without Maps,* p. 263.

52. "The Dark Enemy," *The Spectator,* CLVII (October 2, 1936), 556.

53. *The Lawless Roads*, p. 286.

54. This and following quotations from Ronald Matthews *Mon ami Graham Greene*, pp. 61-2.

55. The habit continued. He writes in *In Search of a Character*, p. 75, "The interest I always feel in dreams, not only my own dreams but the dreams of my characters, is probably the result of my having been psycho-analyzed at the age of sixteen."

56. "The Revolver in the Corner Cupboard," *The Lost Childhood*, p. 174.

57. *Ibid.*

58. "A Stranger in the Theatre," *Picture Post* (April 18, 1953), p. 19.

59. John Russell, "The Enlisted Man," *The Listener*, XLV (April 26, 1951), pp. 673-4.

60. "The Burden of Childhood," *The Lost Childhood*, pp. 74-5.

61. "The Turn of the Screw," *The Spectator*, CLXVI (June 20, 1941), 651.

62. "Herbert Read," *The Lost Childhood*, p. 138.

63. *Journey Without Maps*, p. 278.

64. "Fiction," *The Spectator*, CLIII (August 10, 1934), 201.

65. "Cinema," *ibid.*, CLVI (May 1, 1936), 791.

66. "Fiction," *ibid.*, CL (June 30, 1933), 956.

67. *The Lawless Roads*, p. 4.

68. "The Lost Childhood," *The Lost Childhood*, p. 17.

3

MAURIAC: POET INTO NOVELIST

*

In the introduction to *Commencements d'une vie* Mauriac admits that the intensity of his childhood experience was heightened by the habit of self-dramatization. "As a child I played at being solitary and misunderstood," he writes, "and it was the most fascinating of games. Perhaps I found it so because I instinctively knew that much more than a game was involved, a preparation in fact, an exercise for becoming a writer. To enjoy watching oneself suffer is the obvious sign of a literary vocation."[1] It is the change of that instinctive sense of vocation into conscious purpose that I wish to trace in this chapter, furnishing biographical background and evidence from the novels of the period, but still focusing on those elements which determine the character of Mauriac's creative vision.

One of the forces that contributed most to its development was a passionate love of literature. "As a child books were my unique deliverance," Mauriac states, and adds, characteristically, qualifying the idea of escape, "they provided me with the image of my own confusion and anxieties."[2] There was nothing exceptional in his early "vora-

cious appetite"[3] for books. Like any child, he read indis-
criminately, and his mother, apart from making sure that
what he read was "safe" (as often as not sanctioned by the
Bibliothèque Rose), did nothing to guide him or shape his
taste. Mauriac thinks that among the children's classics of
his time the novels of Zénaïde Fleuriot had the greatest influence.[4] It is hard to say just what these stories of the mis-
adventures and heartbreaks of little aristocrats in Brittany
could have given him beyond some insight into the pleasure
of invention, but they impressed him enough to set him
writing numerous imitations of them at the age of ten.[5]

Despite this precocious start, the form of the novel was
not to tempt Mauriac seriously for almost twenty more
years, and during this time his literary taste was being
formed by his reading in French classics. At Grand-Lebrun
he was introduced to Pascal and Racine who were to affect
him profoundly, not so much by providing him with literary
models as by furnishing him with a point of view. Referring
to the strict religious practice of his mother and to the dramatic extremes of fear and love which colored family piety,
Mauriac says that he was well prepared to fall under the
spell of Pascal.[6] The Brunschvicg school edition of *les Pen-
sées* has never left his bedside, and he refers to Pascal as
"the writer to whom I owe the most, who has most permanently left his mark upon me, and who has been my master
since my sixteenth year."[7]

If Pascal's influence was capital in shaping his religious
attitude, Racine's was even more important in forming his
artistic outlook. Mauriac states that he knows Racine "from
the inside," and from his first encounter with the plays in
the school curriculum he felt that he had been penetrated
by Racine's tragic sense "to the very marrow-bones."[8] He
assures us that on an adolescent level the Racinian type of
conflict between conscience and the passions was lived out
with great intensity in a religious college like his own.[9]

And in a poem in *L'Adieu à l'adolescence* he says that at sixteen Racine's heroines awakened him to the life of the passions.[10] When he seriously began to write, he found that his
novels proceeded directly from Racine's dramas, and he
has often acknowledged that Racine's characters, Phèdre
in particular, have served as inspiration for his own creation.[11] Moreover, as he advanced in his literary career he
felt that Racine's problems as a Catholic writer, led by his
artistic vocation to delineate the passions, tallied so closely
with his own difficulties that when, in 1926, he was asked to
write a biography, the method he employed was to reconstruct Racine's interior life by thinking constantly of his
own.[12]

It was really lyric poetry, however, that first captured
Mauriac's imagination and fixed his desire to write. In his
lonely days at Grand-Lebrun he fortified his solitude with
poetry: "I interposed between myself and reality all the
lyricism of the last century. Lamartine, Musset, Vigny...."[13]
Mauriac's father, alone among his family, had been well-
read, and it was in his library that, at fifteen, he discovered
Baudelaire and Rimbaud, whose books had hitherto been
classed as *les mauvais livres*.[14] The former led him out of
childhood into the fallen world, into "the world of sin."[15]
The latter represented to his growing dislike of the bourgeois climate of Bordeaux, and the indifference of his next
of kin, the romantic image of the artist in revolt. Yet despite
the fact that the influence of both poets came early and remained a strong undercurrent, the experience that they
dealt with remained foreign to him, and their full effect
on him was delayed.

When he began to write poetry himself during his last
years at Grand-Lebrun, he turned to more modest regional
models. In Francis Jammes he discovered tender and simple
love of the Girondin countryside, of that nature which had
remained his own first love, even beyond his love of books.

"Nothing can change the fact of my indebtedness to him in that secret order of things that is at the very heart of one's inspiration," Mauriac writes.

His verse . . . may not have modified my vision of the world, but it taught me that I could express it in the plainest terms without falling back on the clichés of romanticism. Jammes revealed to me that to write would mean directly expressing what I felt with all the fervour of a country-bred child. He showed me the path which was to become my own, and which was to lead me through the tangible world of nature to the world of human passion. Already at college I knew from Racine that there was nothing more wonderful than to be able to give the passions visible form in invented character. . . . But through Jammes I discovered that human feelings and the moods of nature would fuse together in the novels I would write, and that it would be my special artistic province to so combine them.[16]

In the works of another poet of the southwest, Maurice de Guérin, whom Mauriac felt he knew "from the inside,"[17] he found an even more intense expression of this communion with the natural world. "De Guérin not only made us sensitive to the beauty of external nature as the great romantics had done," he writes of himself and two young poet friends, André Lafon and Jean de la Ville de Mirmont, "he initiated us to the mute passions of the earth. He gave to our frail and humiliated adolescence the giddy certitude that we were the conscience of the vegetal world. It was through us that the trees tortured by the Atlantic wind and the hills shadowed by the flying clouds knew themselves. . . ."[18]

But although Mauriac felt himself in close correspondence with nature, he was prevented by the Jansenist in him, by the influence of Pascal, from following de Guérin in his paganism. And while sympathizing with de Guérin's romantic idealism and his rejection of the compromises of the adult world, one side of his nature was ambitious for success and esteem; he was drawn by the doctrine of Barrès and his *culte du moi* to exalt his own individuality and to covet the glory and influence that usually accompany the careers of professional writers in France. On the positive side of the balance he writes of Barrès: "Without the influence of this disciple of Pascal, everything human would never have become for me the object of such an ardent curiosity."[19] More critically, he speaks of himself in his twenties as being "the perfect little Barrèsian,"[20] conditioned by "the ruminations of a scrupulous Catholicism to read Barrès's breviary of egotism like an open book."[21]

Mauriac's early fiction resounds with echoes of his literary favorites and current reading. In the course of his first short novel, *Young Man in Chains* (1913), the twenty-year-old hero, Jean-Paul Johanet, finds occasion to quote from Jammes, Pascal, Verlaine, Laforgue, Balzac, LaFontaine (and Mauriac), and to refer respectfully to Chateaubriand, Lacordaire, Montalembert, Henri Perreyve, Baudelaire, Huysmans, Barrès, Maeterlinck, Romain Rolland, Gide and Claudel. Although Mauriac himself was saturated in literature at this time, he was nervously aware of the dangers of such over-exposure. In fact, the central theme of the novel is the conflict between the power of literature over the hero and the call to a life of action, and through the character of Jean-Paul, Mauriac analyzes his own situation as he hesitated in his mid-twenties on the threshold of a life of letters.

"He swims in a tide of books and spends long afternoons alone analysing his empty, complicated little mind," one of the characters says of Jean-Paul, a remark which must have given Mauriac a shiver of self-contemptuous delight. Jean-Paul who "throughout a quiet and lonely childhood . . . had got into the habit of watching himself live," believes his only happiness to lie "in examining myself by the light of what I find in the books I most adore." His cousin, Marthe, warns him that he is a victim of his reading, that he takes his books too seriously, that he talks like a book, and his only rejoinder is to assert complacently: "You're right,

Marthe, I've got printer's ink in my veins instead of blood!"

Jean-Paul's infatuation with literature is not innocuous. It sustains him in a self-centered universe and in a kind of emotional vacuum which often borders on despair. One of his friends, Vincent Hiéron, a rather smug young religious zealot, analyzes Jean-Paul's trouble in the following terms: "The love of books, when all's said and done, Jean-Paul, is just love of oneself. One reads only those authors in whom one sees oneself reflected. But worshipping himself, a man fails to live because he is his own prisoner. Before any of us can truly live he must renounce self. . . ." And he tries to win Jean-Paul's enthusiasm for an altruistic Christian-Socialist movement called *Amour et Foi* to which he is committed.

He briefly succeeds, and Jean-Paul becomes an ardent disciple. But accompanying, and perhaps growing out of, his love of literature is an acid self-critical sense which he finds he cannot help turning on the idealistic "Cause" of *Amour et Foi*. His cynicism results in his expulsion from the movement. Having failed "to free himself from himself" and "live" in a spiritual sense, Jean-Paul seeks escape by trying to lose himself in the pleasures of the body. He takes a mistress and lives a life of forced gaiety in Paris. But again he is too self-conscious to succeed. He experiences nothing but an "artificial passion" which is "pieced together . . . from odds and ends of literary memories," and in the end is forced to see himself as "an exile even from the world of human love."

Finally he is rescued from this impasse by an act of Grace, by "the awakening of his religious consciousness." At first, true to his habit of self-examination, he is skeptical of its validity, and wonders if he was "just yielding to it with the shrewdness, the ability he always had to fabricate emotions, to deceive himself." But this time he senses a difference: "At this moment, of all the petty dodges learnt from books, nothing remained." The conversion is a lasting one.

His interior change is seconded externally by Marthe's patient love which is now revealed to him, and the young man in chains discovers that "on that day when my thoughts became centered upon Marthe with a tender and a fixed concern, I began to be delivered from myself."

The genuine part of this novel is not the liberation but the chains. Jean-Paul's conversion is literature, contrived to round out the novel. His doubts about being able to come to terms with reality, the curse of incessant introspection, and his mistrust of the literary quality of all his experience reveal the true preoccupations of the young author. These themes run like an obsessive undercurrent through the next three novels. I have already mentioned the curious disability of Jacques, hero of *The Stuff of Youth* (1914), who cannot react spontaneously to those who love him, but must wait for the intervention of death, either real or figurative, before he can shape a suitable emotional response. The narrator in his fourth novel, *Questions of Precedence* (1921), is one of the same species and speaks of "those of my race who suffer from the melancholy mania of worshiping that part of themselves that is already dead. They are alive with memories, images, and anterior sensations like badly embalmed corpses." This same character refers to himself elsewhere as to "one whom reading has dispensed from living." And Edward Dupont-Gunther, a major figure in the intervening novel, *Flesh and Blood* (1914-1920), is a brooding, self-absorbed young man like Jean-Paul who is addicted to literature and has so feeble a hold on reality that, following his morbid penchant, he is led to commit suicide.

In these various characterizations Mauriac explored his own conscience. Unlike Jean-Paul after his conversion, he was by no means free from the prison of himself. He saw that, committed to the passive life of a writer, liberation in art or in action, as he had invented it for Jacques's father, the South Seas painter in *The Stuff of Youth,* or for Augustin, hero of *Questions of Precedence* (like Rimbaud, Augustin abandons himself to an inconspicuous and laborious life in Africa), would never be his except in imagination. At about the same time, or a little earlier, he must have given up hopes of a direct religious vocation. Jacques in *The Stuff of Youth* speaks of a Jesuit priest as having "infected me with his own passion for souls." But he adds, "his attitude was one of absolute detachment. I, on the other hand, though I did not know it, was less moved by love than by curiosity." Mauriac, aware of this distinction, decided, as for himself, that he would try to surpass Jacques's mere inquisitiveness, or at any rate, if he was to remain a prisoner it would not be to the kind of listless and sickly curiosity that had ruined Edward in *Flesh and Blood*. Short of a vocation to the religious life, in his fiction he would try to give the passion for self-analysis and the "taste for the delicious pleasure which comes from probing into the intricacies of human souls"[22] a Christian orientation.

At the time of Jean-Paul Johanet's conversion, his friend Vincent invokes the enduring power of a Catholic childhood over one's adult life and refers to it as to an imprisonment of a different kind. "No man can serve two masters," he apostrophizes, adding in his preachy way, "Is it not *that* truth which now torments you? You cannot escape it. It holds you prisoner. . . ." This same truth was to torment Mauriac far into his career, as will be seen in a later chapter, but at least he had fixed a goal for himself. Years later, writing of this period in his life he expressed his attitude in these words: "I took stock of my resources. And my first decision was, whatever happened, never to let go the hand of God . . . I determined that I would no longer let questions of faith arise for me, but that my destiny should be played out in the borderland between nature and Grace, and that I would resign myself to live in the shadow that the cross throws over a human life."[23]

Resigned to his faith, he also resigned himself to a life of literary introspection. "We all belong to the heritage of

Rousseau,"[24] he wrote, and felt that the greatness and the peril of a literary vocation lay in audacious and sincere self-revelation which must, however, be undertaken with the maximum of lucidity and the minimum of self-indulgence. To write, for an artist of his kind, would be not so much deliverance as surrender of himself: on the one hand to the exigencies of his art, on the other to the curiosity of his public. This sort of self-exposure would require the greatest self-knowledge and the greatest self-discipline. "The perfection of art," he wrote, "is to take those morbid inclinations which threatened to destroy you, isolate them, contain them, and make them serve, on the contrary, to release in you a vital, life-giving power."[25]

It was in these terms that Mauriac began to voice the debate between the idea of a life devoted to action and a life devoted to literature. Much more of a struggle is implied in his attempts to resolve it than in the simple intervention of Grace that dispels Jean-Paul's difficulties. Not only was this sense of strain to be felt in every succeeding examination of his literary vocation, but it was also to nourish many of the conflicts of his forthcoming fiction.

Young Man in Chains is partly based on the private journal which Mauriac kept during his last year at Grand-Lebrun, and he recognizes in Jean-Paul the most authentic characterization of his four early novels.[26] The hero's experiences not only reveal the state of his author's mind, but also provide a point of departure for a brief review of some of the actual circumstances of Mauriac's literary debut. The part of the novel which deals with Amour et Foi is a fictionalized account of Mauriac's association with the Sillon movement under the direction of Marc Sangnier (Jérome in the novel) before its condemnation by Rome in 1906. The rest of the novel is drawn from his first impressions of Paris where he had gone in 1906, after completing a licence ès lettres at the University of Bordeaux, with the intention of preparing a diploma at the École des Chartes. A small inheritance made him financially independent, however, and after qualifying in the entrance examinations, he decided to abandon his studies and devote himself entirely to literature. For three years he led a leisurely and introspective life, much like that of the hero of his novel. He busied himself with the affairs of a Catholic students' group, Cercle Montalembert, and published a few poems and critical articles in its review. On the side he began to make contacts which would later permit him to enter the thorny labyrinth of Parisian literary society. During his third year in Paris he attracted the attention of C.-F. Caillard, editor of *La Revue du Temps Présent,* who gave him the job of reviewing poetry for the magazine and sponsored the publication of his first volume of verse, *Les Mains Jointes,* which appeared in November, 1909, when Mauriac had just turned twenty-four.

In later years Mauriac judged this verse very severely, writing that he had "stepped on to the literary scene an angelic cherubim, fresh from the sacristy,"[27] and deploring the facility of its "spineless" technique, as well as the timid sentimentality of its religious outlook.[28] When the book was reprinted in March, 1910, however, it was enthusiastically reviewed by one of Mauriac's adolescent idols, none other than Maurice Barrès, who forecast that his future would be "easy, open, assured and glorious."[29]

Barrès's approval was an important first step in the fulfillment of this prophecy. From that time on, more and more doors were open to Mauriac; he began to frequent literary circles and to publish in better known reviews. In May, 1911, a second volume of verse, *L'Adieu à l'adolescence,* appeared; in November of the same year he contributed his first fiction (a chapter from what was to be *The Stuff of Youth*) to *La Revue Hebdomadaire.* This was followed by the serialization of *Young Man in Chains* in the *Mercure de France* in June, 1912, and by a second installment of *The Stuff of Youth* in the *Revue de Paris* in October. After this he published little more verse.[30] By the age of twenty-six the change from poet to novelist was well begun.

This metamorphosis, for all that it is a common one, deserves some attention. "If I am first of all a poet," Mauriac wrote in the year of his Nobel prize, "and that is something that I, at any rate, have never questioned, I have never deliberately betrayed poetry for the novel." And yet, though the poetic quality of Mauriac's prose is indisputable, it is a fact that, as Mauriac admits, "it was fiction and not poetry which released in me that irresistible revelation of the inmost self, that cry which a man in the grips of inspiration cannot hold back."[31]

What exactly is the relationship between the lyrical and the narrative mode of expression in Mauriac's experience? On the surface the change from one to the other seems largely to be an effect of age. As an adolescent, interested in nothing so much as himself, Mauriac sought to define his sensations by finding their reflection in nature. He made a fetish of his solitude and his sense of difference, and this decided the subject and the mood for most of his early poetry. As revealed in the heroes of his first novels, he felt himself to be alone, even in love, and his soul-searching, his joys and his griefs were almost invariably private and self-centered. While with one side of himself he believed in the universal validity of his experience, with another he held as fervent a faith in his own singularity. Like the romantic poet, he remade the world in his own image and became self-consciously immanent in everything that he created, while the exterior world tended to fade or be transformed by the uniqueness of his own subjective vision.

In retrospect, Mauriac speaks of himself at this time as being under the spell of "a certain type of romanticism which at my age seems to be the very height of absurdity and foolishness."[32] Although he still acknowledges his debt to his early masters, Jammes and de Guérin, he describes the truth of their work as "the truth of sensation." And while it is too simple to suggest that his change in view from romanticism to realism was made through a transfer of allegiance from one poet to another, his description of Baudelaire, "who was my hero as a young man," points up the change in emphasis:

Baudelaire is the poet of the real, so little romantic that the very language created by his poetry for its purpose is the nearest thing to prose that any poet has ventured to use, the most "figurative"—to use the modern jargon, always strictly controlled by the object. . . . Whatever its nature, Baudelaire saw it with an unswerving eye, smelt it, touched it, and showed it *sub specie aeternitatis* as Van Gogh did his kitchen chair.[33]

A change in interest of this order stimulated Mauriac's growing interest in fiction in his mid-twenties. Though the poet in him was still very much alive, he began to shed some of his romantic self-centeredness in his first experiments in prose. He began to see his lonely childhood in perspective as an object, not just as a theme. He recalled in detail the facts and people of his early years, as well as his own moods and emotions, now somewhat objectified in memory. He remembered the fascination with which he had listened to the adult members of his family as a child. He speaks of having been "passionately interested in grown-ups," because they were, to his eyes, deeply engaged in the drama of living, and, even more—since to him they seemed to be close to death—dangerously involved in the drama of salvation. He recalled, too, their stories of local and family history, "of which I have made great use in my work," and he now feels that his own narrative instinct was cultivated by listening to these family raconteurs.[34] From these elements he began to build up his first novels.

The transition from poet to novelist was a gradual one however. It is carried on throughout the first four novels, and in them one can observe a developing process of objec-

tification, particularly in regard to the creation of charac-
ted. *Young Man in Chains,* Mauriac's first novel, is little
more than a transcription into prose of Mauriac's self-
analysis in verse. Jean-Paul is patently a self-portrait and
the only significant character in the novel, eclipsing all the
other figures who exist only as signposts and sounding-
boards for his own development. The author is not yet disengaged from his hero whose self-questionings remain
fluid, imprecise, and troublesome beyond the requirements
of the characterization. And although Mauriac employs the
third person narrative technique in an attempt to distance
himself from his subject, it is constantly being interrupted
by telltale interior monologue in which the author continues his own unresolved debate.

In his second novel, *The Stuff of Youth,* which is again
autobiographical, Mauriac risked a first person narrator.
But this time he described a period further in the past, his
adolescence in Bordeaux, and this gave him some necessary
perspective. Here for the first time he also discovered that
the scenes of his childhood could furnish him with the
objective detail which would give strength and color to
his fiction. As a result, this book was much more successful
than the first. If it is less ambitious, it is less pretentious.
It is relaxed and droll, and is one of the few of Mauriac's
works which seems to have been written in a mood of easy,
fresh enjoyment. Jacques, the young hero, again holds the
center of the stage and is the most fully realized of the
characters. In retrospect Mauriac speaks of the others as
being "fabricated."[35] Jacques's father, who only plays an indirect role, is, as has already been mentioned, a literary
concoction made up of equal parts of Gauguin and Rimbaud. His libertine uncle is also a stiff and unnatural creation, conceived in theory but not in flesh.[36] But the old
women and Jacques's teasing young cousin, Camille,[37]
though only partial portraits, are drawn with a freedom and
confidence which betray the pleasure Mauriac took in their

invention. He may now be too sensitive to their "fabricated" quality because he remembers the book, with the impatience typical of any author reviewing his juvenilia, as being largely derivative and written in imitation of Jammes's *Clara d'Ellébeuse*.[38] But it is a good imitation, and slight and anecdotal though the novel may be, it is a successful exercise in the creation of half a dozen clearly differentiated types of character.

The Stuff of Youth is the last of what one might call the "idyllic" early work, which includes the first two novels and the two early volumes of verse. The war interrupted the composition of the next novel, *Flesh and Blood*, and the finished book bears the marks of a hardening of attitude that I will examine fully in a later chapter. In this novel one can distinguish a definite attempt to be more adventurous in the creation of character. Both of the principals in *Flesh and Blood*, Claude Favereau, the ex-seminarian of peasant stock, and Edward Dupont-Gunther, the effete young chatelain who offsets him, are created from material outside the range of Mauriac's own immediate experience. The former shares something of his author's sensibility, but his background and his reactions are his own. The latter is an even more conspicuous example of Mauriac's desire to transcend the limitations of the autobiographical novel. Edward's background is Protestant (he and his sister Mary are two of the very few Protestants in Mauriac's fiction), and in further search of a reality external to himself Mauriac modeled Edward's suicide on the death of Barrès's nephew, Charles Demange.[39]

Despite this progress in objectification, the novel belongs to an intermediary stage between the autobiographical and introspective novel and the confident and objective handling of narrative. Before he is able to distribute his interest convincingly among many characters, a young author will often single out two of them who quite transparently embody different sides of his own nature. That is the case in

Flesh and Blood where the two young men represent two aspects of their author's character, very like Pierre Gornac and Bob Lagave in *Lines of Life,* though in the later novel they are treated much more successfully. Claude develops out of Mauriac's country heritage. Edward, the young bourgeois intellectual, reproduces the figure that Mauriac cut in his early years in Paris. But in bringing the two selves into fictional conflict Mauriac marked a definite advance in characterization, and in this novel he succeeded in dramatizing his own private life much more effectively than he had been able to do with the earlier autobiographical technique.

The next novel, *Questions of Precedence,* illustrates a further step in Mauriac's increasing skill in drawing character objectively. As in *The Stuff of Youth,* Mauriac uses the first person point of view, but the "I" of *Questions of Precedence* has lost nearly all autobiographical connections. He is conceived dramatically. Although he is able to view ironically the vice of social snobbery, he himself is firmly caught in its toils, and it brings about his own ruin. The melancholic lucidity with which he reviews his own past is matched by his author's detached handling of character as character. Here, for the first time, Mauriac fully achieves that transposition of himself in fictional terms instead of the mere transcription of his own character and problems which had mainly decided the characterization in the previous novels.

Mauriac relegates *Questions of Precedence* to his juvenilia because one of its main characters, Augustin, is fabricated—"a mixture," he allows, "of Rimbaud and *Grand Meaulnes,* the typical *poète maudit.*"[40] But besides the successful treatment of the narrator, the novel also contains in the person of Florence, his sister, Mauriac's most mature female characterization to date. Marthe, Camille, and May of the first three novels tend to be the same kind of ephemeral young heroines in sun hats, who patiently suffer the vagaries of the young men they love, play the piano, and sing Du Parc's *Invitation au Voyage* like nightingales. There is a new vein of realism in Mauriac's treatment of May in *Flesh and Blood* when he describes her revulsion, then mute acquiescence, and finally unexpected happiness in the marriage of convenience that is imposed on her. But it took Mauriac a long time to outgrow a kind of chivalrous softness in regard to women and to begin that gallery of tragic heroines that was to make him famous. Florence is the first of these. Born with a taste for self-degradation, marked out for suffering, doomed to be a prisoner of the flesh, seeking her lost purity in an adolescent lover, she stands in direct line with the tormented heroines of the major novels: Gisèle de Plailly of *The River of Fire*, Maria Cross of *The Desert of Love*, and Thérèse Desqueyroux.

Another sign of growing confidence in the fictional medium and of growing objectivity in the treatment of character is Mauriac's increasing use of satire. He had shown promise of this talent in a scene or two of *Young Man in Chains*, particularly when demonstrating the vanity of Jérome Servet. *The Stuff of Youth* contains a vein of wry humor in his portrayal of "the redoubtable trinity" of old women who surround the young hero, and *Flesh and Blood* contains his first full-scale caricature in Mme. Gonzales, one of that coarse, domineering, ruthless breed of maternal monsters who were to populate his later fiction.

It is interesting to pause for a moment at this characterization. Mme. Gonzales is Dupont-Gunther senior's ex-mistress who has hung on, leech-like, to manage his affairs and to see what further she can extract from him. It is she who drives his daughter, May, by blackmail, into a loveless match with a richly landed neighbor. She schemes, meanwhile, to trap the father into a late marriage with her own pliable and succulent daughter, Edith. When her plans miscarry and Edith runs off with the son, Edward, she imper-

turbably follows them to Paris to engineer a profitable con-
cubinage for her daughter. It is a safe guess that "the Gonzales" is a postwar creation. She is described in the broad-
est possible terms, and Mauriac misses no opportunity of
underlining her viciousness and vulgarity. Yet she thrives
on her creator's distaste and exists more substantially than
many other characters of this period who are closely and
delicately adjusted to Mauriac's own temperament. Her
machinations provide a strong plot line on which to display
the emotions of the other characters; she is a further example of Mauriac's decision to expand his range of characterization; and she is the first illustration of the fact that
hatred as well as sympathy can be a potent primary stimulus to creation.

In the following *Questions of Precedence* Mauriac's satire is even more effective. Here it is not concentrated on
one character but is directed against the whole social fabric,
the cloth from which all the characters are cut. Since the
object of the criticism is more general and the satire is
rendered dramatically through the pen of the narrator, it
loses the tone of personal animosity which had given vigor,
at the expense of overemphasis, to his caricature of Mme.
Gonzales. When *Questions of Precedence* was reprinted in
1928, Mauriac prefaced it by an apology stating that he
now felt he had put too much malice into his picture of
Bordeaux society. But it is more reasonable to doubt the
validity of the retraction than that of the satire, for the
novel remains an expert piece of fiction, more finished than
anything that he had yet done, and its sting is no sharper
than that of later novels such as *The Knot of Vipers* or *A
Woman of the Pharisees.*

In terms of structure *Questions of Precedence* was also
more objective. It had fewer of the lyrical qualities of the
previous fiction and, on the contrary, showed many affinities to the most objective of all forms, the dramatic—per-

haps a reflection of the fact that at this time Mauriac was reviewing plays for *La Revue Hebdomadaire*. With its constant use of irony, its carefully constructed scenes of reversal and recognition, its small cast, and its tightness of situation, *Questions of Precedence* was the most Racinean of the early works. In this respect as well as in the other details that we have been examining, it could as easily be classed the first of his major novels as the last of his juvenilia. It is the first of Mauriac's novels in which the pattern and tone of his mature fiction are fully evident.

To concentrate on Mauriac's growing skill in the art of objectification when reviewing these early novels takes in only part of the creative process, however. Had he been born a novelist and not a poet, the loss to his fiction would have been incalculable. One must remember that even at his career's end he still considers himself a poet, and writes of his poem *Atys* as "the least disappointing of anything I have written."[41] If he turned from "the truth of sensation" of his early romantic verse to a harder, more realistic view, it was still under the patronage of a poet, and he describes himself at this time as "moving deliberately in the direction of Baudelaire."[42] And speaking of the importance of poetry to him at the age when he was writing his first novels, he says: "Prose, even imaginative prose, was without value in my eyes unless it had a deep top-soil of poetry."[43] While serving a valuable and necessary apprenticeship in the art of the novel, then, his poetic faculty was not suppressed. It is nearer the truth to say that it was being assimilated to his new narrative skills. The two coexist rather awkwardly in *Young Man in Chains,* whose chief claim to the title of poetic novel could be summed up in the fact that its hero is a poet and in its analysis of his introspective and impressionable temperament. Mauriac's poetic sensibility is put actively to work in the next novel, however, for in *The Stuff of Youth* he discovers the importance of atmosphere and hereafter relies heavily on the evocative quality of childhood memories to give color and density to his prose:

Vaguely, in the dusk, I could see the Ceres on the mantelpiece, the little jewel-case set with moonstones, the portrait of Pius IX —all the objects with which I had been familiar since my childhood. Many were already wrapped in pages from *La Croix* and *l'Univers.* In this confined paradise . . . religious-minded and ageing women, with no poetry in their hearts had, all unwittingly, taught me the meaning of poetry.

In *Flesh and Blood,* a novel in which, Mauriac esteems, "the poet in me is fully present,"[44] he succeeds for the first time in that poetic transference of the moods and emotions of his characters into seasonal and climatic states which was to become his stylistic trademark:

Their conversations took place, as a rule, at the hour of the day when siesta empties the fields, and the sun forces men and beasts into their lairs, there to sleep, while it is left sole master of the vines and dusty roads. But the two had no fear of him: maybe, they even blessed the collusive blaze and fierceness which enveloped them in an enchanted solitude holding them isolated at the heart of a universal furnace.

And even a novel like *Questions of Precedence,* which does not depend so much on natural setting, is shot through with passages of great lyric beauty permitted by the first person narrative technique which is so well suited to Mauriac's genius:

In this fisherman's hut, between the harbour and the ocean, I have gone to ground like a sick animal. I am hiding my nakedness. Bare, whitewashed walls, a sterile beach on which there is nothing but empty oyster-shells, sandy sea-wrack and dead jellyfish, an empty sky where, when the sun goes down, only a few clouds move apart, and, at times, the smoke of an invisible ocean liner—everything here combines to teach me the lesson of destitution. I am remaking myself in the image of this arid universe. Often I lie naked on the sands, or under the pines which seem so unreal that they give no shade. They hedge my body in, living torches of resin which, at times, under the August sun, go up in flames together.

Finally, we find this drive of the lyrical impulse through the narrative form even in a skill as proper to the craft of fiction as the creation of character. The gain in objectivity that we have been tracing in this regard cannot be considered as an end in itself; rather it must be seen as a necessary corrective to those lyrical and subjective tendencies which had first marked Mauriac out as a poet. He would never be an objective writer in the sense that the social-historian is. He deserts the camp of Balzac and Bourget who "studied man as a function of family and society,"[45] and writes: "Nothing tempts me less than a work of fiction in which two opposed conceptions of society are at odds."[46] He would never use the science of psychology as an end in itself, and states in Le Roman: "We doubt, today, whether there is a science of the mind. What we dread more than anything is to introduce the processes of science into the novel."[47] Although he learned the art of caricature, he would never be principally a satirist. One has only to compare Mme. Gonzales with Félicité Cazenave, the mother-monster in Genetrix three years later, to see how incidental Mauriac's interest was in this sub-order of the comic genre. The former is a ruthless caricature; the latter a full-fledged character. Hatred is replaced by horror in his portrait of Félicité Cazenave, and Mauriac shows his true colors, not as a comic writer but as a tragic realist in the later novel. "There is irony but no satire in M. Mauriac's work,"[48] writes Greene, referring to the third and most famous character of this type, Brigitte Pian in A Woman of the Pharisees.

In the best of his characterizations Mauriac strikes a dynamic balance between subjectivity and objectivity, between identification with his fictional creatures and detachment from them. He might learn from the disciplines of objectivity how to create convincingly not only characters who resembled him in some way but also a wide variety of types drawn from outside his own immediate experience. But in so doing he felt he must describe these characters "from the inside," must "draw [them] out of his own substance."[49] And he brought to the most objectively conceived of the characters in these early novels—to Florence, for instance, in *Questions of Precedence*—the same intense and deeply personal concern for his subject as marked the best of his own lyric poetry. To have gained proficiency in the technique of objectivity was, in the end, to have mastered a device which would permit him to penetrate even further into his own private world.

NOTES TO CHAPTER 3

1. "Commencements d'une vie," *Oeuvres Complètes*, IV, 128. (*Oeuvres Complètes* is hereafter cited as *O.C.*)
2. *Ibid.*, p. 141.
3. *Mémoires Intérieurs*, p. 66.
4. Interviews with Jean Amrouche.
5. *Ibid.*
6. *Ibid.*
7. *Ce que je crois* (Paris, 1963), p. 144.
8. "Préface," *O.C.*, VIII, ii.
9. Interviews with Jean Amrouche.
10. "Dès le college . . .," *O.C.*, VI, 375-6.
11. "Préface," *O.C.*, IX, iv. Also *Mémoires Intérieurs*, p. 158.
12. "Préface," *O.C.*, VIII, i-ii. In much the same way, many years later, he found an inspiration for his own career as a journalist in the example of Pascal of *Les Provinciales;* see *Ce que je crois*, p. 144.
13. "Commencements d'une vie," *O.C.*, IV, 146.
14. Interviews with Jean Amrouche.
15. *Ibid.*
16. "Préface," Francis Jammes, *Clara d'Ellébeuse* (Paris, 1958), pp. 17-18.
17. "Préface," *O.C.*, VIII, iii.
18. "Avant-propos," Maurice de Guérin, *Le Cahier Vert* (Paris, 1947), p. 1.
19. "Discours de réception à l'Académie française," *O.C.*, VIII, 436.
20. "Préface," André Lafon, *L'Élève Gilles* (Paris, 1956), p. v.

21. "Mes premières années à Paris," *Le Figaro* (February 24, 1940), p. 1.

22. *Young Man in Chains* (London, 1961), p. 79.

23. "La Rencontre avec Barrès," *O.C.*, IV, 189.

24. "Hommage à Charles Du Bos," *Qu'est-ce que la littérature* (Paris, 1945), p. 125.

25. "Le Jeune homme," *O.C.*, IV, 477.

26. "Préface," *O.C.*, X, i.

27. "Dieu et Mammon," *O.C.*, VII, 289.

28. "Les Mains jointes," *O.C.*, VI, 323.

29. "La Rencontre avec Barrès," *O.C.*, IV, 208.

30. Mauriac did, however, continue to write poetry. Titles include: *Le Disparu* (1918), *Huit Poèmes* (1924), *Orages* (1925), *Le Sang d'Atys* (1940).

31. "Vue sur mes romans," *Le Figaro* (November 15, 1952), p. 7.

32. *Mémoires Intérieurs*, p. 46.

33. *Ibid.*, p. 47.

34. Interviews with Jean Amrouche.

35. "Préface," *O.C.*, X, ii.

36. In *Mémoires Intérieurs* Mauriac mentions a great-uncle, "an old loose-living bachelor," who may have been a model for this character, though Mauriac never knew him.

37. Also a portrait from life.

38. "Préface," *O.C.*, I, i.

39. "Préface," *O.C.*, X, ii.

40. *Ibid.*

41. *Mémoires Intérieurs*, p. 55.

42. *Ibid.*

43. *Ibid.*, p. 44.

44. "Préface," *O.C.*, X, i.

45. "Le Roman," *O.C.*, VIII, 271.

46. *Mémoires Intérieurs*, p. 240.

47. "Le Roman," *O.C.*, VIII, 271.

48. "François Mauriac," *The Lost Childhood*, p. 72.

49. "Le Province," *O.C.*, IV, 476.

4

GREENE: ROMANCE TO REALISM

Greene owed even more than Mauriac to the early influence of other writers, and for two reasons. First, his
childhood did not present him with the same kind of rigidly defined and self-contained universe that Mauriac had
found ready-made in his own bourgeois, Catholic and provincial environment. Although both childhoods were
marked by the same kind of "private symbols" and "oppressive images"[1] and experiences, for Greene they remained largely personal and lacked the strong external
frame of reference. Instinctively he was led, on the one
hand, to stage his own adventures, on the other, to seek in
literature what he did not find in life, that patterning of
experience which would give body to his own confused
but acute sensations, which would lend them the significance of legend. Second, his early works are more literary
in inspiration due to the simple fact that he was ten years
younger than Mauriac when he began to publish at the professional rhythm of one novel a year. In the circumstances
it was natural that he should draw heavily on what he could
learn from other novelists to bolster up his own experience.

"Perhaps it is only in childhood that books have any real influence on our lives,"[2] Greene writes in his "Personal Prologue" to *The Lost Childhood,* and one must begin any study of his indebtedness to literature by examining his own account of his early reading. In contrast to Mauriac's classical formation and love of poetry, Greene's earliest and most lasting preference was for novels of adventure. In the "Personal Prologue," which was originally entitled "Heroes Are Made in Childhood,"[3] he cites R. M. Ballantyne, Percy Westerman, Captain Brereton, Stanley Weyman, Captain Gilson, Anthony Hope and Rider Haggard as his boyhood favorites. He also gives examples of scenes from these novels that found their way into his own fiction and suggests how these books possibly influenced his future.

But he singles out one novel in particular, Marjorie Bowen's *The Viper of Milan,* which precipitated a crisis and gave life "a new slant on its journey towards death." It is easy to see the superficial fascination for Greene at the age of fourteen in this violent tale of warfare, bloodshed and treachery in Renaissance Italy. It is perfectly successful in its own genre, a rapid narrative of sensational courage and crimes, told with zest, cunning and variety. Characters are set out with a quick and vivid stroke; dialogue is clipped and dramatic; and the action which turns now on fantastic coincidence, now on the trusted devices of poisoned potions, wells and rings, of dungeons, hidden doors and secret passages under the fortress walls, is as full of suspense and excitement as the palpitating reader could desire.

What set this novel apart from the other melodramatic fiction in which he was steeped, however, was the fact, as Greene explains it, that under the surface agitation of the plot and the flamboyant coloring was a somber and steady view of human nature. Unlike the books that he had read before which let him escape into dreams of heroic exploits, *The Viper of Milan* led back to reality and helped to "colour and explain the terrible living world of the stone stairs and the never quiet dormitory." Although she relied for her plot on the conventional struggle between good and evil, Miss Bowen refused the usual melodramatic solution of long-suffering virtue rewarded and villainy crushed by nemesis. Mastino della Scala, Duke of Verona, who champions the good in the novel, begins as a traditionally peerless hero but in the end is blackmailed into betraying his friends and finally becomes a failure even in duplicity. His enemy, Visconti the Viper, tyrant of Milan, is an inhuman virtuoso in terrorism and treachery. Finally, when all who oppose him are either murdered, corrupted, or driven into madness or suicide, Visconti himself perishes, but his death, far from satisfying poetic justice, occurs as a haphazard twist of fate at the hands of a spiteful underling, and the novel closes on a note of confusion and ruin. The reality of evil, the vulnerability of the good, the sense of doom that hangs over success, "human nature not black and white but black and grey, I read all that in *The Viper of Milan*," writes Greene, "and I looked around and saw that it was so. . . . From that moment I began to write. All other possible futures slid away. . . . Imitation after imitation of Miss Bowen's magnificent novel went into exercise books. . . . She had given me my pattern—religion might later explain it to me in other terms, but the pattern was already there. . . . It was as if I had been supplied once and for all with a subject."

There are reasons to doubt Greene's seriousness in this account of Marjorie Bowen's influence. He once allowed that in the essay he was "merely engaged in a little mild baiting of intellectuals,"[4] and it is extremely improbable that at fourteen anything so conscious as a pattern emerged from his reading of this novel. Still, one can accept as fact that *The Viper of Milan* sparked his desire to write. And one can take his word for the numerous imitations that followed, "stories of sixteenth-century Italy or twelfth-century England marked with enormous brutality and a despairing romanticism," for his first three published novels and brief descriptions that he has given of three earlier unpublished ones[5] bear the same general characteristics. In fact, during the first indecisive years as a novelist, Greene was within an ace of becoming a writer of historical romance.

One other important literary influence turned his first experiments in fiction in the direction of romance: that of R. L. Stevenson, who not only satisfied his taste for adventure stories but appealed to him strongly on personal grounds, for Greene's grandmother and Stevenson had been first cousins. Although he has never directly acknowledged this influence, Greene has written several articles on Stevenson and has referred admiringly to him in a dozen others; he has known his work intimately since adolescence, and at one time he intended to write a Stevenson biography. There is no question that he would have been well suited to the task, for Stevenson represented many of his own chief interests. He was a popular writer who, nevertheless, held the highest regard for the intricacies of his craft; he had treated the adventure story and the historical romance as serious genres, and he had succeeded in what Greene aspired to do as a young writer, had elevated this type of popular fiction to the level of art. Whenever he took up Stevenson's cause in the margin of his early literary criticism, Greene was really pleading his own, for he deeply shared Stevenson's concern for fine writing as well as his taste for excitement, violence, and the grotesque.

It is also interesting to note that Greene attributed to Stevenson the same underlying realism of attitude that he claims he found in *The Viper of Milan*. In *Kidnapped* he distinguishes "that 'darkness of despair and a sort of anger at the world' which when we were young dragged us with [the hero] through the heather."[6] He emphasizes Stevenson's "grim moral brackground,"[7] and writes: "If a morality does emerge from his novels—or rather from omissions in his novels—it is founded on an emotional disgust."[8] Debunking the legend of Stevenson's optimism, he reads the novels as tales of heroic failure, of realistic disillusionment in romantic settings, of evil, vigorous and convincing, and he turns attention particularly to the novels of the last six years when Stevenson's "fine dandified talent began to shed its disguising graces, the granite to show through."[9]

Here again, one must be careful of chronology and state that while this aspect of Stevenson's work may have appealed to Greene subconsciously when he first read the novels and may have confirmed an attitude, as Miss Bowen's novel had done, this sort of analysis and disengagement of a pattern belongs to a later period. From the evidence of Greene's first three novels one can say that what chiefly interested him in Stevenson at this time was the alternating play between his desire for high romance and his underlying sense of a grimmer reality.

The Man Within (1929), Greene's first published novel, is a historical romance which deals with the smuggling trade and is set in late eighteenth-century England. Although it is in no sense autobiographical like Mauriac's first novels, it does reveal many of Greene's early creative preoccupations, and in particular his hesitation between realism and romance. Francis Andrews, the young hero, is Greene's embodiment of a favorite Stevenson theme, that of the divided mind. A quotation from Sir Thomas Browne: "There's another man within me who's angry with me," keys up this study of the double-natured hero and throughout the novel in different ways Greene keeps his predicament constantly before the reader's attention. On one level the duality is given a hereditary origin, and Andrews discerns in himself "the vague romantic longings" of his mother contrasted with the "lust, blasphemy and cowardice" of his brutish and sensual father. In another sense the conflict is rooted in the hero's childhood experience, school representing the ugly reality, and beauty of different sorts and dreams of adventure representing his romantic side. In a third way, since his mother and father are both dead, this internal opposition is exteriorized in his relations with other characters in the drama. Carlyon, the present master of his father's smuggling ship, is the incarnation of romance, and the intermingling of these several levels of conflict is well illustrated in Andrews' first meeting with him on a moor above the school:

> ... the stranger turned to him and said, "The school. I'm looking for the school." It was as though he had mentioned the word prison to an escaped convict. "I've come from there," Andrews said. "It's down there."
>
> "One can't see the sun set from there," Carlyon remarked, and had the air in those few words of condemning the whole institution, masters, boys, buildings. . . . "Do you like it?"
>
> "I hate it," he said.
>
> "Why do you stay?" the question, quietly put, was stunning to the boy in its implication of free will.
>
> "It's worse at home," he said. "My mother's dead."
>
> "You should run away," the stranger said carelessly and turning his back stared again at the sunset. Andrews watched him. At that moment his heart, barren of any object of affection, was ready open to hero worship.

In fact Carlyon has come seeking Andrews to announce his father's death and to offer him a chance of escape by joining him in a smuggler's life. Andrews accepts and finds that Carlyon does not disappoint his hopes. "He was brave, adventurous, and yet he loved music and the things which I loved, colours, scents, all that part of me which I could not speak of at school or to my father." But the theme of betrayal and divided allegiances—taken over directly from Greene's own childhood—intervenes to foil Andrews of romantic escape. He also finds that the ship is haunted by his father's ghost, that it is just another image of the hell of school, and he grows to hate impotently "the sneers, the racket, the infernal sea, world without end." Finally, his hatred of the life overrides his admiration for Carlyon and drives him, in an act of rebellion, to betray the smugglers to the customs men.

This act shows up Carlyon in a critical light. He is now seen as "a romantic with his face in the clouds, who hated any who gave him contact with a grubby earth," as the quixotic follower of "a foolish sentimental blind dream of adventure." Andrews' betrayal shatters this dream and reveals his life as a smuggler not to be one of "adventure, courage, high stakes" but "a dull, dirty game."

Andrews, however, gets no satisfaction from his rebellion, for in revolting against the ship and his father he is really revolting against part of his own nature, just as his betrayal of Carlyon is a betrayal of his mother, the romantic side in him. In this sense his flight through the fog across the Sussex downs, pursued by Carlyon and wanted by the excise officers, is really an attempt to escape from himself.

As the story develops, Andrews' divided nature is expressed on a final level as a conflict between the spirit and the flesh, the former representing the romantic element, the latter, the realistic. He falls in love with the girl Elizabeth who shelters him during his flight, but betrays this love almost immediately by sleeping with Lucy, another man's mistress who lustily represents the body's pleasure. This new betrayal convinces Andrews that a cynical attitude (in this case towards sex) is just as unbearable as Carlyon's romanticism, for after his night with Lucy, Andrews leaves her, overcome by a feeling which he describes as "a terror of life, of going on soiling himself and repenting and soiling himself again."

By this time Andrews' internal turmoil is too complex for him to resolve himself. Indeed, near the end of the novel he admits: "It is as though there were about six different people inside me. They all urge different things. I don't know which is myself," an inadvertent admission on the part of the author that the theme of the divided mind was getting rather out of hand. But Greene rescues his hero by giving Elizabeth the role of mediating between the warring elements in his character. She holds "the promise of his two selves at one." Her sanity is contrasted to Carlyon's (and Andrews') romanticism; her purity with Lucy's (and Andrews') sensuality; her love with his hatred; her calm with his excitability; her quiet faith with his cowardice and doubt. In fact she represents too many antitheses to Andrews' already much divided mind to ever become a strong character herself. She remains a vague, idealized creature whose role will be described more fully in the chapter dealing with religious themes. For the time it is enough to say that her vitality, like Marthe's in *Young Man in Chains,* dwindles beside the oppressive reality of the hero's confusion.

In the end Andrews' internal debate closes in the impasse of a double suicide, his own and Elizabeth's, if anything, a solution which borders on "the despairing romanticism" of Greene's earliest fiction. The fact is that Greene had not yet resolved the conflicting demands of realism and romance himself, and the same debate was to animate his next two novels.

Before following up the fictional continuation of this internal argument, I would like to examine briefly the texture of *The Man Within.* Although Greene was able to objectify some of his childhood experiences in fictional terms in this novel, the fabric of the story is often so thin that his own obsessions show transparently through. The haunting fears of his prison, the desire to escape, the sense of the inevitability of betrayal and failure are the strong components of that basic drive which, according to Greene, characterizes "every creative writer worth our consideration, every writer who can be called in the wide eighteenth-century use of the term a poet [as] a victim: a man given over to an obsession."[10] But in *The Man Within,* Andrews carries Greene's obsessions too openly, his self-questionings take up too much of the novel and, like Jean-Paul Johanet's, tend to be a direct transcription of the author's own confused concerns. And while Greene is more successful than Mauriac in his creation of credible and self-contained minor figures, they, too, tend to be projections of different sides of his own nature. In general, the problem of objectification presented itself in somewhat different terms for Greene, however, and to illustrate this it is useful to refer to Stevenson again.

In a study of Stevenson's novels David Daiches writes: "He had difficulty in his earlier work in coming to terms with his insights and his skills, in knowing how to distribute the burden of meaning between the direction of the narrative line and the actual fabric and quality of the line itself."[11] Without suggesting direct influence, one can claim on the grounds of temperamental affinity that Greene's early difficulties in fictional creation were of the same order. His instinctive impulse was to tell an adventurous tale, and his novel succeeds when, as in the chase across the downs, or in the courtroom and bedroom scenes which take up the middle third of the novel, his insights are carried directly into action. But in the rest of the novel he so loaded the narrative with poetic qualities, in vocabulary, "sensibility" and personal significance, that it flounders badly.

This concern for fine writing was not a reprehensible fault. "Contrary to what is often thought," Daiches says of Stevenson, "it is not the fault of a man with nothing to say and lots of fancy ways of saying it, but of a man with more to say than he quite knows how to handle."[12] It is also another instance of the intrusion of lyric qualities into the narrative medium at an early stage in the novelist's career, as we have observed for Mauriac. At twenty Greene had a penchant for poetic prose and poetic fiction. He found reason to praise Walter de la Mare's short stories because they were "packed with imagery."[13] Of John Masefield's novel, *Sard Harker,* he wrote in *The Oxford Outlook:* "It is a tale of gross improbability for that is the common ingredient of poetry. Without its improbability it would be a shilling shocker, without its poetry it would be beauty wasted."[14] He was a poet himself at the time and in his last year at Oxford published a collection of verse entitled *Babbling April* (1925). The temptation to introduce a poetic quality into his own fiction with the unfortunate result of overwriting could be illustrated almost anywhere in his first novel. Take for instance his descriptions of fire and candlelight in Chapter IV, when Andrews returns to the safety and peace of Elizabeth's cottage:

A large fire burnt with a kind of subdued ferocity and its red rays, instead of bearing a light, spilt blacker pools of darkness in the room (page 47).

the flicker of flames played up and down her body like the dazed, groping fingers of a lover (page 47).

He twisted his figure into odd distorted shapes, so that every part of him might receive a blessing from gracefully gesticulating hands of flame . . . (page 48).

A gap of shadow separated them, and the flickering of the flames made useless but persistent efforts to cross it . . . (page 53).

Slowly [the candle flames] rose higher and higher making little aspiring peaks of flame pierce the shadows. Slowly they rose higher and small haloes formed round their summits, a powdery glow like motes in sunlight. Cloaked from all draughts by the surrounding mist they burnt straight upwards, tapering to a point as fine as a needle. The shadows were driven back into the corners of the room where they crouched darkly like sulking dogs rebuked (page 54).

he advanced to the fire and let the heat and flame stain his hands a red gold . . . (page 64).

She smiled at the tendrils of the fire uncurling themselves and folding again in bud (page 66).

"You are free," she whispered, her eyes watching him . . . through the gold mist which the flames of the fire shed (page 68).

This kind of cataloguing, of course, grossly misrepresents the total texture of the narrative, but it does point up the poetic excesses I have referred to. Obviously the intent is to supercharge the atmosphere with emotion for this important encounter, but Greene has overloaded the passage with intensity. The play of light and shadow is too vaporous itself to be convincing as an objective correlative for the emotions. And as it is nearly the only image he uses in this scene—the interior of the cottage and the appearance of the characters are never described in detail but remain bathed in a kind of immaterial unreality—one is led to recall Greene's admission of an inert aesthetic sense and to judge the overemphasis as an attempt to force significance into the story. In later novels where concrete detail abounds and furnishes a rich background, Greene's frequent use of imagery is unobtrusive; significance is carried in the fabric of the narrative line rather than applied externally, and atmosphere, filtered through a wry, oblique point of view, is rendered much more tellingly than by this headlong direct method.

Its one justification might be that the impulsiveness in the writing is intended to reflect Andrews' impulsive, romantic mind. He is not a poet like Mauriac's first hero, but he tends to take the same exalted, rather literary view of his own experiences. He is often seen "engaged in the favourite process of dramatizing his own actions"; he frequently imitates gestures and turns of phrase which he has picked up from the stage, and his "sentimental and melodramatic instincts" are the equivalent, in terms of the adventure novel, of the self-scrutinizing habits of Mauriac's young French hero.

An identical weakness marks both characterizations. The author has only been able to "live in the skin"[15] of his character by making him very much like himself. There is no doubt that Greene has endowed him, not only with experiences like his own, but also with his own state of mind. Despite its historical trappings *The Man Within* is as much a novel about Greene's early sensibility as *Young Man in Chains* is about Mauriac's. Andrews' habit of "dramatizing his actions," which Mauriac described as "the obvious sign of a literary vocation," is certainly one which Greene shared, and, finally, the impulsiveness and romantic overstress in the writing is as much Greene's as his character's.

A few years later Greene was able to criticize another writer for "the poetizing of experience" which he described as "a failure to use the senses . . . the acceptance of sight and sound and smell at second hand,"[16] and for trying to give poetic value to fiction by the use in prose of "the worn word counters of verse in its decadence."[17] He could speak with authority because he had been guilty of the same fault. It is this weakness which he distinguishes in the young Stevenson when he writes of "the dead flesh—including the dreadful B.B.C. smoothness of his early style,"[18] contrasting it to the "granite" quality of his mature fiction, or when he perceives in his work a change from "the romantic fancy" which inspired the early novels to "the realistic imagination"[19] operating in the late ones.

At twenty-six, however, at the time of Greene's second novel, *The Name of Action* (1930), the debate between romance and realism was still open. Through Andrews, Greene had tried to find a sanction for his own sense of melodrama and his own desire for romance. True, Andrews was not satisfied by the conventional rewards of melodrama which Henry James once described as "a distribution at the last of prizes, pensions, husbands, wives, babies, millions, appended paragraphs and cheerful remarks."[20] But even though he was too complex a character to enjoy conventional romantic bliss, his end was still a victory for a perverse kind of romanticism, and he surmounted his disillusionment with life by entering into the adventure of death. In *The Name of Action,* a much simpler novel which stands to *The Man Within* as Greene's later entertainments do to his serious novels, Greene experimented with another idealistic young hero, but this time one whose hopes for romance were checked by disillusionment at every turn.

Perhaps the best introduction to the theme of the novel is the passage in Hamlet's soliloquy from which the title is taken:

> Thus conscience does make cowards of us all . . .
> And enterprises of great pith and moment
> With this regard their currents turn away
> And lose the name of action.

Though the enterprises in which he sets high hopes do lose their romantic luster, Oliver Chant, hero of the novel, is less plagued by conscience than either Hamlet or Francis Andrews. Nicknamed "Croesus the idealist" by one of the characters, Chant is a rich young Englishman who, as much from a sense of boredom as from any other motive, puts himself and his fortune at the disposition of a revolutionary party in a small Rhineland state whose capital is Trier. He thinks of his mission as "his only hope of escape from a life of which he had grown inexpressibly tired, a life without meaning, without risk and without beauty. In that life there had been nothing worthy of reverence or defence." Arriving in Trier, however, he does not find the release in action that he seeks, discovering instead that the motives of the rebels are founded on self-interest and that their methods are base. He meets Paul Demassener, the dictator he has come to depose, and his wife Anne-Marie, finds here more promising material for his romantic inclinations, and sensing an estrangement between them falls in love with Anne-Marie and exchanges "for the image of himself as the saviour of a city from a not very evident tyranny the more satisfactory image of one who would release Anne-Marie Demassener from a hated contact."

Here too he is disillusioned. Anne-Marie is an adventuress but of a common breed and leads Chant on only because she lacks excitement. After a night of love which fires up his hopes, she refuses to go on with the game and wearily reveals the secret of her surrender to him: that her husband is impotent. Furious at the truth, Chant gets drunk and betrays this secret to the rebels who put it to good use and depose the dictator, not, as Chant had adventurously hoped, by force of the arms which he has bought and smuggled into the country himself at considerable risk, but by a campaign of exposure and public ridicule. The last scene completes the disenchantment of the hero and shows him, a frustrated lover and unwanted savior, leaving Trier on the night train in company with the impotent husband and deposed dictator, the man whom he had come to crush.

It is an advantage in this novel to have simplified the character of the hero. Throughout, Chant is buoyed up by his romantic instincts, and it is only at the end after repeated disappointment that he is allowed anything like the complexity which muddled the mind of Andrews. Other factors make this a better, though less ambitious book. Its setting is contemporary, and its details are taken from the first of Greene's many trips in search of material, this time from his Easter trip to the Rhineland as an undergraduate, expenses paid by the German government. Three sequences in the novel—when Chant runs from the police through the deserted night streets of Trier, when he shakes off a plainclothesman who is shadowing him in Coblentz, and when he bribes a suspicious customs officer into passing over a hidden shipment of arms—three scenes, in short, which do merit the name of action, are handled with as much ingenuity and suspense as similar scenes in any of Greene's later thrillers. Moreover, although most of Greene's obsessional themes are here—fear, flight, betrayal and failure—they are held in check and give intensity to the action without overwhelming it as in *The Man Within*.

With so many of the required elements present, this might well have been Greene's first successful entertainment, and it is profitable to ask where it fell short. Despite the simplification of the hero, the main fault still lies in the characterization. As was the case in his creation of An-

drews, Greene was still unable to visualize a hero much
different from himself, and Oliver Chant is a fairly direct
transcript of the romantic side of his own nature. He mo-
nopolizes the point of view from which the story is told and
so absorbs Greene's imaginative energy that the other characters only develop as projections of different facets of his
character. Thus Joseph Kapper, the rebel leader and writer
of obscene political satires against Demassener, stands for
the sensualist in Chant, while Demassener represents the
idealistic dreamer, and Anne-Marie holds the middle
ground of the realist, positions similar to those held by
Lucy, Carlyon and Elizabeth in *The Man Within*. An ambitious idea, an interesting formula, and, as in the first
novel, the sign of a writer who wishes to put fiction to work
for a serious purpose. But the theory obtrudes, the characters are symbols rather than full-bodied creations, and
the plot which links them, when it is not caught up in the
momentary excitement of events, drags mechanically and
improbably after the initial idea. Had Greene been able to
relax his hold and permit the characters to take on independent life, and dictate their own personalities and his-
tories, he might have brought the novel off. But he had not
yet the confidence or the means to permit this license.

Like *The Man Within* this second novel deals in fictional
form with some of Greene's early creative preoccupations.
It is as much a novel about adventure as a novel of adventure. Chant is continually brooding on what adventure
promises. He hopes that it will break routine, put meaning
into his life, set him among men "who really loved and
hated," and perhaps bring him into contact with the abso-
lutism of "death which dignifies the most unworthy object
with the immortality of no further change." These thoughts,
like Andrews' meditations, to a certain extent reveal character, but they also awkwardly stress the artificiality of the
fiction and artlessly jolt the reader's willing suspension of
disbelief. One wishes that Greene would leave off specu-

lating about the nature of adventure and get on with the story. They are interesting intrusions, however, for through them we can see Greene seeking a justification for his own taste for melodrama and adventure, and one can sense him clinging desperately to Chant's romantic views which, through a kind of naïve and passionate overstatement, have the ring of truth about them. In the end Greene finds them irreconcilable with reality, and Chant is paid off with frustration. But this, too, is deeply felt. It probably reflects second and somewhat jaded thoughts that Greene was beginning to have about a life dedicated to fiction. *The Man Within* had been a minor success. It went into five editions in 1929, and had been published simultaneously in France and America. But his contract with Heinemann's required a novel a year, and everything Greene has said about second novels betrays the difficulties he had with *The Name of Action.* "A first novel sometimes absorbs too much of a writer's vitality," he wrote in 1933. "He has not learnt to harbour his resources, and when it is a success he is driven to write another before he is ready."[21] "A first novel is usually the result of many years' saturation," he wrote a year later, and "a second novel often uses a too immediate experience. The writer has become a professional without learning economy. The intensity of a first novel cannot be repeated. . . ."[22] His adolescent longing for romance was beginning to sour in measure with his discovery that the romance of the novelist's career was as unlikely a fiction. His next novel, *Rumour at Nightfall,* was to be one last strenuous attempt to reconcile some of his romantic yearnings in a novel. When it failed, Greene seriously considered ending his literary career and taking a teaching position in Bangkok.[23] But the seeds of disillusionment had already been sown, and there is little doubt that Greene shared Oliver Chant's disappointment with a world where the adventurer was doomed to discover, even if he never quite believed it himself, "how shabby was the underside of the most selfless success."

As I have suggested, Greene's technique was better matched to his subject in the second, less ambitious novel than in the first. In *Rumour at Nightfall* he lost most of the ground he had gained in *The Name of Action*. This was partly due to the source and setting that Greene chose for this novel. At Oxford he had become interested in the story of an ill-fated Carlist uprising in Spain in the early nineteenth century described in Carlyle's *Life of John Sterling*. In fact, before *Rumour at Nightfall* he had already written a novel on the subject which had been rejected by Heinemann's but which had stirred their interest enough to make them ask for his next, which was to be *The Man Within*. Now, several years later and under pressure to provide a new book, he returned to this subject as to ground already worked over. It was a bad move. Although he had not made much of his own experience in Trier—the journalist's eye was still fogged with poetic vision—the setting for *The Name of Action* did have a certain actuality, and the novel called on his powers of observation and reconstruction from fact. To exchange the contemporary for the historical and to abandon his own experience for a background in literature was to step further back from reality into romance.

As Kenneth Allott points out,[24] another literary influence can be distinguished in *Rumour at Nightfall,* that of Conrad, and particularly the late Conrad of *The Arrow of Gold,* a novel which also takes as its subject Carlist revolutionary activities. How susceptible Greene was to "the heavy hypnotic style"[25] has already been stressed by Greene's admission that he stopped reading Conrad "about 1932 because his influence on me was too great and too disastrous." In *Rumour at Nightfall* a sketchy revolutionary plot pieced out with a love affair is lost in dreary tracts of introspection while the main characters tirelessly analyze their experiences and emotions. The Spanish heroine, Eulelia Monti, is not proficient in her lover's language, so their romance is carried out in a kind of basic English, with Greene, as an unidentified but overinvolved commentator, interpreting the subtleties of intonation and gesture. In another context Allott calls the practice, which he finds common to both Conrad and Greene, "spreading the butter too thick."[26] Although the intent may be honorable, the excess of analysis, usually conducted in vaguely poetic terms, effectively smothers the action.

As for characterization, it is more theoretical than ever. Taking a hint from a criticism by Charles Fenby of *The Name of Action*,[27] Greene tried to make a virtue out of one of the failings in that novel and replaced the hero with a divided mind who perceives his own conflict played out in the clash of personalities around him by twin heroes, each of whom represents one side of a nebulous total nature. The first and last parts of the novel are recorded from the point of view of Francis Chase, an English journalist, who is a skeptic and a rationalist and represents "mind." The middle part is given to his friend Michael Crane, a romantic with mystic leanings, who represents "heart." Perhaps the double point of view might have succeeded, but, caught up in the game Greene extended it even further, assigning to Eulelia Monti the role of "soul" (like Elizabeth she also represents the realist, midway between her mother, a voluptuary, and her father, a saint, and in this, as in her name, is akin to Ollala, the heroine of a Spanish story by Stevenson) and giving to Caveda, the rebel leader, the part of "body." This rough division does not do justice to the complexity of Greene's manipulation of these character-symbols. It does not take into account Chase's fascination to the point of identification with Caveda, Caveda's seduction of Eulelia, her love for Crane, Crane's doubling for Chase, or any of the multiple cross-relationships that spring up between them. But lacking a strong central point of view, this complexity is wasted, and the novel falls into confusion. Again, one might say that these faults are those of "a man with more to say than he quite knows how to handle."

Later Greene might well write of Conrad's *Heart of Dark-*

ness: "The language is too inflated for the situation. Kurtz never comes really alive. It is as if Conrad had taken an episode in his own life and tried to lend it, for the sake of 'literature,' a greater significance than it will hold."[28] The same faults applied to his own handling of the drama in *Rumour at Nightfall*. It was a bad novel, but a good lesson for Greene. Frank Swinnerton reviewed it roughly in *The Evening News*,[29] and Greene has since stated that this review "shocked him out of the cultivation of his hysteria."[30] A rather exaggerated claim, perhaps, for Swinnerton's remarks were not as "scathing"[31] as Greene remembers, but at least they underlined what Greene had begun to sense himself, that it was time to change direction, to free himself from literary influences and to bring his long and worrisome romance with romance to an end, or at least under control.

I want to return later to *Rumour at Nightfall* for, despite its artistic failings, it is a key work for opening the subject of Greene's religious outlook. If *The Name of Action* is an embryonic entertainment, and *The Man Within* in many respects is the prototype of Greene's serious fiction, *Rumour at Nightfall* could be called his first Catholic novel. It contains Greene's first attempt to find a religious basis for his emerging novelist's point of view, and as such contributes some interesting material to the chapter on Catholic themes.

But I do not want to dismiss these three early novels without insisting that the conflict between realism and romance which they explore remains an important theme for Greene. In the novels that immediately follow we will see the pendulum swinging as far in the direction of a disillusioned cynicism in attitude as it had pressed towards an extreme of romanticism in *Rumour at Nightfall*. But even in later novels, the tension between the two attitudes, although it is often submerged and does not break to the surface as in the early novels, is a constant factor in Greene's imagination. It so obsessed him that ten years after *Rumour at Nightfall* Greene returned to the theme and built one of his best entertainments around it. Because the whole problem that we have been examining is recast in fresh and useful terms in this novel, *The Ministry of Fear* (1943), it **is** fitting to close this chapter on Greene's juvenilia by a brief reference to it.

The novel is divided into three "books" entitled "The Happy Man," "The Unhappy Man," and "The Whole Man." Each of these represents one phase in the hero's experience: the first that of Arthur Rowe's hopeful childhood and romantic adolescence, the second his disillusioned and unhappy manhood, the third, his painful acceptance of reality in middle age. The narration is so devised that all three stages are experienced by an adult mind, for Rowe's happiness is due to the fact that he has suffered amnesia from a bomb blast and can remember nothing beyond his eighteenth year. In this state, experience is agreeably simplified. It is the age of idealism again, life is an adventure, the world is an exciting place, good and evil are clear-cut issues, "there is such a thing as truth, and justice is as measured and faultless as a clock. Our heroes are simple: they are brave, they tell the truth, they are good swordsmen and they are never in the long run really defeated." The country nursing home in which Rowe finds himself after the accident is a kind of Arcadian equivalent of his childhood home, and his convalescence there is like reliving his earliest years in the peace and security of provincial England before the 1914 war. But Rowe finally recovers to face the harsh contrast of the modern world, the Pompeian chaos of London in the blitz and the ugly knowledge that he had long before left childhood innocence behind and is, in fact, an acquitted murderer who had poisoned his wife because he could not bear to watch her slowly dying of cancer.

His rediscovery of this unhappy past—unhappy because he had been unable to reconcile the absurdity and suffering

of life with the idea that it should be beautiful and serious
—is delayed, however, while Rowe, his memory still un-
restored, tastes some of the adolescent pleasures of a life
of adventure. He becomes fascinated with one wing of the
nursing home which is forbidden the patients because it is
where the "violent cases" are kept. One night, like a schoolboy "breaking out of dormitory, daring more than he really
wanted to dare, proving himself," he steals out of his room
and down to the sick bay. In contrast to the spruce nursing
home, although separated from it only by a green baize door,
it is run down, dirty and disordered; an evil air hangs about
the place (obviously a fictional reconstruction of Greene's
own school), and Rowe wonders "was *this* the real adult
life to which we came in time?" But instead of leading him
directly back to reality, his discovery puts him on the track
of fresh adventure, for he finds one of his friends imprisoned there and escapes to the London police with his story.

From here excitement quickens rapidly. The doctor in
charge of the hospital turns out to be an enemy agent, and
Rowe finds himself a key figure in helping the police round
up a widespread spy ring. At first launched in this new
adventure he experiences only "a sense of exhilaration,"
he is "happily drunk with danger and action." The ruins of
bombed London strike him as "only a heroic backdrop to
his personal adventure; they had no more reality than the
photographs in a propaganda album. . . . He didn't understand suffering because he had forgotten that he had ever
suffered." But during the chase his memory gradually revives, and with it the unhappy man's knowledge "that adventure didn't follow the literary pattern, that there weren't
always happy endings." He reluctantly begins to feel the
artificiality of "this violent superficial chase, this cardboard
adventure hurtling . . . along the edge of the profound natural common experiences of men." Immaturity struggles
hard: "The sense of adventure struggled with common
sense as though it were on the side of happiness, and com-

mon sense were allied to possible miseries, disappoint-
ments, disclosures." But finally common sense wins a sad
victory, and he learns "the lesson that most people learn
very young that things never work out in the expected way.
This wasn't an exciting adventure, and he wasn't a hero,
and it was even possible that this was not a tragedy." He
learns that "life . . . isn't a detective story," and in the end
finds that "the sense of adventure had leaked away and left
only the sense of human pain."

The unusual experience of reliving former states of mind
takes Rowe beyond his point of departure as an "unhappy
man" to the stage of the "whole man," for he learns to
accept suffering and absurdity and unhappiness and the
mediocrity of life. He sees his mercy killing for what it was
—an act of rebellion—and the unhappy attitude which had
prompted it as just the reverse face of his youthful optimism. He learns, painfully, to come to terms with "the
dingy hole" of reality and discovers that "after all one
could exaggerate the value of happiness."

In his first three novels Greene explored chiefly the first
two states. Like Rowe, at the convalescent home, Oliver
Chant is a happy hero who enters undoubting into an adventure which "promised to be the first Eden, an Eden for
once without the snake," and at the end of the book he is
barely taken over the border into unhappiness. Andrews
is an unhappy hero, young enough still to be haunted by
the dream of heroism but forced, like Rowe, to acknowledge that the heroes of childhood are "dead and betrayed
and forgotten; we cannot recognize the villain and we sus-
pect the hero and the world is a small cramped place."
His refusal of this world and his act of suicide parallel
Rowe's mercy killing. *Rumour at Nightfall* does not take us
much further. Chase, the rationalist, resembles Chant, and
Crane, the romantic, dies a violent death like Andrews before he can form more than a few fleeting ideas about

reality. In short, there are no whole men in Greene's early fiction.

In the next novels there were no happy heroes, nor were there romantic extremes of unhappiness. Greene himself moved towards realism and took his characters with him. And even if he did not immediately reach the attitude of the whole man, that was the direction of his next development.

NOTES TO CHAPTER 4

1. "The Young Dickens," *The Lost Childhood*, p. 53.

2. "The Lost Childhood," *ibid.*, p. 13.

3. "Heroes Are Made in Childhood," *The Listener*, XXXVII (March 27, 1947), pp. 462-3.

4. "The Art of Fiction," *The Paris Review*, No. 3 (Autumn, 1953), p. 39.

5. See John Atkins, *Graham Greene* (London, 1957), pp. 15-16, and Ronald Matthews, *Mon ami Graham Greene* (Paris, 1957), p. 115.

6. "Cinema," *The Spectator*, CLXI (August 5, 1938), 232.

7. "Fiction," *ibid.*, CLIII (October 19, 1934), 578.

8. "Cinema," *ibid.*, CLVIII (April 2, 1937), 619.

9. "From Feathers to Iron," *The Lost Childhood*, p. 66.

10. "Walter de la Mare's Short Stories," *ibid.*, p. 79.

11. David Daiches, *Stevenson and the Art of Fiction* (New York, 1951), p. 11.

12. *Ibid.*

13. "Ding-Dong Bell," *The Oxford Outlook*, VI (June, 1924), 244.

14. "Sard Harker," *ibid.*, VI (December, 1924), 357.

15. *In Search of a Character*, p. 26.

16. "Fiction," *The Spectator*, CLIII (August 24, 1934), 264.

17. "Fiction," *ibid.*, CLII (May 18, 1934), 786.

18. "Cinema," *ibid.*, CLVIII (April 2, 1937), 619.

19. "Fiction," *ibid.*, CLII (June 29, 1934), 1010.

20. Henry James, "The Art of Fiction," *Partial Portraits* (London, 1911), p. 382.

21. "Fiction," *The Spectator*, CL (May 5, 1933), 654.

22. "Fiction," *ibid.*, CLII (June 1, 1934), 864.

23. Matthews, *op. cit.*, p. 142.

24. Kenneth and Miriam Allott, *The Art of Graham Greene*, p. 37.

25. *In Search of a Character*, p. 48.

26. Allott, *op. cit.*, p. 37 ("The phrase is M. C. Bradbrook's").

27. *Ibid.*, p. 44n.

28. *In Search of a Character*, p. 51.

29. Frank Swinnerton, "People we all know," *The Evening News* (November 20, 1931), p. 10.

30. Allott, *op. cit.*, p. 76.

31. *Ibid.*, also see Matthews, *op. cit.*, 144-5, for the text of the review and Greene's later reaction to it.

5

GREENE AND MELODRAMA

Mauriac's apprenticeship in the novel stretched over an eight-year period, so we are able to discern a considerable development from *Young Man in Chains* to *Questions of Precedence*, published when he was thirty-five. Greene's indoctrination was more compressed. In his first three novels he explored the possibilities of historical romance, introspective narrative, and conventionally poetic prose in as many years. In so short a space there is little internal change, and when a change did come in his fiction it was a radical one. Twelve months after *Rumour at Nightfall*, just after he had turned twenty-eight, Greene published his first "entertainment," *Stamboul Train* (1932). It was remarkably different from anything he had done before. Its setting was contemporary. Action, not introspection, adventure, not speculation about it, was the major interest. Greene dropped the device of the divided mind which had embroiled the previous novels, enlarged his cast to a dozen, brought his characters together on the Orient-Express and, using a film technique, kept the point of view, the camera eye, moving rapidly from one to another. It amounted to a fresh start, and as such the novel deserves close examination.

The formula of the train journey imposes a simple, straight-line development on the story. At Ostende, the starting point, short scenes and snatches of dialogue establish a chorus of minor figures, deftly caricatured. Against this background Greene sets two main characters, Myatt, a young Jewish raisin merchant on his way to investigate a shady merger in the Eastern market, and Coral Musker, another passenger who is going "all the way" to join a dance troupe in a Constantinople night club. At each main stop, one or two new characters are introduced and a new thread is woven into the plot. At Cologne the masculine newspaperwoman, Mabel Warren, recognizes in one of the passengers, Paul Czinner, an exiled communist leader who is returning to Belgrade to head a popular uprising, and interest is caught up in the hunt as she tracks him down and tries to trap him into a confession for her paper. At Vienna another theme of pursuit is introduced when Josef Grünlich, a cat burglar, boards the train to escape from the police. The several threads are twisted together at the third stop when the train is held up at the Yugoslav frontier where Czinner is taken by the police with Coral Musker, who is mistaken for his accomplice, and with Grünlich, who is arrested for carrying firearms. Czinner is shot, and his death closes the political intrigue. The thief escapes. Mabel Warren gets her story and saves Coral Musker, taking her back to Cologne as her "companion." The last section of the book brings the remaining passengers safely to Constantinople and the novel neatly to an end. Myatt successfully closes his business deal by merging with one of Mabel Warren's ex-girlfriends, Janet Pardoe, whom he had met on the train and who turns out to be his chief competitor's niece.

From the evidence of Greene's first novels one would say that he had begun his career as a novelist by seizing on

Marjorie Bowen's subject and outlook without reckoning on the importance of the technique that carried them. *Stamboul Train* is the first of his adventure stories to strike the necessary balance between inspiration and artistry, even though somewhat at the expense of the former. The mechanics of the plot are slickly handled. The action is full of suspense and invention. Closely observed detail replaces the former romantic vagueness. Dialogue is abundant and dramatic, revealing more of character through indirection than pages of brooding analysis in *Rumour at Nightfall*. Characters are drawn in a straightforward manner, are absorbed in their own problems, not their author's, and stand with an integrity of their own, independent of everything but their creator's sympathy.

Another important difference is Greene's changed attitude towards adventure. In *Stamboul Train* he accepts the thrills and accidents of plot at face value without apologizing for them or reasoning about the nature or desirability of unusual excitements. If anything, the characters in this novel, unlike their predecessors, are reluctant heroes, taken off guard by adventure, frightened (though not obsessed by fear like Andrews) at the thought of danger and risk. This is clearly seen in their mixed reactions to the experiences that befall them on the journey. For Myatt the trip initially holds no romance. His mind is absorbed with columns of figures and details of the business that awaits to be settled in Istanbul. At first Coral Musker intrudes unwanted on his calculations. Then he begrudgingly accepts the possibility of a quick sexual adventure of the kind he is used to in London. He is surprised to find Coral different, surprised to discover that she is a virgin, surprised almost into thinking that she loves him, and he even makes an unsuccessful attempt to rescue her from the frontier police. But little by little she fades from his memory, and the thought of an adventure in love dissolves in the familiar routine of business, in the affluence and ease of a good

113

hotel in Constantinople, and before the prospect of a profitable liaison with his rival's niece.

Coral herself feels nothing but apprehension at the
thought of the journey which represents only a longer trek
than usual from one poorly paid job to another. At Ostende
she is cold, hungry and sick, embarked on "the unwanted,
dreaded adventure of a foreign land." Her hard life makes
her suspicious of the Jew's kindness, and she gives herself
to him unsentimentally as the inevitably exacted return for
a favor. Hope stirs briefly when she senses something more
than casual pleasure in Myatt's attentions: "Intimacy with
one person could do this—empty the world of friendships
. . . make the ordinary world a little unreal and very unin-
teresting. . . ." But when she is separated from him at the
Yugoslav frontier and is violently thrust into Dr. Czinner's
adventure of which she understands nothing, gradually
and sadly the hope that Myatt will come back for her dies:
"Her thoughts returned with a stupid fidelity to Myatt. . . .
But she was aware all the time that there was no quality in
Myatt to justify her fidelity. . . . She wondered for a moment
whether Dr. Czinner's case was not the same; he had been
too faithful to people who could have been better served by
cunning. She . . . thought again without bitterness or criticism, it just doesn't pay."

Mabel Warren's attitude towards adventure is the hard-
shell journalist's. She knows that if fidelity doesn't pay,
sensationalism does. She has spent her life "forcing dramatic phrases on to the lips of sullen men, pathos into the
mouths of women too overcome with grief to speak at all.
There wasn't a suicide, a murdered woman, a raped child
who had stirred her to the smallest emotions; she was an
artist to examine critically, to watch, to listen: the tears
were for the paper." And though she is briefly stirred to
sympathy for Czinner, she sticks to her job—to get a scoop
for her editor. To her the story is worth a raise to four
pounds a week.

In this descending scale of cynical attitudes towards adventure, Grünlich is the lowest. Occasionally he brags to himself of his ingenuity in escape, but he is too stupid and self-centered to speculate on the nature of his experience and, after all, his motive for embarking on the Orient Express is the most primitive: to save his own skin.

I have left Dr. Czinner to the last because he most nearly resembles Greene's earlier romantic heroes. Yet here again Greene has refused every temptation to provide him with faith in adventure. True, he is returning to Belgrade to lead a revolution and hopes, like Oliver Chant, that it will overthrow tyranny and relieve the poor and oppressed. But he carries his hopes wearily and acts out of a sense of sad devotion and forlorn duty rather than with any heroic flourish. Greene accentuates his age, his tiredness, his longing for rest, and the indignities he has had to suffer as master of a boys' school during his exile in England. Mabel Warren finds that he "reeked of failure." Almost with relief he discovers before reaching Vienna that the revolt has been premature and has already been crushed. And he keeps on to certain capture from a dull desire to share in the failure of the defeated. Even his arrest provides no opportunity for heroism. After sentencing him to death, a bored police officer lets him speak his mind but his only audience is a couple of stupid guards. " 'I think I shall be of more use dead,' " he ends defiantly. "But while he spoke, his clearer mind told him that the chances were few that his death would have any effect." His dying, at any rate, hidden in an empty shed beside Coral Musker who cannot grasp any of the issues at stake, is simply one of ugly, incoherent, unedifying pain. When one compares this end to Andrews' melodramatic suicide or Michael Crane's passing into light in *Rumour at Nightfall,* one can measure the distance Greene had covered. In *Stamboul Train* even the adventure of death is viewed ironically.

The only reason Greene has given for this change is the

shock administered by Swinnerton's review, which, as I have pointed out, is to lay a great deal of responsibility on a not very perceptive piece of criticism. If Swinnerton's sarcasms acted as an irritant, the circumstances surrounding the composition of *Stamboul Train* had as much to do with the change. After the "inexplicable success"[1] of *The Man Within,* the sales of the last two novels had been very small. Greene's contract with Heinemann's was on the point of expiring, and with it his hopes for a literary career. The "entertainment" was conceived to revive them. It was to be a quick book, designed for popular taste. Greene hoped that it would be a financial success, not only as a novel but also as a potential script, and he has admitted that its form and setting were decided with a view to film adaptation.[2]

Writing to these conditions imposed the kind of discipline Greene needed to escape from the esoteric and derivative style of *Rumour at Nightfall.* Obliged to curb his romantic and poetic inclinations to meet the demands of a popular modern formula, he now became acutely aware of the importance of technique to the novelist, and the first of his many book reviews for *The Spectator* which began to appear about this time clearly reflect this new preoccupation. He now abandoned Conrad and took up James.[3] With Percy Lubbock's *The Craft of Fiction* as his guide—a book which exerted "an enormous influence"[4]—Greene began to study James's prefaces and to apply "The Lesson of the Master," seeing the value of a complex technique behind which the writer could deploy the obsessions which drove him to write. "Behind the barbed network of his style," Greene wrote of James, "he could feel really secure himself."[5] Another writer who helped him make the transition from Conrad to James, and from whom he learned a great deal, was Ford Madox Ford. Greene recognized him as a first-rate critic of the novel,[6] as "the best literary editor England has ever had,"[7] and as "incontestably our finest living novelist and perhaps the only novelist since Henry James to contribute much technically to his art."[8] His fidelity to Ford at a time of general critical neglect testifies to his new interest in the mechanics of his craft.

Having taken a firm resolution to submit his inspiration to close technical control, Greene could now look back and draw some useful precepts from his own errors. These he applied in his *Spectator* criticism. We find him, for example, rating "the horde of subjective novels," calling them "novels of escape: delicious day-dreams in which the writer is enabled to utter all his complaints and bafflements aloud."[9] Several times he refers to "that blurred edge which is caused by the author's own emotion about his characters taking the place of the characters' emotions about each other."[10] He finds the defect of one novel to be that "the author shares the hysteria of his subject,"[11] and much later, on the same theme, writes of "the embarrassment caused by the pulse of a private excitement. It is like the effect of a damp enthusiastic handshake from a stranger."[12] In contrast, he praises a novelist for writing "from the level of her characters,"[13] and commends Julian Green for his "sense of control," for that "firm line which he draws around his subject which is never crossed even by the thoughts of his characters."[14] To the damp enthusiastic handshake he opposed "the hard objective tragic sense one expects from Mr. Bates."[15]

He now became particularly wary of the lures of poetic fiction and romance, writing of a Du Maurier novel: "Everyone is more than life-size; every action is overburdened with significance"[16] pronouncing the next week: "symbolism should be insinuated, it should appeal to the reader unconsciously,"[17] condemning "numinous words,"[18] "the finely fleshed phrase,"[19] and "conventionally poetic prose which seems to be struggling between the claims of romantic verse and psychological truth,"[20] and preferring a style which was "bare, lucid, without literary echoes."[21]

This sample of critical opinion, taken within a few years of
Rumour at Nightfall, gives some idea of the change in
Greene's attitude once he had become persuaded that "the
interest in the technicalities of his art . . . can alone prevent
the mind dulling, the imagination losing power. Nothing
else can enable an author to approach each new book with
sustained intellectual excitement."[22]

Paralleling this new emphasis on technique which permitted him to see his own early work objectively came the
crystallization of his novelist's point of view, "that most
precious thing to a writer . . . not the result of mannerisms
but of an inalterable attitude."[23] Disillusionment was the
keynote of his own emerging outlook, and he began to read
disillusionment into all the writers he had learned from.
Now, and not before this, I think he could truly say that he
had assimilated what he had intuitively grasped in Marjorie
Bowen's *The Viper of Milan:* "Shame, cowardice, deception
and disappointment. . . . Human nature not black and white
but black and grey."[24] It was at this time that he began to
uncover the bedrock under the glossy surface of Stevenson's novels. Although he had given up reading Conrad, he
could now assess his value more coolly, seeing him as "a
romantic poet . . . working in the medium of prose fiction"[25]
and distinguishing in his novels "the ironic sense of an
omniscience and of the final unimportance of human life
under the watching eyes."[26]

Even more influential was the fact that he found cor-
roboration for his point of view in the works of his new
masters in technique. "The approach to life is the same
with all these three," Ford Madox Ford had written to
James, Conrad and Stephen Crane; "they show you that
disillusionment is to be found alike at the tea table, in the
slums and on the tented field."[27] And Greene wrote in turn
of Ford that "he had never really believed in human happiness. . . . The little virtue that existed only attracted
evil."[28] In Henry James he discovered "a sense of evil, re-

ligious in its intensity,"[29] and wrote of James's "fine nose for corruption, his persistent tragic awareness of deceit in human relations."[30] "Deception," he concluded, "was Henry James's prevailing theme,"[31] and he described his novels as "a long record of human corruption."[32]

The new sense of solidarity with these writers was very important to Greene, but literary considerations alone rarely determine a writer's style and outlook, and to complete this analysis of the change between *Rumour at Nightfall* and *Stamboul Train* one must look outside literature. "I suppose that most men sooner or later arrive at a stock-taking time of life,"[33] Greene wrote in one of his earliest reviews in April, 1932. "It is a period which coincides with the realization that life is no longer an unlimited adventure." In his own case added years, disappointment, even the threat of failure as a novelist certainly played their part in deciding a more mature attitude. For the first time, too, because of the depression and social unrest at home and in Europe, Greene began to see a reflection of his private anxieties in the world of public affairs. His first three novels had belonged, like Mauriac's, to a lyric phase when he was engrossed in his own drama and was mainly concerned to test the validity of his own perceptions and sensitivity. In *Stamboul Train*, together with the new objectivity in approach gained through greater technical control, there was the first evidence of a social conscience which grew increasingly important in the following novels, a sense that what the author was describing was not just a highly personal matter, but the common lot.[34] "The consciousness of one's time is the shaping and restraining element in creation," he wrote in 1934 in an article attacking aesthetic novelists and "pure" storytelling. "It is like the pressure of air upon the body. . . . I can imagine no prose . . . which does not suffer by its divorce from social consciousness."[35]

Finally, in *Stamboul Train* the sense of disillusionment itself seems to have dropped from the theoretical level where it tended to be high-pitched and overstated to what one might call the level of practical suffering. Greene's characters are saved from being simply caricatures in this novel by a central tenderness in their author's attitude towards them. All the rebuffs Myatt has suffered because of his Jewish blood; Mabel Warren's grotesque, hopeless infatuation with Janet Pardoe; the cheapness and roughness that has been Coral Musker's daily diet; Czinner's long experience of deception and failure—the author's sensitivity to all these things conditions the sensationalism, artificiality and violence of the adventure on the Orient Express. It is through their inadequacies that the characters come to life, through their unhappiness that we find a means of sympathizing with them. They have all been hurt by life, and this is an experience, one feels, that Greene himself, for all his precocious "terror of life," must have first felt deeply sometime after the writing of *Rumour at Nightfall.*

In his own terminology, Greene had moved into the phase of "The Unhappy Man." In the next novels he continued to explore the lives of characters who, like the passengers on the Stamboul train, were caught up in an unwanted adventure. To consolidate his new attitude and point of view, he experimented in different techniques of objectivity. Under the tutelage of James and Ford he also became much more form-conscious. His development along these lines, as well as his changing concept of the relationship between realism and poetry in fiction, can be traced by analyzing his next novel and his literary criticism of the period.

The design of *It's a Battlefield* (1934) was more complex than the straight linear development of the train journey. The scene was London, the pattern a spiral. On the periphery—on the "outer circle" as Greene calls it with double intent, referring to the London underground and inferring Dante's hell—lie the impersonal institutions, the prison, the match factory, the newspaper office. As Greene describes each of these places, which he does with great vigor and irony, he closes the circumference by underlining the similarities between them. The divisions in the prison—rather like those of a boys' school—Block A for new boys, special privileges in Block C for seniors, are reduplicated in the factory where the silence imposed by the roaring machines parallels the silence imposed by the prison authorities. The assembly-line automation in the factory is compared to the mechanical processing of news in the offices of a great daily where Conder, the journalist, watches his exclusive story "disappear in the hands of a messenger down the stairs. Soon it would be leaden type and soon a column of print, and twenty-four hours later it would be pulp." Individual destinies swallowed up in the machinery of modern society is the unstated theme which is carried in this descriptive technique.

After situating three main characters in these surroundings, Greene turns the reader's attention to the inner circles of the city and to the interplay in the lives of eight people from widely different milieus, all of whom are concerned with the fate of a communist bus driver who has killed a constable in a party clash with the police and is sentenced to be hanged. Greene traces the movements of these characters with careful accuracy, street by street, describing the different quarters of the city in great detail, emphasizing with the slight technical pressure of a repeated phrase or a shared observation the places where their trajectories cross.

Little by little coincidence draws the characters closer together and at the same time Greene draws us gradually down to the inmost circle, into the loneliness of each individual mind. Yet this loneliness, too, is a link, a shared characteristic. To take but one example—the most outstanding perhaps—Conrad Drover, the condemned man's brother, who is driven by desperation and frustration to take an insane kind of revenge on the law, is continually though subtly likened to his intended victim, the Assistant Commissioner of Police. Both men are bachelors leading solitary lives, hesitant and awkward in their relations with others, clinging doggedly to their jobs as the only security in a confusing and hostile world. Between Drover in his glass-walled cubicle in the insurance office—feeling the resentment of the junior clerks, perplexed in his relations with his brother's wife, moved to act but not knowing how —and the Assistant Commissioner in his office in the Yard —nagged by his knowledge of his subordinates' dislike, uncertain of his responsibilities in the Drover case, unable to meet the mind of his only friend, Caroline Bury—there is a bond which draws them irresistibly together in the climax of the story. It is a bond of unhappiness, uncertainty and loneliness, in short, a bond of common humanity which they both share, incidentally, with the condemned man in his prison cell. This is just one example, but all the coincidental contacts between characters in the novel are strengthened by similar bonds. In this way the design of the novel becomes more than just a clever device imposed externally because it functions as a metaphor for Greene's meaning. In *It's a Battlefield*, by means of structure and a consistent if unstated point of view, he achieved the kind of artistic success that he had tried to realize in the early novels by direct statement and the use of a poetic vocabulary.

By the time of *It's a Battlefield*, Greene had left behind any doubts he had had about devoting his life to literature and was working very hard to build up a reputation. It is not commonly known just how industrious he was at this time. In the two and a half years from the appearance of *Stamboul Train* in December, 1932 to the publication of *England Made Me* in June, 1935, he wrote two novels, started a third, prepared a volume of short stories, edited a collection of essays entitled *The Old School*, went on a three-months' expedition on foot into the jungles of Liberia to get material for a travel book, *Journey Without Maps*, and found time to review over two hundred books for *The Spectator*, whose "Fiction" chronicle he wrote every other week for a year and a half during this period.[36]

These reviews, as I have already stated, are an interesting running commentary on his own current work, for Greene's is a creative writer's criticism and he is prone to see his own artistic interests reflected in the work of other novelists. Beginning on a somewhat superficial level, he quite often paid tribute to a book he liked by borrowing a name from it for one of his own characters. Thus Mr. Kalebdjian, the Armenian hotel manager in *Stamboul Train*, is taken from G. Reitlinger's *A Tower of Skulls*, which Greene considered to be "the most amusing travel book since E. Waugh's *Labels*."[37] And Baines, a West-African builder referred to in Leonard Barnes's *Zulu Paraclete*,[38] gave his name to the hero of Greene's long short story "The Basement Room." Other examples are of greater consequence. He was impressed by George Soloveytchik's biography of the Swedish industrialist *Ivar Kreuger*[39] and used many details from it to build up one of the main characters, Krogh the match king, in *England Made Me*. Some time before *It's a Battlefield*, he enthusiastically reviewed William Marsh's *Company K* and quoted a long passage from its preface, in which Marsh spoke of arranging the contents of his book on a wheel and spinning the wheel until the different parts "were recreated and became part of the wheel, flowing towards each other, and into each other; blurring and then blending together in a composite whole, an unending circle of pain."[40] Greene may not have borrowed Marsh's pattern for *It's a Battlefield*, but there is a similarity; and there is no doubt that he read this book with close attention, for in the same review he wrote admiringly of "the skill which even minor German novelists seem to possess of letting contemporary affairs into their novels without sacrificing a pattern." He prefaced *It's a Battlefield* by a quotation from Kingslake; but another from *The Gates of Hell*, a Catholic spy story by Eric von Kühnelt-Leddihn, which he gave at length in a *Spectator* review in December, 1933, might have served as well:

The enemy is camped not only in front of us, but within us, so that our battlefield is doubled. . . . And the saddest part of it is that we are all merely a fragment of a sector of the infinite firing line; we never see the end. One day or another we are born, in the midst of a hail of shots; somewhere or other we find ourselves placed in the firing line; we battle for a few decades; and then in some way we go down under fire.[41]

He not only drew material and inspiration from other books and from his own immediate experience (a trip to Scandinavia which he reported on in *Living Age* in January, 1934[42] gave him the setting for *England Made Me*, and impressions of his first airplane flight gave him another scene for the novel), he also turned his hand to portraits from life. Caroline Bury in *It's a Battlefield* is modeled on the literary patroness Lady Ottoline Morell, and Mr. Surrogate in the same novel owes his name to *Brave New World* and takes certain traits of character from John Middleton Murry. These various examples show how eclectic Greene had become once he abandoned the historical novel and turned his attention outward to the contemporary scene.

His concern for objectivity is also revealed in his general critical approach. Several times in these reviews he used Conrad's definition of art: "A single-minded attempt to render the highest kind of justice to the visible universe."[43] He also quoted Chekov: "Fiction is called artistic because it draws life as it actually is. . . . A writer is not a cosmetician, not an entertainer: he is a man bound under contract by awareness of his duty and his conscience."[44] And he approved Henry James's statement: "Catching the very note and trick, the strange irregular rhythm of life, that is the attempt whose strenuous force keeps Fiction upon her feet."[45]

And here it is appropriate to clear up a misapprehension. Although Greene called certain of his novels "entertainments," designating by the word books that "do not carry a message,"[46] it is wrong to underestimate on this score the seriousness of his artistic purpose which remained consistently high. In his reviews he belabored the writers of "popular" fiction, distinguished between true novelists and "entertainment purveyors,"[47] and fell in with Ford Madox Ford's suggestion that critics should use the word "nuvels" to describe stories they could not treat seriously as art.[48] This is what Greene had to say as early as 1933 on the subject of fictional entertainment in the vulgar sense:

It is odd at first thought that stories written purely for entertainment are almost invariably dull; less odd when one considers that the aim of fiction is to present the truth as honestly as possible, that the mind persistently demands in a story something it can recognize as truth, while the aim of the entertainer is very different (sometimes flattery, sometimes excitement) and his methods are almost invariably deceitful.[49]

Whatever he wrote, novel or entertainment, Greene's aim remained "to present the truth as honestly as possible," and the novel remained for him "the most important of contemporary art forms."[50]

But for all his emphasis on objective truth he recognized too that "verisimilitude is not enough"[51] for a work of art. "Is it wrong to demand of a novel poetic value?" he asked. "I can think of no novel that has survived more than a few publishing seasons without it," and he praised Duhamel's *Le Notaire du Havre*, finding that "what is said is always strictly relevant and true to objective life but the words echo, they have the evocative quality of poetry."[52] In the same vein he wrote of "the accumulation of objective detail (in Chekov) of which the real importance is that it precedes a sudden abandonment of objectivity."[53] He felt that it was not enough for an artist "to render the highest kind of justice to the visible universe" unless the word "visible" included the private vision,[54] and he defined as the final justice of James's art not his realism but his sense of pity, " 'The poetry is in the pity.' "[55] He now cited as "qualities without which a novel cannot survive: a deep poetic sensibility and extreme technical ability."[56]

To clarify what Greene understood by poetic value in fiction at this time will lead us to consider several other formative influences on his work and will introduce some new terminology. It will show a shift in interest from romantic to metaphysical poetry and from the nineteenth century novel of adventures to Jacobean melodrama. Concurrently, the problem of how to control melodramatic material arises, and this in turn leads to a preliminary discussion of the importance of a consistent poetic, not to say religious point of view against which to display the melodramatic material. But to introduce these questions in Greene's own terms, I would like to quote a rather long passage from a review of Conrad Aiken's *The Great Circle:*

The method of the novelist and the poet is more similar than is generally allowed; the same form of criticism is often applicable to both. Henry James found it possible to criticize *The Ring and the Book* as a novel, and it would be impossible to treat *A la recherche du temps perdu* or *The Waves* without reference to their poetic content. So the best explanation of Mr. Aiken's subtle and important novel will be found in Mr. Eliot's essay on "The Metaphysical Poets":

". . . it appears likely that poets in our civilization, as it exists at present, must be difficult. Our civilization comprehends a great variety and complexity, and this variety and complexity, playing upon a refined sensibility, must produce various and complex results. The poet must become more and more comprehensive, more allusive, more indirect, in order to force, to dislocate if necessary, language into his meaning. . . . Hence we get something which looks very much like conceit—we get, in fact, a method curiously similar to that of the metaphysical poets."

As Mr. Eliot found that the way to revitalize contemporary poetry, which was dying of the romantic tradition, was to go

back to earlier and unexhausted influences, so Mr. Aiken, aware
of the equally blind alley into which the novel had been led . . .
has chosen, instead of the verbal experiments of Mr. Joyce, to
cast back to the metaphysical poets, the Jacobean dramatists. . . .

After mentioning some of the possible models—Ford,
Tourneur, Webster—Greene concluded: "This is to beat
a new road; one man cannot do it, and it is to be hoped that
Mr. Aiken will find fellow workers."[57]
Let us follow up the several strands of Greene's thought
in this passage. First there can be little doubt that he considered himself one of the fellow workers. In his next review of an Aiken novel, this time *King Coffin* (1935), he
restated his admiration—"he is perhaps the most exciting,
the most finally satisfying of modern novelists"—and
passed him into the company of James: " 'Henry James
went ahead fearlessly, irretrievably into regions where few
are found who care to follow him,' " he wrote, quoting
Herbert Read, and added, "Mr. Aiken is one of the few."[58]
Greene, in his own way, was another. He described
James as "a metaphysical poet working in the medium of
prose fiction,"[59] and found in his work the combination of
"a deep poetic sensibility and extreme technical ability."
It was from James that he had learned the need, as Eliot
stated it, to become "more comprehensive, more allusive,
more indirect," and James's novels, too, could be described
as poetic in terms of Ford Madox Ford's definition, as representing, "not the power melodiously to arrange words but
the power to suggest human values."[60] But as much as he
owed to James, there was a rift between them of more than
years. James was mundane, punctilious, intellectual, theatrical; Greene's instinctive inclinations were popular, racy,
melodramatic, cinematic. And while Greene could profit-
ably use James's example to check his own early impulsiveness, once he had gained a certain technical mastery himself, he was to look elsewhere for literary models closer to
the root of his own inspiration.

It is for this reason that he was drawn so strongly to the Jacobean dramatists. They supplied violence and excitement together with a complex and vivid style which reposed on a metaphysical foundation. Greene had been attracted to seventeenth-century literature as early as his Oxford days, and his *Spectator* reviews reveal him to be something of a specialist in the period. In 1924 he had compared Walter de la Mare's prose style to Webster's[61] and had written of the seventeenth century as "the only period in our literature where the intellect definitely plays a small part as compared with the emotions and we do not feel the lack."[62] In 1934 he returned to this comparison and described de la Mare's *A Froward Child* as Jacobean in style and Jacobean in its horror.[63] Later still, in his short literary history, *British Dramatists* (1942), he implied a parallel between modern times and the chaotic early years of the seventeenth century—"violent, mad, miserable, without point,"—writing of the early Webster, Ford and Tourneur as "a group who share a kind of dark horror, a violent moral anarchy which seems to have followed the Elizabethan age like a headache after a feast." He particularly singled out the later Webster "because he emerges . . . far enough from the darkened intellectual world to organize." Organizing meant not only describing this world in vivid realistic detail—he praised Webster's "surrealistic style . . . the keen, pointed oddity of his dialogue"—but also, in the metaphysical sense, describing it in the light of the most basic common concerns of human existence which, although they might not be expressed in terms of a creed, were religious in nature. Greene described Bosolo in *The Duchess of Malfi* as "an exile who has not quite forgotten, a prisoner who knows by his own fate that there is such a thing as liberty— that is why Webster is an incomparably finer dramatist than Tourneur."[64] He struck the same note in reviewing a third of Walter de la Mare's books, *The Wind Blows Over*, in 1936:

Death is more inevitable than social change and causes more hourly misery than poverty, and we should welcome one artist who is less concerned with politics than with human fate. Our awareness of life bears a direct relation to our awareness of its end and to those of us . . . who have pushed the future into the background, the injustices, miseries, inequalities lying over life must be the present reality. But that will not alter the fact that it is *we* who are escaping, who are not listening to the deepest human instinct . . . who are deceiving ourselves by thinking death less important than a change in government.[65]

Finally, in an earlier article he had made the same point in slightly different terms, objecting to the aesthetic novelists because they were incapable of introducing into their work "the ruling passion of their time." "To remove the moral consciousness from the Victorian novel, which in effect the aesthetic novelist did," he wrote, "was to leave it weak indeed, as weak as the Jacobean play without its questionings on death and eternity."[66]

Questions of influence are delicate matters and it is tempting to overstress Greene's indebtedness to the Jacobeans. But this much is certain, that, in a modern idiom, Greene's subject was equivalent to theirs, and that he attempted to approach it in the same manner. The common problem centers in the term, melodrama, and Greene gave a good deal of thought to a suitable definition of the genre, to its limitations, and to means of enriching and controlling it. In a film review in *The Fortnightly* in 1936 he aired the problem in these terms:

Perhaps . . . the term melodrama should only be used disparagingly for failure: for violence insufficiently explained. *Othello* uses melodramatic material but it is not a melodrama. Now the stage has to transform melodramatic material by depth of characterization or by placing the individual drama in its general setting. It is less the characterization of *The Duchess of Malfi* than the vividness of the corrupt Italian scene which "explains" the violent material. . . .

And deploring the poverty of language on the modern stage Greene suggested that the cinema, which was largely taken up with melodramatic material, also possessed the means of transforming it.

It is easier to work in pictures than in words and the film possesses an advantage over the stage when genius is absent. . . . The camera, because it can note with more exactness and vividness than the prose of most living playwrights the atmosphere of mean streets and waterfront cafés and cheap lodgings, gives the story its setting, its authenticity, the violence is explained and therefore ceases to be melodramatic.[67]

That was one aspect of the problem. The artist, in this case Hitchcock, needed "a documentary eye" to transform his melodramatic material, and we have seen how in the early thirties Greene was concerned to train his own vision in this discipline. From *Stamboul Train* on, his novels are crowded with sharply etched detail, often presented without comment as a kind of literary montage. And paralleling this new attention to the facts of his novel (which did not exclude a vigorous display of social consciousness), was a new emphasis on character. Perhaps "depth of characterization" is not quite the right term to apply to this aspect of Greene's art in these early novels, but he was becoming interested in portraying character objectively, not just as a projection of his own private problems. In a preface to R. K. Narayan's *The Bachelor of Arts,* Greene praises his "complete objectivity," stating: "This complete freedom from comment is the boldest gamble a novelist can take. If he allows himself to take sides, moralize, propagandize, he can easily achieve extra-literary interest, but if he follows Mr. Narayan's method, he stakes all on his creative power. His characters must live, or else the book has no claim whatever on our interest."[68]

There was yet another way, besides the creation of a vivid and realistic general setting or attention to character, in which Greene felt that the artist could "transform" melodramatic material, and it takes us back from the question of objective disciplines to that of the poetic quality which Greene required in prose fiction. The artist could enrich his melodrama by setting it in a philosophical or religious framework. This is what Chapman did with his "difficult metaphysical treatment of melodrama."[69] Webster and Walter de la Mare had done the same. And Greene examines this method most thoroughly in an essay on Henry James written in 1935 in which he pays the master the compliment of treating him as a fellow worker in melodrama. "Life is violent and art has to reflect that violence," Greene wrote.

The novel by its nature is dramatic, but it need not be melodramatic, and James's problem was to admit violence without becoming violent. He mustn't let violence lend the tone (that is melodrama): violence must draw its tone from the rest of life; it must be subdued, and it must not, above all, be sudden and inexplicable. The violence he worked with was not accidental; it was corrupt . . .[70]

This deep-seated sense of corruption, this "sense of evil religious in its intensity," was one of the two premises on which Greene based his definition of James as "a metaphysical poet working in the medium of prose fiction." The other, related intimately to it, was James's ability to subject his personal obsessive vision to meticulous artistic control. In the same essay Greene compared James to Hardy:

Hardy wrote as he pleased, just as any popular novelist does, quite unaware of the particular problems of his art, and yet it is Hardy who gives the impression of being cramped, of being forced into melodramatic laocoon attitudes, so that we begin to appreciate his novels only for the passages where the poet subdues the novelist. In James the poet and novelist were inseparable.

One name remains in the margin of this discussion of poetic qualities in fiction, but it is not the least important:

that of T. S. Eliot. Greene considered his to be the only contemporary talent capable of writing for the stage with a vividness to match Webster's.[71] He had first read Eliot at Oxford and admired his poetic technique, referring to it as an example of literary montage.[72] Like many others of his generation he absorbed something of Eliot's point of view, and critics in the mid-thirties frequently drew attention to the similarities between the Greeneland of his novels and Eliot's *Waste Land*. But Eliot's criticism was even more interesting to Greene. He stated directly what Greene had been obliged to read between the lines in James: the importance to the creative writer of a strong religious sense. Greene was particularly impressed by *After Strange Gods* which he reviewed for *Life and Letters* in April, 1934,[73] and from which he quoted passages in several subsequent articles. The gist of these was the same and coincided with his conclusions about the Jacobeans: that the strength of metaphysical poets lay in the fact that they had retained a spiritual dimension in their work, and that the loss of this dimension in life and literature in modern times was a crippling one. In his own creative work Greene, like Eliot before him, was to be satisfied for some time simply to describe the wasteland of an irreligious age. But when he did turn to the open treatment of Catholic themes in his fiction, it was as though to illustrate some of Eliot's critical pronouncements. And when, in 1938, he began to give his own critical articles a theological orientation,[74] he again had Eliot's example in mind.

All these elements contributed to the slow formulation of Greene's own style, though all are not immediately apparent in the next novels. In *England Made Me* (1935), for example, which followed *It's a Battlefield* by little more than a year, Greene seems to have returned to some of the obsessional themes and stilted devices of his juvenilia. The pattern of the novel has none of the complexity of the previous one; the number of major characters is reduced to three, and Kate Farrant and her twin brother Anthony represent two sides of one nature something in the manner of *Rumour at Nightfall;* breaking with realism he also makes frequent use of interior monologue, and the novel contains many echoes of his own childhood and adolescent experience.

In reworking these elements from the early novels, however, Greene now applied those precautionary techniques which he had learned would guarantee his story as story and prevent it from becoming little more than melodramatic self-exposure. His progress can be gauged by comparing this novel with his apprentice works. Although Anthony and Kate, for example, may complement one another—she has reliability, efficiency, he has charm; he is clever, she is stable: "He was more than her brother; he was the ghost that warned her, look what you have escaped . . . he was pain . . . he was fear, despair, disgrace"—they exist as individuals. They are drawn together by affection, love, a sense of responsibility, but they exist as separate entities to be so joined, not as mysteriously discoordinated halves of a split personality like Francis Chase and Michael Crane. Their individuality is assured by the detail in which Greene describes their background (Chase and Crane have no past), and it is the same concentration on the bric-à-brac of their present lives (Crane and Chase exist in a limbo of vaguely defined Spanish mountains and nondescript inn courtyards) which gives them necessary objectivity as characters.

The same is true of the other major figure in the novel, Erik Krogh, the Swedish industrialist whose mistress Kate is. At an earlier time he would have been a purely symbolic figure, as was dictator Paul Demassener in his cardboard décor in *The Name of Action.* But by the time of *England Made Me* Greene had profited from his experience in creating somewhat similar types and was able to compound this new character out of Myatt and Czinner from *Stamboul Train* and the Assistant Commissioner in *It's a Battlefield,* together with certain details taken from the life of Ivar Kreuger. Although more sparsely furnished, his life too has density of specification, and he comes sufficiently alive to surprise us often by unexpected reactions.

It is necessary for him to have this vitality for in the plan of the book he is, through characteristics of stiffness, solitude and success, the counterweight to Anthony's charm, facile friendliness and perpetual failure, while Kate holds the balance between them: "She was like a dark tunnel connecting two landscapes." " 'Here' was the twin dials on the gas meter, the dirty pane, the long-leaved plant, the paper fan in the empty fireplace; 'here' was the scented pillow, the familiar photographs, the pawned bags, the empty pockets, home. . . . And 'there' was the glassy cleanliness, the latest fashionable sculpture, the soundproof floors and dictaphones and pewter ash-trays and Erik in his silent room listening to reports from Warsaw, Amsterdam, Paris and Berlin."

To further fill out Krogh's character and prevent him from becoming just one corner of an unconventional triangle, Greene links him to the devoted, unscrupulous cockney thug, Fred Hall, his only remaining tie with his own working class past. In a similar way he reinforces Anthony's shabbiness by associating him with the spider-like little ex-Harrovian, the journalist Minty. But it must be emphasized that, unlike Kapper and Demassener in *The Name of Action*, Hall and Minty exist not as projections of the main characters but as full-fleshed individuals.

By the time of *England Made Me* Greene's style was capable of containing his personal vision. He would go on experimenting and perfecting his technique, but from now on a general form has been developed within the limits of which he will concentrate his talent. (He once defined style as "a confession of limitations" and wrote: "A novelist's technique is always in part a method of avoiding what he finds impossible.")[75] Future development in his work centers mainly around his use of a religious basis for his novelist's point of view. And before examining this aspect of his work I would like to summarize, drawing illustrations from *England Made Me*, those characteristics which crystallized in the novels of the early thirties and which would provide the structural framework for the fiction to follow.

Greene's novel is generally built up on several different levels—political, sociological, psychological—and interest is carried forward on all these planes as they intersect and interact on their way to a complex climax. So it is in *England Made Me* that a shady business deal Krogh is trying to push through on the international market, a young worker's reaction to an injustice his father has suffered in one of Krogh's factories, the risks Kate takes because of her love for her brother, Anthony's sense of exile and homesickness which lead him to desert Kate for Loo (a chance acquaintance from Coventry) and to betray Krogh's secrets to Minty—all sustain interest separately yet all contribute to the final crisis.

It is also a continuing characteristic that these several levels of interest are presented in their most sensational, not to say melodramatic aspects: the political in terms of intrigue, the sociological in terms of violence and crime; the psychological in terms of sex. Quite candidly Greene makes his first appeal with the material of melodrama and the popular thriller, in this way continuing to indulge that taste for excitement and adventure which dominated his earliest work and nourished his desire to write.

But if the excitement remains, Greene leaves the tradition of the thriller and transforms his melodramatic material. He had always refused the successful hero of melodrama and romance. After *Rumour at Nightfall* his characters were even denied romantic despair. Anthony Farrant is one of a long line of "seedy adventurers" and his shabbiness and hollowness and falsity are a kind of check against even failure swelling to heroic proportions.

135

From the time of *Stamboul Train* this seediness is a controlling constant not only in character but in setting. No matter how exotic the locale of the novel (its strangeness calculated to attract like the other sensationalist bait), by revealing its underside Greene naturalizes it and gives it the significance of a general setting by bringing it into his own particular universe. This is done with special purpose in *England Made Me* where the cheap, shoddy, sentimental confusion of Minty's and Anthony's rooms, baggage and minds—of the England that made them—is contrasted to the neat, cold efficiency of Swedish art and life.

An accumulation of vivid detail marks all Greene's work. And it is interesting to note that one of the methods he uses for introducing it in this novel is not naturalistic documentation but can be better described in the terms which he used to approve Arthur Calder-Marshall's technique in *At Sea* (1934), in which the thought sequences he wrote "are closer to the soliloquies of Jacobean drama than to Mr. Joyce's 'stream of consciousness.' "[76] This surrealist treatment of detail is not only an antidote to romantic indeterminateness, but it also helps to establish atmosphere and to circumvent melodrama by placing the individual drama in the setting of the author's point of view.

Here and hereafter Greene also shows the same respect for the individuality of his characters as for the details of their lives. They usually represent a wide spectrum of human life from multiple points of view. But instead of standing for conflicting ideologies or different facets of human nature as they tended to do in his early fiction—the many in the one—he now lets them stand independently in all their eccentricity and seeks to find—the one in the many— the bond of common humanity that unites them. Anthony's sympathy for the young Swedish worker, Andersen; Kate's thoughts of Krogh: "He's one of us, fighting for his own security like one of us, he's not the future, he's not self-sufficient, just one of us, out of his proper place"; Krogh's dependence on Hall, Anthony's on Loo or Minty—classify all these characters as failures and exiles. They are exiles from happiness, failures in love, imprisoned in loneliness, isolated on the battlefield, uncertain travelers on an adventure that they do not understand.

But here Greene's artistic point of view verges on the philosophical, and its development can be better studied if it is disengaged from technical considerations. And after I have traced the parallel development of Mauriac's mature style and general point of view in the next chapter, I will return to examine the religious background of the two novelists as it influences their creative work.

NOTES TO CHAPTER 5

1. "Author's Note," *The Man Within*, Uniform Edition (London, 1952).

2. Ronald Matthews, *Mon ami Graham Greene* (Paris, 1957), p. 150.

3. Greene's first critical reference to James is in "Servants of the Novel," *The Spectator*, CXLIX (August 20, 1932), 238-9.

4. "Lettre-Préface," Paul Rostenne, *Graham Greene: Témoin des temps tragiques* (Paris, 1949), p. 11.

5. "Walter de la Mare's Short Stories," *The Lost Childhood*, p. 79.

6. "The Facts of Fiction," *The Spectator*, CXLVIII (January 23, 1932), 117. This is the first of many references to Ford.

7. "Ford Madox Ford," *The Lost Childhood*, p. 90.

8. "The Landowner in Revolt," *The London Mercury*, XXXV (February, 1937), 422-3.

9. "Fiction," *The Spectator*, CLI (October 20, 1933), 538.

10. "Fiction Chronicle," *ibid.*, CLI (October 6, 1933), 455.

11. "Inflation," *ibid.*, CXLVIII (June 4, 1932), 807.

12. "Thunder in the Air," *ibid.*, CLIX (August 6, 1937), 252.

13. "Fiction," *ibid.*, CLI (August 11, 1933), 198.

14. "Fiction," *ibid.*, CL (February 10, 1933), 194-6.

15. "Thunder in the Air," *ibid.*, CLIX (August 6, 1937), 252.

16. "Fiction," *ibid.*, CL (April 7, 1933), 508.

17. "Fiction," *ibid.*, CL (April 21, 1933), 579.

18. "Fiction," *ibid.*, CLII (May 18, 1934), 786.

19. "The Seedcake and the Lovely Lady," *Life and Letters*, X (August, 1934), 524.

20. "Fiction," *The Spectator*, CLI (December 1, 1933), 820.

21. "Fiction," *ibid.*, CL (April 7, 1933), 508.

22. "Fiction," *ibid.*, CLI (November 3, 1933), 638.

23. "Short Stories," *ibid.*, CLVII (October 9, 1936), 606.

24. "The Lost Childhood," *The Lost Childhood,* pp. 15-16.

25. "Fielding and Sterne," *ibid.*, p. 60.

26. "Remembering Mr. Jones," *ibid.*, p. 99.

27. F. M. Ford, "The Old Man," *The Question of Henry James,* ed. F. W. Dupee (New York, 1947), p. 70.

28. "Ford Madox Ford," *The Lost Childhood,* pp. 90-91.

29. "Henry James: The Private Universe," *ibid.*, p. 21.

30. "Background to Henry James," *The Spectator,* CLIII (September 28, 1934), 446.

31. "Fiction," *ibid.*, CL (May 5, 1933), 654.

32. "Henry James: The Private Universe," *The Lost Childhood,* p. 21.

33. "Taking Stock," *The Spectator,* CXLVIII (April 2, 1932), 485.

34. "The Job of the Writer," Interview with Philip Toynbee, *The Observer* (September 15, 1957), p. 3.

35. "The Seedcake and the Lovely Lady," *Life and Letters,* X (August, 1934), 517, 521.

36. This pace continued. For the sake of statistics, in the ten years from 1932 to 1942 he published 44 essays and stories in the *Spectator* alone, plus 384 review articles covering 860 books, films and plays.

37. "The Unsentimental Journey," *The Spectator,* CXLVIII (June 11, 1932), 837.

38. "The Waste Land," *ibid.*, CLIV (June 7, 1935), 986.

39. "Gold Bricks," *ibid.*, CL (March 3, 1933), 308.

40. "Fiction," *ibid.*, CL (April 7, 1933), 508.

41. "Fiction" *ibid.*, CLI (December 15, 1933), 910.

42. "Oslo and Stockholm," *The Living Age,* CCCXLV (January, 1934), 424-6.

43. "Spanish Gold," *The Spectator,* CLIV (June 21, 1935), 1076. "Henry James," *The English Novelists,* ed. Derek Verschoyle (London, 1936), p. 231.

44. "Fiction," *The Spectator,* CLI (September 22, 1933), 380.

45. "The Seedcake and the Lovely Lady," *Life and Letters,* X (August, 1934), 517.

46. "The Art of Fiction," *The Paris Review,* No. 3 (Autumn, 1953), p. 32.

47. "Fiction," *The Spectator,* CLII (June 1, 1934), 864.

48. "Cinema," *ibid.*, CLV (July 26, 1935), 150.

49. "Fiction," *ibid.*, CLI (September 22, 1933), 380.

50. "Creative Reading," *ibid.*, CLIV (February 15, 1935), 256.

51. "Fiction," *ibid.*, CLII (April 6, 1934), 551.

52. "Fiction," *ibid.*, CLII (May 18, 1934), 786.

53. "Short Stories," *ibid.*, CLII (March 16, 1934), 424.

54. "Henry James: The Private Universe," *The Lost Childhood*, p. 21.

55. *Ibid.*, p. 29.

56. "Fiction," *The Spectator*, CLII (May 18, 1934), 786.

57. "Fiction," *ibid.*, CLI (October 20, 1933), 538.

58. "Arabia Deserta," *ibid.*, CLV (November 8, 1935), 788.

59. "Fielding and Sterne," *The Lost Childhood*, p. 60.

60. "Cinema," *The Spectator*, CLVIII (February 26, 1937), 356.

61. "Ding-Dong Bell," *The Oxford Outlook*, VI (June, 1924), 244.

62. "Verse in Bloom," *ibid.*, VII (February, 1925), 106. Review signed Hilary Trench.

63. "Short Stories," *The Spectator*, CLIII (Book Supplement, November 23, 1934), 28.

64. *British Dramatists* (London, 1942), pp. 23-4.

65. "The Dark Evening," *The Spectator*, CLVII (October 2, 1936), 556.

66. "The Seedcake and the Lovely Lady," *Life and Letters*, X (August, 1934), 524.

67. "Middle-brow Film," *The Fortnightly Review*, CXXXIX (March, 1936), 304-5.

68. "Preface," R. K. Narayan, *The Bachelor of Arts* (London, 1937), pp. vii-viii.

69. *British Dramatists*, p. 22.

70. "The Lesson of the Master," *The Spectator*, CLIV (April 26, 1935), 698.

71. "Middle-brow Film," *The Fortnightly Review*, CXXXIX (March, 1936), 304.

72. "The Cinema," *The Spectator*, CLV (September 27, 1935), 462.

73. "After Strange Gods," *Life and Letters*, X (April, 1934), 111-13.

74. "The Art of Fiction," *The Paris Review*, No. 3 (Autumn, 1953), p. 38.

75. "The Seedcake and the Lovely Lady," *Life and Letters*, X (August, 1934), 519.

76. "Fiction," *The Spectator*, CLIII (September 7, 1934), 336.

6

MAURIAC AND *LE ROMAN NOIR*

One of the links between Greene and Mauriac is the sharp division between their juvenilia and the first of their mature novels, in Greene the break between *Rumour at Nightfall* and *Stamboul Train,* in Mauriac a less dramatic but nonetheless decisive change which declares itself in *A Kiss for the Leper* (1922). Mauriac has called this novel the first of his books which he does not blush to acknowledge. His blushes may in part rise from his memory of the chorus of mockery that greeted his first published works. Rachilde in the *Mercure de France* described the hero of *Young Man in Chains* as "a young calf," another critic called him "a foetus," and Paul Souday gave up a full page in *Le Temps* to nip this tender young talent in the bud.[1] The most favorable of the early reviews must have been just as hard to swallow, for they tended to be of the pious variety and praised Mauriac as champion of "prudence and delicacy" against "the outrageous intemperance in expression" of certain female novelists.[2]

There was indeed little in either of his first two novels to suggest that Mauriac would shortly become an expert in *le roman noir* to rival Colette herself. His second, *The Stuff of Youth*, could not have ruffled the susceptibilities of even his most straight-laced readers. A new cynicism began to enter *Flesh and Blood*, however, largely due to the fact that its composition spanned the years 1914-1920.

At the beginning of the war Mauriac was mobilized in the *Service de Santé*, and until he was discharged for reasons of health in the spring of 1917 he did ambulance duty on the Western Front and in Salonica. He has not written much of the war, but a few journal entries from these years reveal the change he felt it was working in him. The following passage from the spring of 1916 is one of these: "I was that type of young Frenchman who studies for his examinations, stands for a long while with his forehead pressed to the window pane, leafs through anthologies. . . . But all that is over. All that is finished."[3] A little earlier that year he had decided, as an antidote to what he was experiencing, to bury himself in the study of one of his favorite poets, "to relive the life of Maurice de Guérin."[4] Yet a few months later, he wrote in a passage of his journal addressed to André Lafon, a friend and fellow poet with whom he closely identified de Guérin: "The war has killed everything you loved. You need feel no regret for this world, André . . . where your gentleness has become a crime."[5]

André Lafon had been killed in 1915 as had Jean de la Ville de Mirmont, another intimate friend and poet who had shared Mauriac's literary hopes and enthusiasms since Bordeaux days. This loss deepened Mauriac's hatred of the war and hastened the end of the lyric, the Guérinean phase in his own work. There is little doubt that these deaths had as much to do with the change from sad nostalgia to passionate melancholy in Mauriac's works as any of his own experiences of the war.

Mauriac also suffered generally from "the massacre of an élite,"[6] the loss of some of the most vigorous and original writers of the younger generation—Alain-Fournier, Ernest

Psichari, and Charles Péguy, to mention only a few whose work Mauriac admired. This blow was felt widely, but especially in Catholic circles. Just before the war Mauriac, André Lafon, and some other young Catholic friends had started a campaign "to spiritualize contemporary letters."[7] Through a new literary review, *Cahiers de l'Amitié de France*, for which Mauriac was general secretary, and through an organization of Catholic writers to be known as *Société St. Augustin*, they had hoped to launch a Catholic renaissance in the arts like the one which had been stimulated by Chateaubriand's *Génie du Christianisme* a century earlier. At the outbreak of war the group disbanded. By 1918 it had been so crippled by the deaths of active members and potential leaders that it never reassembled. The survivors found it impossible to regain their initial spirit of militant optimism. And in the general mood of postwar disillusionment and bitterness, they wrote off their plans for a Catholic revival as one more war casualty.

It was not surprising in these circumstances that Mauriac should seek literary affiliations elsewhere, nor that he should gravitate towards the strong group of writers who published in *La Nouvelle Revue Française* (cited hereafter as *N.R.F.*), which for some time had been the boldest new literary review in the country. Ever since its foundation in 1909 Mauriac had read it avidly, "even to the advertisements," he writes. "In literature it was my gospel."[8] After a four-year suspension during the war, the review started up again under the editorship of one of Mauriac's acquaintances from Bordeaux, later to become his close friend, Jacques Rivière. Under his direction it continued its reputation for daring experiment, liberal opinion and artistic freedom, and in the early postwar years Mauriac's chief ambition was to associate himself actively with this group.

To this end he began to take a much more professional attitude towards his work. He reviewed more widely for various publications and brought out his first book of critical essays under the title *De quelques coeurs inquiets* in 1920. He became drama critic for the *Revue Hebdomadaire* and wrote thirty-five theater reviews for this weekly from 1920 to 1923. Besides publishing nine novels, in the next ten years he wrote a dozen book-length essays on moral, religious and literary subjects, two biographies, a book of short stories, and a new volume of verse. His industry was rewarded. With its notice of *Flesh and Blood* in December, 1920, the *N.R.F.* began a series of increasingly enthusiastic reviews of his successive novels. *The River of Fire* was serialized in its pages beginning in December, 1922, and thereafter Mauriac was asked to write frequent reviews of current fiction for the magazine, and became its regular drama critic for the first half of 1925. These are the bare facts of his introduction to "the group with which I felt myself to be in closest sympathy."[9]

About the time of *A Kiss for the Leper* then, Mauriac found himself a somewhat senior member (he was thirty-seven) of the postwar generation. He had set his feet in a new path and could look back aggressively on his long apprenticeship as to a time when he had been "bogged down."[10] And indeed, his rise to fame during the next decade, from *Grand Prix du Roman* of the Academy in 1925 to a seat in the Academy itself in 1933, was little short of meteoric. In identifying himself with the avant-garde he now came under the sway of its current gods. He refers to himself as being "profoundly sensitive to the atmosphere of the generation of which Gide, Marcel Proust and Freud were the intellectual leaders,"[11] as being "infected"[12] by the spirit of his age. "Almost despite himself, a novelist is a witness," he writes, "who records the most secret collective tendencies."[13] Although he disagreed fundamentally with many of the views of Gide, Proust and Freud, and never ceased to harry them from a Catholic position, he found their influence inescapable.

In another sense, however, this contact was a liberation,

for it enabled Mauriac to free himself from provincialism and to feel that he was taken up in the main intellectual current of his times, even if only to swim against it. And while I do not intend to deal extensively with the influence of these three writers, they do provide, as Mauriac says of Gide, "a point of reference and comparison"[14] for the analysis of the novels of the twenties that follows. It is appropriate at first, then, to review briefly the characteristics which Mauriac shares with these writers.

Mauriac's first reference to Gide dates from 1910.[15] He exchanged letters with him in 1912,[16] knew him later as a friend, and throughout his career considered his work, both critical and creative, of highest importance. Mauriac saw in Gide "a case of terrible sincerity"[17] and felt that through his influence, in his novels and in the *N.R.F.*, "the passion of sincerity"[18] had become "the virtue of our generation."[19] Gide's role, he allowed, was "to throw light into the dark abyss of human nature and to collaborate in our examination of conscience."[20] He was aware that "this compulsion to dissimulate nothing of oneself" might be "a false sincerity—the most subtle form of lie,"[21] might be "nothing but a fiction and a mental concept,"[22] and he suspected that Gide's doctrine of total abandon to experience might lead to "dreary eroticism."[23] But he also capitalized on the artistic licence secured by Gide, to ferret out the most equivocal themes and subjects for his own novels, and deeply shared Gide's penchant for daring introspection. "The thing that is peculiar to modern man," he wrote, "is his taste for suffering, and for suffering in the dark. . . . We have made ourselves a bed of our own anguish."[24]

The example of Proust supported this assessment. Mauriac called him "a prisoner of the self,"[25] admired the audacity of his exploration of the inner world, and approved his method of observing life, "not from behind his monocle," like Paul Bourget, but by making it "surge up within himself."[26] He had met Proust in 1918,[27] and while

144

writing *Questions of Precedence* had decided to use *Du Côté de Chez Swann* "not as a model but as a stimulant to help me to get out everything I have to say."[28] More generally, he felt indebted to Proust for having opened a whole new field of investigation to the modern novelist: "He flatters us with the hope," wrote Mauriac, "that in violating the most secret part of the human being we will advance in knowledge even further than the men of genius who have preceded us."[29]

Freud, whose work had first been interpreted to the French public in the *N.R.F.* in the early twenties, supplied the modern perspective for the novelist's research. Independently Mauriac had come to believe that "Christianity does not take sex seriously enough into account,"[30] and had written that "the mystery of salvation lies in the mystery of the flesh."[31] In his novels he was to conduct a long and detailed analysis of sexual aberration, and although he wrote of "the exaggerated importance" that his generation had given to physical love, and spoke of "our partiality for considering everything in this light, for explaining everything by it,"[32] he did not claim to be innocent of the charge himself.

"Collective or private passions are at the source of every work of inspiration,"[33] Mauriac writes. While it is certain that private passions dominate his own inspiration, he was also deeply involved in the collective concerns of his generation, and the interaction of these two forces can be observed in the following survey of themes of the seven major novels from *A Kiss for the Leper* (1922) to *Lines of Life* (1928) which make up the canon of Mauriac's *roman noir*.

The most clear-cut case of a novel exploiting the theme of sexual passion is *The River of Fire* (1923). This is a study in eroticism, of a casual but insistent carnality in the hero, Daniel Trassis, and of a possessive sensuality in his victim, Gisèle de Plailly. Mauriac had sensitively followed the innocent first stirrings of desire in May Dupont-Gunther in *Flesh and Blood*. Florence in *Questions of Precedence* was a more extreme heroine who had "surrendered to the exigencies of the flesh," who, "obsessed by a craving for the gutter—for her own utter degradation," had taken a succession of lovers and had fallen prey to a strange infatuation with an adolescent. But her self-abandonment is listless, and her neurotic fascination for young Jean Queyries is contrived and unconvincing beside the abnormal sexual passion which holds Gisèle in its grip. Despite her own self-knowledge, despite the firm intervention of a friend, Lucile de Villeron, who is keenly aware of her weakness, despite an uncharacteristic reluctance to act which afflicts Daniel Trassis as his chances for seduction grow certain, Gisèle plunges into the river of fire, abandons herself to "the fury for self-destruction." And her drama is heightened and seconded not only by Daniel's avidity in the chase but, in Mauriac's characteristic fashion, by the collaboration of the whole of nature urging surrender:

In the country, in the season of sunlight and storms, the flesh is subject to the universal law. To fight against it in oneself is to claim the power to hold back the tides, to stop the flowing waters, to hold in check the movements of rivers—of those that chatter gaily down the hills, of those that, all unseen, swell the growing plants with sap.

It is rare that Mauriac lets passion go so far as fulfillment. There is only one *River of Fire* among his novels; there are several which might have been called *The Desert of Love*. His most withering study of sexual frustration is in the novel we have already examined, *A Kiss for the Leper,* where the poor passion born of the marriage of convenience between Jean and Noémie goes through progressive stages of humiliation, disgust, frigidity. But no affair in these novels of the twenties, however passionate, escapes its full measure of anguish and remorse. It is characteristic of his heroes and heroines to suffer all the pangs of love without ever making more than one awkward and embarrassing contact with the beloved which, while it carries all their hopes, irremediably blights them. Thus Dr. Courrèges' long rehearsed declaration of love to Maria Cross in *The Desert of Love* (1925) crumbles into professional platitudes. Through a tactless and brutal gesture, his son, Raymond, also forfeits the chance of enjoying Maria's love. And the disgust which his clumsy assault inspires in her not only chokes off her desire for him but makes Maria want to end her life, so completely had she given herself to him in imagination. The same type of incident is repeated in *Lines of Life* where Raymond's counterpart, young Bob Lagave, makes a drunken pass at middle-aged Elizabeth Gornac. Although her first reaction is one of revulsion and indignation, she discovers, after Bob's accidental death, the full weight of her emotional involvement. "From this profound disruption of all her being, there emerged now into the light of day a love which lay buried in her flesh, which she carried within her like a pregnant woman who does not know at first that she is bearing in her womb a living seed." But her passion is stillborn and after bringing it painfully to light she relapses into sterility: "Elizabeth Gornac had again become one of those dead who are carried down the stream of life."

Referring to Maria Cross and Elizabeth Gornac leads one to consider a peculiar twist to Mauriac's delineation of passion. Nearly all his heroines are attracted to adolescents. Florence, the first of these, elects to be the dupe of her passion in *Questions of Precedence* and chooses young Jean Queyries, the double of her former love, Augustin, in preference to the true Augustin ten years older. "Each for the other was a ghost," writes the narrator, "and each had loved only an ephemeral grace, the spring-time of an hour, that one moment of time when every living being is a god: oh, youth so quickly gone!" Maria Cross falls in love with the image she constructs of Raymond Courrèges as a pure and timid boy, hence her disillusionment when she discovers him to be attracted to her by nothing but animal appetite. In *Lines of Life* Bob Lagave's fascination over his Parisian friends is described in these terms: "What they loved in him was their own tarnished youth, now at its last gasp, or already dead, everything which they had lost forever and could now dotingly see reflected in this young creature's ephemeral bloom. It was in some sort of a religion . . . a mystery of which they were the initiates, with its rites, its sacred formulae, its liturgy. Nothing had any value in their eyes but this charm which nothing could replace, which was lost to them forever." And Gisèle in *The River of Fire*, speaking of this desire from the male point of view, says: "It is almost as though men seek in us their own lost innocence."

Pushed to its extreme, this infatuation with adolescence on the part of the woman becomes the terrible maternal passion of *Genetrix* (1923). The mother-complex is never treated as openly or as brutally again after this novel, but it is worth noting that most Mauriac heroines are frustrated of opportunities for maternal affection: Florence is childless; Maria Cross has just lost her six-year-old son, and Elizabeth Gornac cannot love her cold and prudish son Pierre whom she continually contrasts with Bob Lagave. The reverse is also consistent: Mauriac's adolescent heroes are either motherless or sons of mothers who are narrow-minded and insensitive. In fact, anything approaching normality in mother-son relationships in these novels seems only to occur between the elderly and the middle aged, between Dr. Courrèges and his mother, for instance, or between old Maria Lagave and her son Augustin in *Lines of Life*.

When considering the aberrations in love in Mauriac's fiction, one should return to examine in its perspective a phenomenon that was observed earlier: Mauriac's association of love and death. "I loved his memory more than I loved him!" the narrator in *Questions of Precedence* realizes when he meets Augustin again after a lapse of ten years. Instances of love reaching its full stature only after the death of one of the partners are scattered throughout these novels. Noémie in *A Kiss for the Leper* cannot conquer the disgust she feels for her husband until he is under sentence of death, and afterwards remains faithful to his memory. Elizabeth Gornac only realizes her passion for Bob Lagave after he is killed in an automobile accident. And the most striking instance of this ultimate frustration of love is provided in *Genetrix* where Fernand Cazenave frees himself from the domination of his mother's love, which had ruined his marriage, by cherishing the memory of his dead wife, only to find that by her own death his mother again triumphs over his wife and regains the ascendant in his affection.

Faced by a survey like this of sexual themes in Mauriac's novels of the twenties, by such a grim and tortured representation of passion, it is easy to sympathize with Françoise Mallet-Joris' objection that Mauriac never shows a healthy sexual relationship in his fiction.[34] Love, which is an impossible search after lost youth; which, when on rare occasions it comes to the act, is little short of bestiality, later flagellated by remorse; which is never fully consummated except after death—all the evidence necessary to bring down a verdict of the most astringent Jansenism seems ready here to hand. One might choose as epigraph for this part of Mauriac's work the harsh words of Pascal that he has often cited: "Marriage is the lowest of all Christian states, vile and unpleasing to God,"[35] or the passage from Bossuet which he uses to preface *The River of Fire*: "Oh God . . . who shall dare speak of this profound and shameful wound that nature bears, of the lust which binds the spirit to the flesh by bonds which are at once so tender and so violent."

But it is relatively useless to docket these novels with the tag "Jansenistic." Rather than halt the analysis here one should try to penetrate below appearances and discover what leads Mauriac to describe passion in these terms. If one considers the repetitive themes in his fiction, it is obvious that he uses physical love only as a symbol for more basic convictions about the human condition. In illustrating this I will draw evidence from one novel alone, *The Desert of Love,* although any other major one would serve as well.

The frustrated passion of Raymond, Dr. Courrèges and Maria Cross stands, in fact, for a larger frustration: the impossibility of real contact between any two human beings. It is not only that the Doctor's love for Maria is fumbling and incoherent, unrealized and even unexpressed; he is also incapable of reaching his son, Raymond. "The practitioner, who a few moments later would be speaking eloquently, authoritatively, to his helpers and his students, had been vainly seeking, for months, some word that should provoke a response from this being of his own flesh and blood. How was he ever to succeed in blazing a path to this heart which was bristling with defences? . . . This powerlessness to give expression to his feelings was his habitual martyrdom." The same gulf separates the Doctor at times even from his mother: "How could he expect this old lady to understand the music that sounded so deep down in her son's heart, with its lacerating discords? He was of another race than hers, being of another sex. They were separated more surely than people living on two different planets." And when he has resigned himself to repress his passion for Maria Cross, to have done with suffering, "with beating, like a prisoner, against the walls of his cell," and seeks to find some comfort in renewing contact with his wife, the same impenetrable barrier rises between them: "From somewhere beyond the wretched fabric of words that she had built up, from somewhere beyond the wall that her vulgarity had erected, with ant-like patience, day by day, Lucie Courrèges could hear the stifled cry of a man who was buried alive, the shout of an imprisoned miner, and deep within herself, too, another voice replied to his, a sudden tenderness fluttered."

But Lucie's movement of intuitive tenderness, too, is frustrated, and all that the last quotation suggests, is that the doctor's case is not singular, and that the family itself, instead of being the symbol of a fertile solidarity is better represented by the central image of the book, each of its members lost and alone in the desert of love. Maria Cross, too, is alone. Her situation, "without husband, children, friends," ostracized in Bordeaux because she is a kept woman, dramatizes her interior solitude by placing it in a social setting. And in another context Mauriac speaks of "the desert which separates classes as surely from one another as it does individuals."

This nightmarish sentiment of incommunicability is at the root of all the mutations of normal love in this and other novels. Passion is blindly followed because it promises a release from solitude. Hope of contact constantly denied, or even frustrated in the act itself, refuses to die but swells into the possessive instinct. The life of the imagination in these circumstances becomes unnaturally active, easily turns morbid, or feeds on impossible dreams of innocence and youth regained.

Undoubtedly Freudian theory has influenced Mauriac's treatment of the passions, but he has interpreted it in his own fashion, putting it to the service of his most intimate personal vision, using it as a symbol to express one of those fundamental obsessions of which, Greene writes, the creative writer is a victim.

That Mauriac has chosen such an important field of imagery as that of sexuality to embody this sense of inescapable solitude suggests how profoundly it affects his imagination. In fact the sentiment of the complexity and mystery of each individual destiny shapes his whole approach to the creative act. In *The Desert of Love* the doctor expresses his author's dilemma: "Which of us is skilled enough to compress a whole inner world into a few words? How is it possible to detach from the moving flow of consciousness one particular sensation rather than another? One can tell nothing unless one tells all." And Mauriac again makes one of his characters speak for him when in *Thérèse Desqueyroux* (1927) the heroine wonders how she should explain herself to her husband: "What should she tell him? What should be her first confession? Could mere words ever make comprehensible that confused, inevitable conglomeration of desires, determinations and actions unforeseen? . . . Bernard . . . was never satisfied until he had labelled, ranged, and set aside each separate emotion, ignoring their gradations, the subtle nexus of their interchange. How make him see with his own eyes that world of shifting forms in which Thérèse had lived and suffered?" Of course, these questions are rhetorical. It is the novelist's job to find the means by which Thérèse shall explain herself, if not to her husband, at least to the reader. But it is significant that Mauriac so deeply feels the difficulty, not just of explaining, but of preserving the mystery of Thérèse's personality. So deeply in fact that he betrays himself into taking the reader momentarily into his artistic confidence.

Together with the haunting sensation of inevitable solitude stands another instinctive conviction that heightens the tragic tension of Mauriac's view of human destiny: that although we may never make successful contact with others, their influence on our lives is indelible and incalculable. "We are, all of us, moulded and remoulded by those who have loved us," he writes in *The Desert of Love*, "and though that love may pass, we remain none the less *their* work—a work that very likely they do not recognize, and which is never exactly what they intended. No love, no friendship can ever cross the path of our destiny without leaving some mark upon it forever." And in *The River of Fire* he states: "Can we ever wholly escape from the influence of those who feel for us a deep and burning love? Those who love us leave on our characters a more lasting mark than those we love."

A third basic concept that shapes Mauriac's creative vision is the thought that his heroes and heroines are not only marked for life by their unhappy passions or by the hopeless love that others bear them but that, further back, their destinies are shaped by other complex and uncontrollable factors. "By the time we are beginning to grow up the future is wholly formed in us," he states in *The Desert of Love.* "On the threshold of manhood the bets have already been played; nothing more can be staked. Inclinations planted in our flesh even before birth are inextricably confused with the innocence of our early years, but only when we have reached man's estate do they suddenly put forth their monstrous flowers."

In summary, what one might call the triple bondage of Mauriac's tragic figures, not only in *The Desert of Love* but in all the novels we have been examining, could be stated in these terms: They are condemned to a solitude to which they cannot resign themselves: they are the victims of those they despairingly love or of those who love them but whose love they cannot return; and they are cast in this destiny by undecipherable forces which they have not willed and cannot change.

These are basic themes in Mauriac's fiction, early and late. The titles of his novels—*Young Man in Chains, The Desert of Love, Lines of Life, The Loved and the Unloved*—provide a capsule commentary on this aspect of his work. As we have seen, the same preoccupations echo through his account of his own childhood like a buried leitmotif. Indeed, these obsessive themes spring from such a primary source in Mauriac that what he once said of Gide might be applied to himself. "Gide, like Jean-Jacques and Chateaubriand," he writes in *Mémoires Intérieurs,* "will live on only in those books of his which treat directly of himself: *Si le grain ne meurt* and the *Journal,* because it is he who interests us, and not the creatures of his invention. But I was forgetting that he remains the one and only subject of his imaginative books: *L'Immoraliste* is he: *La Porte étroite* describes the cerebral love on which he built the painful ambiguity of his life. . . . His presence in everything he wrote gives a lasting quality to his work."[36] But one must make certain reservations when applying the sense of these words to Mauriac. One cannot question that the matter of his fiction comes from the deepest levels of his own experience (conscious and unconscious), nor can one mistake the genuine note of anguished concern in the novels that bespeaks that complete sincerity towards oneself which Mauriac felt he shared with Gide. But although the drama in his novels may be inspired by his own besetting obsessions, it remains dramatic. In a sense that Gide does not, Mauriac remains a novelist, a creator of character. The creatures of his invention do interest us as much if not more than their creator. There is usually a thorough fictional transposition in his work. Thérèse is not Mauriac; Mauriac becomes Thérèse, Dr. Courrèges and Bob Lagave; and even his most personal insights are related in his fiction to a reality external to himself.

This can be seen if one investigates some of the causes that Mauriac gives for what we have called the triple bondage of his characters. Though they may seem to be shackled in loneliness and lovelessness by their author's Jansenistic sense of predestination, there are always other factors present in the novel which account for and fix their fate. For the sake of detail, I would like again to consider these external forces in one novel alone, *Thérèse Desqueyroux,* simply adding that one might apply the same observations to any other of Mauriac's major novels.

Thérèse is a typical Mauriac heroine, "condemned to an eternity of loneliness," "fated to carry loneliness about with her as a leper carries his scabs." Although she does not visualize release in terms of physical love, in her isolation she dreams of making a human contact that would free her. Her "salvation" lies in the hands of her husband, Bernard. "If only he would take her in his arms and ask no questions. If only she could rest her head on a human shoulder, could weep knowing the comfort of a warm and human presence!" But though she feels that this "one gesture and one only would solve everything," she knows that "Bernard would never make it." Like so many other of Mauriac's heroines, Thérèse is condemned to the desert of love. Even as a girl she knew that relations between two people were made up mainly of suffering. "I suffered and made others suffer too, I delighted in the pain I caused—and knew at the hands of my friends." And in a passage already quoted, Mauriac suggests that in the purity of her childhood her criminal adult life was already being formed. "Our destiny, once we begin to isolate it, is like those plants which we can never dig up with all their roots intact. . . . Even our childhood is, in a sense, an end, a completion."

But besides this *a priori* condemnation, there are other reasons for Thérèse's sentence to a life of solitude. In fact, what seals her destiny is the aridity of her environment. She is passionate, curious and imaginative by nature, yet finds herself surrounded by people who are inert, materialistic, submissive to the dull routine of their lives. Her husband belongs to "the blind implacable race of simple souls"; he is one of those "who are incapable of love." Like the older generation, he is guided by the belief that "property is the most solid good this life can show, and that the only true value of existence is earthly possessions." He gives great importance to the idea of family and family honor, but only because this institution is the surest custodian of wealth, and indeed, his marriage to Thérèse, like every other one described in the novel, is purely a business proposition.

The fact that Thérèse becomes a criminal (through a complex series of circumstances she is led, partly by accident, to attempt to poison her husband) puts her at the mercy of these hostile forces. She feels "the whole powerful machinery of the family" set in motion to crush her. Among the many images which describe her punishment, in one of the most vivid she sees "in imagination the cage with its innumerable bars, each of which was a living person, a cage full of eyes and ears in which she would have to spend the whole of her life, her chin on her knees, her arms clasped about her legs, waiting for death." She is only preserved for the sake of the family name and because she bears a Desqueyroux child: "I lost all sense of being an individual person. In the eyes of the family I was merely a species of vine-shoot. All that mattered was the fruit of my womb."

The inquisition of the family is tacitly upheld by a suspicious, narrow-minded, reactionary society which is represented as "a vast smooth surface of ice beneath which the minds of all here are frozen." And the metaphor continues to include Thérèse. . . . "Through an occasional hole the water shows black. That means that someone has disappeared after a violent struggle. But the crust reforms above it. . . . Here, as elsewhere, the destiny of each one of us is unique, yet one must submit to the dreary common lot. A few resist and that accounts for those dramas which the family agrees to keep shrouded in silence. . . ." And out beyond society the mournful landscape of heath and forest stands for the encircling aridity.

All this is thrown into relief by the fact that Thérèse is a criminal and an outcast. But is her imprisonment the result of, or the cause of, her crime? Judged by the standards of family and society she is a monster, but in the novel Mauriac reverses the judgment and condemns family and

society as monstrous. Thérèse's crime is, in the end, that
she is different, that surrounded by people "who really
know nothing whatever about love," whose lives are "remarkably like death," she is one of the passionate, one of
those "who are really alive." And this, as much as any overt
act of hers, condemns her to ennui, to solitude, to the impression of being encaged, of being "a trapped animal," of
tasting "death in life." One cannot call Mauriac a social
novelist, or an objective chronicler of the life and times of
his segment of provincial society; but he does interpret the
drama of his tormented heroes and heroines in terms of
family and society. And setting his novels firmly in this
framework differentiates his mature technique and point of
view from that of his earlier novels. Like Greene, in another
tradition and with other means, he applied the necessary
lesson of objectivity. But, again like Greene, he used the
process for a poetic end, not a sociological one. He took certain characteristics of the race of bourgeois Girondin land-
owners that he knew well to clothe his personal vision, just
as he made seasonal and climatic changes in this part of
the country reflect the interior dramas of his characters.

Once again, one is impressed by his dependence on the
past and on childhood experience. He has, as he says of
Proust, not observed the world from the position of a privileged and detached commentator, but has made it "surge up
within himself." He has recreated it from the rich sources
of memory. Yet Proust has a certain objectivity that Mauriac lacks, and comparing the two sends one back to consider what we have called the essentially lyric quality of
Mauriac's creation. "Beginning with *A Kiss for the Leper*
and *Genetrix,*" writes Mauriac, "no character in my novels
will be drawn from the books of other authors, nor, from
this time on, will I ever again attempt a self-portrait in one
of my novels, because I will be everywhere present in these
creatures which have issued from me, and this presence,
which has been held against me, will be the hallmark of

their authenticity."[37] Elsewhere he has stated that "none of the characters in *A Kiss for the Leper* is invented," but adds, "it is their destiny that I invent."[38] This projection of himself into the living model, the personal stamp he imposes on his description of landscape (which remains, nonetheless, an accurate portrayal), the special use he makes of his observations of provincial society—or for that matter of Freudian psychology—this marriage, in short, of his own imaginative vision and objective reality, "this mysterious union between the artist and the real world,"[39] is the essence of his poetry and the secret of his art.

This is a good place to challenge some misreadings of his work. Judging Mauriac solely from a documentary point of view, critics like Martin Jarrett-Kerr or Joseph Majault have easy sport of listing repetitions in his work,[40] repetitions of scenes, situations, character types, even of certain phrases and sentences. In fact, repetitions so abound in Mauriac's fiction that to beat them up and shoot them down with the blunderbuss accusation that they are "careless echoes"[41] can hardly be called sport. But if one considers them not as indicative of a "failure in imagination"[42] but as consciously accepted limitations, they give some valuable insight into his creative method. The mere repetition of place and family names in his work suggests the narrow limits of his field of investigation. But this is not a criticism, for we do not expect of Mauriac an exhaustive Balzacian reconstruction of his province as much as an intense and personal evocation of scenes which have long been familiar to him and which have a private poetic significance. We should not be surprised, then, to find the stream La Hure in half a dozen different novels, to discover that he uses *Le Lion Rouge* as the name of an inn with certain emotional connotations in several novels, or to find incidents, rooms, objects and people taken over straight from his own childhood and transposed, not once but many times, in his fiction. To accuse him of lack of invention because he makes repeated use of these elements is as futile as convicting him of monotony because his descriptions of nature are limited to his native vineyards, heaths and forests.

The fact is that Mauriac is not a writer who renews himself by accumulating new experience. He must have lived with his subject for a long time, must have made it part of himself before he can bring it to life in his fiction. This can be seen most dramatically in his creation of character. Mauriac has referred to Maria Cross as "a sketch for the character whom I already carried in me and who was to become Thérèse Desqueyroux,"[43] and we have traced certain traits of Thérèse's character back even further to heroines of the earlier novels, to Florence in *Questions of Precedence*, and Gisèle of *The River of Fire*. Not only did Thérèse take form very slowly in Mauriac's imagination, she is also a famous example of a character who lived on in her creator long afterwards. Even after she had been lodged in a novel in 1927, he was led to introduce her briefly into *That Which Was Lost* (1930), to write two short stories, "Thérèse at the Hotel" and "Thérèse and the Doctor" (1933) about her as "attempts to 'sound' the obscure periods of her life,"[44] and finally to devote another entire novel, *The End of the Night* (1935) to trying to imagine her end. "Wearied of ten long years within my brain she craved for death,"[45] is the way Mauriac expresses it. This long parturition is typical of his creation. Some minor characters are fixed statically in his memory and he simply reverts to them when he needs them. There is nearly always a peasant servant in the novels which are situated in the Girondin countryside. Often he scarcely bothers to change her name; in *Genetrix* she is called Marie de Lados, in *Lines of Life*, Maria Lagave, and in a slightly different role in *The Unknown Sea* she is called Maria Cavaillès. Other characters are introduced briefly in one novel and they develop to play a major role in the next: Daniel Trasis, mentioned in *A Kiss for the Leper* becomes Daniel Trassis, hero of *The*

River of Fire. One of his Parisian friends, Raymond
Courrège, becomes Raymond Courrèges in *The Desert of
Love.* Jean Péloueyre is not only hero of *A Kiss for the
Leper* but is mentioned as one of Daniel Trassis's childhood
friends in *The River of Fire*, and the Péloueyre family appears somewhere in the background of nearly every one
of the following books.

Obviously such repetitions are not inadvertent but correspond to some active inner necessity. Mauriac does not
write a *roman fleuve* but works with a limited number of
elements, a few decors and a family of characters which he
reassembles in different combinations in novel after novel.
And in the long run these self-imposed restrictions testify
more to his sincerity as an artist than to a lack of invention.

The same thing is true of Mauriac's themes. He works, as
Greene once said of Conrad, with a few simple ideas.
"These ideas are not enough for a reformer," Greene wrote,
"but they are amply sufficient for an artist."[46] Mauriac's
novels of the twenties support this observation. The few
simple themes that we have been considering in this chapter cross and recross each other in various combinations,
now dominant, now set in a minor key. So frequently do
they recur in the novels from *A Kiss for the Leper* to *Lines
of Life* that one can scarcely speak of "development" in his
fiction. For the sake of clarity one might say that in each
of the earlier of these novels Mauriac treats one theme in
particular: *A Kiss for the Leper*—sexual frustration; *Genetrix*—maternal domination; *The River of Fire*—eroticism;
The Enemy—the adolescent lover—while in the three late
novels of the period, in *The Desert of Love, Thérèse
Desqueyroux*, and *Lines of Life*, these themes are all present in some degree in each novel, are interwoven, are handled more subtly and are complicated by the introduction
of new material. But that is an oversimplification. And if
one considers, as we have done, the underlying themes in
his work, it is the unity of his fictional universe that im-
presses one, and not its superficial variety.

This unity will be further stressed when we come to examine the following novels. It is particularly evident in the novels of the middle and late thirties where, despite the fact that his wish is to renew himself by experimenting in the techniques of the English novel, the same patterns, themes and characters recur with such force and persistency that in the last novels of all he finally reverts to the style of the novels of the twenties.

Rather than speak of development, it is fairer to quote Mauriac himself who writes: "With *A Kiss for the Leper* I found my style,"[47] giving to "style" the global sense of the novel's theme, characters and setting. This chapter has set out some of the fixed characteristics of that style in Mauriac's mature fiction, in what can roughly be called his *roman noir*. But throughout the analysis I have made one significant omission, so significant, in fact, that so far I have only been able to give a partial idea of his creative vision. I have expressly neglected to speak of these novels in terms of Mauriac's religious insights and convictions. But having shown their general configuration, the letter of his art, as it were, I can now turn to examine its spirit in comparing the Catholic themes in his fiction with those of Graham Greene.

NOTES TO CHAPTER 6

1. "Ma rencontre avec le 'Mercure,' " *Mercure de France,* No. 999-1000 (December 1, 1946), 187.

2. C.-F. Caillard, "Les Poèmes," *Revue du Temps Présent* (December 2, 1909), p. 385.

3. "Journal d'un homme de trente ans," *Oeuvres Complètes,* IV, 228. (*Oeuvres Complètes* is hereafter cited as *O.C.*)

4. *Ibid.,* p. 227.

5. *Ibid.,* p. 232-3.

6. H. Clouard, *Histoire de la littérature française du symbolisme à nos jours,* II (Paris, 1947), 7.

7. "La Rencontre avec Barrès," *O.C.,* IV, 198.

8. *Ibid.,* p. 201.

9. *Ibid.,* p. 202.

10. "Préface," *O.C.,* VI, iii.

11. *Paroles en Espagne* (Paris, 1930), p. 55.

12. *Le Tourment de Jacques Rivière* (Paris, 1926), p. 33.

13. *Paroles en Espagne*, p. 55.

14. "Hommage à Charles du Bos," *Qu'est-ce que la littérature* (Paris, 1945), p. 115.

15. "Notes sur le *Dominique* de Fromentin," *Revue Montalembert* (March 25, 1910), p. 208.

16. *La Mort d'André Gide* (Paris, 1952), p. 30.

17. "Préface," A. Gide, *Lafcadio* (Paris, 1924), p. 7.

18. "La Vie et la mort d'un poète," *O.C.*, IV, 405.

19. "La Vie de Jean Racine," *O.C.*, VIII, 58.

20. "Préface," A. Gide, *Lafcadio* (Paris, 1924), p. 12.

21. "La Vie et la mort d'un poète," *O.C.*, IV, 405-6.

22. *Ibid.*, p. 406.

23. *Ibid.*, p. 403.

24. "René Bazin," *O.C.*, VIII, 485.

25. "La Vie et la mort d'un poète," *O.C.*, IV, 407.

26. "Du côté de chez Proust," *O.C.*, IV, 276.

27. *Ibid.*, p. 277.

28. "Journal d'un homme de trente ans," *O.C.*, IV, 250.

29. "Le Roman," *O.C.*, VIII, 273.

30. "Dieu et Mammon" *O.C.*, VII, 329.

31. "Journal d'un homme de trente ans," *O.C.*, IV, 262.

32. *Paroles en Espagne*, p. 55.

33. "Préface," *Trois Récits* (Paris, 1929), p. xxvii.

34. Françoise Mallet-Joris, "Les personnages féminins dans l'oeuvre de François Mauriac," preface to François Mauriac, *Le Désert de l'amour* (Paris, 1959), p. 35.

35. *The Desert of Love and The Enemy* (London, 1949), p. 194.

36. *Mémoires Intérieurs*, p. 177.

37. "Préface," *O.C.*, X, ii.

38. "Préface," *O.C.*, I, ii.

39. "Le Romancier et ses personnages," *O.C.*, VIII, 288.

40. See Martin Jarrett-Kerr, *Mauriac* (London, 1954), pp. 25 ff.; Joseph Majault, *Mauriac et l'art du roman* (Paris, 1946), pp. 108-10, 153-4.

41. Martin Jarrett-Kerr, *op. cit.*, p. 25.

42. *Ibid.*, p. 28.

43. "Préface," *O.C.*, II, iii.

44. "Preface to 'Thérèse and the Doctor,'" *Thérèse* (London, 1947), p. 118.

45. "Preface to 'The End of the Night,'" *Thérèse*, p. 163.

46. "Cinema," *The Spectator*, CLIV (February 14, 1936), 254.

47. "Préface," *O.C.*, I, ii.

7

CATHOLIC THEMES:
THE DIVERS MOVEMENTS
OF NATURE AND GRACE

At the height of their careers both Mauriac and Greene
turned to an overt treatment of Catholic themes in their
fiction. Mauriac recognizes three of the novels which immediately follow *Lines of Life*—*That Which Was Lost*
(1930), *The Knot of Vipers* (1932), and *The Dark Angels*
(1936)—as "the only novels of mine that unreservedly
merit the title of 'Catholic novels.' "[1] Greene's Catholic fiction includes the four major novels from 1938 to 1951—
*Brighton Rock, The Power and the Glory, The Heart of the
Matter*, and *The End of the Affair*.

The decision to experiment with religious themes was
prompted in each case by a complex combination of circumstances. The change in Mauriac's fiction was associated
with what he calls "a religious crisis" which built up "between 1925 and 1930 and reached its peak in *Souffrances et
Bonheur du chrétien*."[2] In its original form, this essay,
which was published the same year as *Lines of Life*, was
part of a series in which a number of contemporary writers
had been asked to comment on texts from the classics. It
was a commissioned work, the author who had been as-

signed to Mauriac was Bossuet, and the essay was at first called *Supplément au traité de la concupiscence de Bossuet*. It also appeared in October, 1928 in *La Nouvelle Revue Française* under the short title *Souffrances du chrétien*.

It dealt in general terms with themes already enunciated in Mauriac's fiction: with man's solitude, his servitude to the passions, and with the inevitable failure of his inevitable pursuit of pleasure. Mauriac opposed to his diagnosis of the ills of modern man the harsh strictures of Catholic morality as set out by Bossuet, and closed his essay with the bitter observation: "The least sin is a crime against God and that is why Christianity condemns all men to become saints."[3] Abstracted from the concrete context of the novel, the note of habitual anguish was pitched even higher than usual, and it reflected a keenly felt personal debate. "Once the work was finished," writes Mauriac, "it remained unresolved, a solemn question planted in the middle of my life. Around a work of circumstance, a commissioned task, a whole destiny crystallized out."[4]

Most of the essays during the next two years (there were no novels), echo the apparent incompatibility between the claims of the flesh and the spirit, between nature and Grace, which tormented Mauriac at this time. Writing a biography of Racine (1928), he reviewed the whole problem in literary terms, opposing to the writer's obligation to paint a convincing picture of the passions, the Christian's obligation to avoid provoking scandal and to beware of endangering the souls of his readers. He concluded that it was not given to every writer to follow Racine's example and burn his books. "Racine did not know the meaning of religious anxiety," he wrote, "and found his faith again when he needed it."[5] And for his own part he contrasted to the demands of his faith the exigence of the literary vocation which compelled the writer to write. "We have yet to see the miracle of a writer whom God has reduced to silence,"[6] he commented wryly.

Gide seized on the ambiguity in Mauriac's attitude and

wrote him an open letter to congratulate him on having struck "a reassuring compromise" which permitted him "to love God without losing sight of Mammon."[7] This malicious challenge provoked a book-length reply from Mauriac, *Dieu et Mammon* (1929), in which he reviewed his religious education and the present state of his faith and traced its relationship to his work as a novelist. In this apologia he took up many points he had made in an earlier critical study, *Le Roman* (1928), in which he had dealt with the theory of the novel and the responsibility of the Catholic novelist.

Finally the crisis passed when Mauriac experienced what has been called "a conversion within the faith."[8] He published an essay *Bonheur du chrétien* in the *N.R.F.* in April, 1929, in which he spoke of having known "the joy of a soul who has found peace in a single night." He denounced his "*parti pris* of equivocation," his "determination not to make a choice"[9] between God and Mammon. He wrote that he now believed the law of the spirit to be identical with the law of the flesh sanctified in the Eucharist, and claimed that the whole debate of the Catholic novelist now resolved itself for him in one decision: to purify the source of his inspiration.[10] He reworked a novel begun in 1928, which had tentatively been called *Pygmalion* and which was to have treated the theme of incest,[11] and published it in 1930 as *That Which Was Lost,* his first "Catholic" novel. In 1931 he published *Souffrances* and *Bonheur du chrétien* together in one volume, making some important omissions which partly drew the sting of the former, dropping, for example, the closing passage on the Christian's being condemned to sanctity and substituting Léon Bloy's: "There is only one sadness, not to be a saint."[12] The sense had not changed, but the attitude was quite different.

Although the "conversion" may have had great personal significance, when Mauriac turned to fiction again the change was not recorded in his novels as much as one might expect. They did not vary greatly in theme or in tone from those that went before and, again, the unity of Mauriac's vision was the striking thing, not the development. His general subject was still the world, the flesh and the devil, and there were, as usual, more vipers than doves among his characters. To be sure, certain Catholic themes were now purposely made explicit, but to overemphasize the importance of the crisis of conscience and its resolution in 1928-1930 is to put Mauriac's work into a false perspective. Although I will deal with the Catholic novels in due course then, one of my main concerns in this chapter will be to deal with the continuing religious qualities in Mauriac's fiction, in the *roman noirs* and Catholic novels alike.

The same caution is necessary when studying Greene's Catholic novels. Suddenly, in 1938, with little warning, *Brighton Rock* appeared, a novel which was almost belligerently religious in theme. One is at first tempted to look for a crisis to explain the new emphasis, but on close examination one finds a number of mixed elements contributing to it, and reading carefully back one discovers in the earlier novels many indications of a movement in this direction.

We have already examined some of the factors which forecast this development: Greene's interest in the metaphysical background of the Jacobean dramatists, for instance, supported by Eliot's critical injunctions. Indeed, Eliot's statement,

Most people are only a very little alive; and to awaken them to the spiritual is a very great responsibility; it is only when they are so awakened that they are capable of real Good, but at the same time they become first capable of Evil,

which Greene had quoted in an early review,[13] might have been the direct inspiration for the theme of *Brighton Rock*.

But there were other non-literary influences. One was the trip that Greene made to the interior of Liberia in the first months of 1935. Writing of this experience later, he defined the fascination of Africa as "a religious fascination: the country offers the European an opportunity of living continuously in the presence of the supernatural. The secret societies, as it were, sacramentalize the whole of life . . ."[14] and his avowed purpose in exploring the interior was to get below the "cerebral"[15] level of modern civilization to the more primitive religious roots of human experience.

By the time of a second voyage of exploration to Mexico three years later, his open engagement in Catholic matters was firmly established. He had undertaken the expedition to report on religious persecution in the southern Mexican states for Longmans Green. It was, therefore, a commissioned venture, but the experience moved him deeply, and he has admitted that he first began to "feel" his faith at about this time.[16] What he learned in Mexico did not influence *Brighton Rock,* for he was correcting proof for that novel at the time, but it did give him the material and the Catholic attitude for two of his best books, *The Lawless Roads,* a travel book account of the voyage, and *The Power and the Glory,* the novel that grew out of it.

Between the two trips a gradual confirmation of purpose took place. Greene (who is a convert) explains that in a practical sense growing familiarity with Catholics and Catholicism gave him the necessary confidence to treat religious themes in his fiction.[17] In late 1936, as if following Eliot's dictum, "Literary criticism should be completed by criticism from a definite ethical and theological standpoint,"[18] he began expressly to give his literary reviews in *The Tablet* and *The Spectator* a religious orientation.[19] Finally, there is the question of Mauriac's influence.

As stated in the introduction, I do not wish to press the case for direct influence because the evidence is not convincing. But one can say that Greene's first reading of Mauriac just preceded the first open application of Catholicism in his criticism and fiction.

Also, as we have already seen, Greene was in the habit

of reading with an eye to finding support for his current creative interests, and it may be said that in the mid-thirties Mauriac's novels were better suited to match these than the work of any contemporary English novelist.

The only modern English Catholic who seems to have intrigued Greene is Frederick Rolfe. In 1934 and 1935, when Rolfe's work enjoyed a brief posthumous vogue, he wrote three reviews on this eccentric novelist, self-styled Baron Corvo, who, incongruously in the middle of the solid Edwardian age, had been obsessed in his life and work with a kind of medieval spirituality. Discovering Rolfe, Greene wrote, made one aware of "eternal issues, of the struggle between good and evil, between vice that really demands to be called satanic and virtue of a kind that can only be called heavenly."[20] Here was an example of a man who was really "alive" in Eliot's sense because his realities were less material than spiritual, and Greene wrote that his life illustrated the paradox that "the greatest saints have been men with more than a normal capacity for evil, and the most vicious men have sometimes narrowly evaded sanctity."[21] But it was Rolfe's life that interested Greene more than his art, and to find a novelist who could treat these themes with a technical skill equal to the intensity of his religious vision he had to look outside England. He had to look beyond Rolfe, and even beyond James, for although he had done his best to accentuate James's sense of evil, in the end he had to admit that "neither a philosophy nor a creed ever emerged from his religious sense."[22] In contrast, Greene wrote that "the French novelist continues an uninterrupted tradition of Christian state of mind, thought and style,"[23] and singling out in Mauriac's novels the presence of forces of good and evil that penetrated them and gave an extra dimension to character, he deplored the fact that "in general this sense of the supernatural is banished from the English novel."[24] Undoubtedly, his reading of Mauriac in the early thirties helped to encourage him to change the plan of *Brighton Rock* (which he had begun in 1937 as a simple thriller) and to recast it as a spiritual drama dealing with the metaphysical implications of crime.

Greene's decision to give a Catholic emphasis to his point of view cannot be attributed, however, to a single influence. In fact, his religious sensibility was active long before the appearance of his first "Catholic" novel, and it is necessary now to trace this sensibility back to its origins, comparing it, when appropriate, with Mauriac's religious outlook.

One should immediately note an important difference between the two writers' experience of Catholicism. Greene is a convert; Mauriac was born a Catholic. "That is the drama of my life," Mauriac writes in *Dieu et Mammon,* comparing his religious education to that of two famous French converts, Psichari and Maritain, "I was born in it; I did not choose it; this religion was imposed on me from the day of my birth. Many others have been born in it and have swiftly escaped from it because the inoculation of Faith did not 'take' on them. But I belong to that race of people who, born in Catholicism, realise in earliest manhood that they will never be able to escape from it."[25] To be, as Mauriac puts it later, "a prisoner"[26] of his faith may at first seem to imply a static quality in belief as opposed to the idea of dramatic change usually associated with conversion. But despite the encircling stability, religious questions within the faith always presented themselves to Mauriac's imagination in dramatic terms; and in the chapter in *Dieu et Mammon* where he traces his own spiritual autobiography he describes various stages of infatuation and rebellion, of "sensual devotion"[27] and nagging scruples, of surface doubts and periods of missionary fervor.

These personal conflicts provided themes for several early novels; the state of internal tension they represent found its way into the conscience of all his major heroes; and his saturation in Catholic thought, symbolism and precept gave him a fixed standard for judging the destinies of his characters whether religious concerns entered openly into their stories or not.

Graham Greene's introduction to Catholicism was quite different. Officially, his conversion in 1926 was occasioned by his marriage to a Catholic. He has implied that it was little short of a convenient arrangement,[28] has written that he is "a Catholic with an intellectual if not an emotional belief in Catholic dogma,"[29] and has constantly played down all references to his entry into the Church. His religious background prior to conversion was that of a public school Anglicanism which left no impression on him greater than one of mild scorn. It is also true that none of the novels before *Brighton Rock* (possible exception made for *Rumour at Nightfall*) clearly foreshadows the religious preoccupations of his major novels, and Greene enjoys quoting a letter he received from a Dutch priest who wrote to him about *The Power and the Glory:* "I suppose that even if you are not a Catholic, you are not too hostile to us."[30] But discounting such humorous reticence and tuning to the right wave-length, one can pick up some interesting rumors of religious preoccupations even as early as his juvenilia.

Although no Catholics figure in Greene's first novel, *The Man Within,* Elizabeth is a Christian and Andrews is fascinated by her faith which gives her a courage, calm, and what he is pleased to call "a sanity" which he is lacking. One can see in Greene's rather too reverent portrait of his first heroine an oblique tribute to his newly adopted faith. Andrews' deferential attitude towards Elizabeth is briefly echoed in Oliver Chant's admiration for Frau Weber, a minor character in *The Name of Action* who is praised for the "calm, tender, unquestioning" love she bears her husband and the faith she puts in him and in Providence which makes her "a good wife and a good Catholic." And in the person of Eulelia Monti in *Rumour at Nightfall* Greene again equates a heroine's realistic grasp of the subtleties of love to her familiarity with the mysteries of religion.

In these early novels the Christian heroine always plays opposite a skeptical young hero which permits Greene to underline, rather self-consciously, some of the tantalizing paradoxes of doctrine which he had certainly stumbled over himself during his instruction. Thus Andrews is led to think of Elizabeth's disinterested charity as being "the cold neutrality" of "this damned Christianity." And in later conversations with her, in the same vein of irate mockery, he is led to question many of the articles of her faith: her belief in an afterlife, in the Devil, in the cult of the dead, in the efficacy of prayer, and her moral code based on the concept of self-sacrifice. In short, he is irrepressibly attracted by her belief "in God and all that" and not a little envious.

Although religious questions do not play so large a part in *The Name of Action,* Oliver Chant is fascinated and mystified by a faith he does not share which is no longer unspecified Christianity but Catholicism. A statue of the Madonna on top of the Jesuit seminary sets him puzzling about the strange "unearthly and tender ideal" that she represents. The heroine, Anne-Marie, is a Catholic (which perhaps accounts for her realistic attitude towards love and life), but not overly pious; she does not hesitate to give Chant a lovers' rendezvous in The Church of Our Lady. Here, in contrast to her indifference, Chant is very conscious of being in a place "where God was not a cloudy aspiration but a concrete hope or fear," and he is struck by the "understanding of pain, tenderness and mystery" which he reads in the faces of old women doing the stations of the cross. These incidental references and such a scrap of dialogue as this:

"Have you done nothing wrong, Frau Weber?"
"Yes, but I have been forgiven."
"Are you certain of even that?"
"You are not a Catholic, Herr Chant, I can see that."

which echoes the question and answer formula of the Penny Catechism, betray the convert sensibility.

This is even more pronounced in *Rumour at Nightfall.*

This time two agnostic heroes are plunged into the element of a Catholic country. Through the mind of Francis Chase, the more materialistic of the twin heroes, Greene often compares Anglicanism with Spanish Catholicism.

[There] a gentle, sentimentally sad ringing across the fields, the respectable slow footsteps in the porch, the gossip across the tombstones, and inside the drone of undisturbing prayer. Here men and women would be kneeling on the flags, their faces lifted in adoration of the raised Host, containing what they believed to be the living flesh and blood of God. . . .

Chase's certainties are contrasted to Eulelia's. What he wants from life is success, money, friends; " 'I am certain of what death is—the end.' He suspected that her certainties were very different, made up of crosses and crucifixes, beads and prayers, tortures, flames, fear. . . . She would not be satisfied with the world as it is."

Michael Crane, it will be remembered, represents "heart" to Chase's "mind," and he is more sympathetic to Eulelia's Catholicism. He contrasts Chase's educated uncertainty to the vulgar belief of a Spanish informer: "His friend was, in some sort, the modern world. He was a sceptic who was not even easy about his materialism. But this pimp had a faith, even if it was a wrong faith, and a believer of any kind is a worthy opponent." Gradually, through his exposure to Spanish faith and through his love for Eulelia, Crane becomes a believer. His conversion is staged during another lovers' tryst in a church. I will quote several passages from this scene because of the interesting foretaste they give of some of the themes that Greene develops in the later "Catholic" novels.

It was easy there in the dark, where time did not enter, and the only human voice seemed burdened already with the horror of eternal life, to believe in a living God that men might eat like bread and a soul that could be condemned to consciousness forever. . . .

If there is a God, he thought, if that wafer is flesh and blood, enduring at every communion the actual pain of Calvary, the torture of the nails and the torment of the thief's mockery, a thousand years foreshortened into this moment, may one be allowed to pity God? . . . He felt the inclination to pray, to beseech God on his knees to put an end to His eternal torment, to cease to overwhelm man with such an enormous debt.

A little later Crane thinks of God "risking sacrilege . . . for the sake of humanity," and in the church he sees "a priest brooding on the death of a sinner, the Virgin disclosing to the insentient dark her pierced heart, the Son of God hanging in torture from the cross, paying in agony for His mother's grief, who paid in turn with hers, a circle of endless torment. For whose sake? For mine?" Crane wonders. And after confessing himself to Eulelia, he has a vision of the two of them united in love and faith and joined in "the endless circle of God and the mother of God." This kind of personal exposition of Catholicism, undertaken as much, one feels, for Greene's own benefit as for that of his non-Catholic readers, is the early and rather clumsy expression of a lasting fascination with religious questions.

Mauriac's early novels also contained a good deal of documentary evidence in favor of Catholicism, and in two novels, *Flesh and Blood* and *The Enemy,* he used Protestants or agnostics as foils for his Catholic heroes. In Mauriac's case this fictional testimony was prompted by the missionary zeal of the prewar years rather than by the curiosity of the convert, but the net result was the same. There was the same vein of Catholic snobbery and the same theoretical approach to certain aspects of dogma not yet very well assimilated to plot or character. There was the same failure to amplify and dramatize the religious implications of the story beyond the use of a few striking ideas and a few melodramatic but superficial effects.

To mark the similarities while at the same time respecting the differences between the two, one might compare their first novels, each of which deals with a conversion spurred on by a woman's love. Both *The Man Within* and *Young Man in Chains* are introspective and overwritten, their subject a drama of conscience. Both heroes succumb to the temptations of the flesh and afterwards are won over to a more enduring kind of love sanctioned by religious faith. In each case this love remains chaste and is not put to the test of experience, but both young authors obviously feel bound to plump for the superior merits of a Christian romance.

But here the differences begin to demand recognition. Jean-Paul's conversion is a conversion within the faith, and he discovers after his false liberty of revolt that he is "a prisoner of his Catholic childhood." His whole drama is cast within the compass of Catholicism and Mauriac's description of *Amour et Foi* is documentation of an internal rift. By contrast, in Greene's novel, Elizabeth's faith is an island in the middle of an essentially irreligious society. Although there is little to choose between the heroes as far as hesitations and scruples are concerned, *The Man Within* is marked throughout by the heightening of theme and exaggeration of conflict typical of historical romance, while Mauriac stays within the limits of his own stricter tradition. Thus *Young Man in Chains* ends in a realistic fade-out with the sense that Marthe's mute and long-suffering love has finally saved and will go on saving Jean-Paul from himself. With exactly the same message (Elizabeth is Andrews' salvation), Greene closes *The Man Within* in a blustering melodramatic manner. Marthe's patient suffering becomes Elizabeth's self-sacrifice through suicide, and Jean-Paul's slow recognition of her love is carried violently into action in Greene's novel by Andrews' self-surrender and self-accusation as Elizabeth's murderer and the suggestion of his death by his own hand.

But these similarities in the realm of Catholic themes

consciously chosen with a documentary or propaganda purpose lie on a relatively shallow level. It is more interesting and significant to trace, in these and later novels, those aspects of Catholicism which are not dictated by a sense of curiosity or obligation but which are closely accorded to very basic creative instincts. And here one must re-examine the distinction made between Greene as a convert and Mauriac as a "cradle" Catholic, and seriously question Greene's assertion that he adheres to the faith by intelligence alone.

In several autobiographical pieces, Greene hints, on the contrary, at a very early stirring of religious sensibility. The "Prologue" to his Mexican travel book contains one such revelation. *The Lawless Roads* begins with a montage of two border scenes, one set on the frontier between "the empty, sinless, graceless world"[31] of the United States and violent, shabby, primitive Catholic Mexico; the other, taken from one of Greene's most urgent childhood memories, set on the border between home and school. The first border scene prompts these thoughts:

The world is all of a piece, of course; it is engaged everywhere in the same subterranean struggle, lying like a tiny neutral state, with whom no one ever observes his treaties, between two eternities of pain and—God knows the opposite of pain, not we. . . . There is no peace anywhere where there is human life but there are, I told myself, quiet and active sectors of the line. Russia, Spain, Mexico—there's no fraternization on Christmas morning in those parts. . . . But where the eagles are gathered together, it is not unnatural to find the Son of Man as well. So many years have passed in England since the war began between faith and anarchy: we live in an ugly indifference.[32]

This meditation is closely linked in the essay to Greene's account of his own first awareness of the conflict in the intimate symbols of his childhood. As a boy of thirteen he has escaped from a compulsory school concert to the family croquet lawn which lies on the frontier between the two countries of home and school. "It was an hour of release," he writes,

and also an hour of prayer. One became aware of God with an intensity—music lay on the air; anything might happen before it became necessary to join the crowd across the border. There was no inevitability anywhere. . . . And so faith came to one— shapelessly, without dogma, a presence above a croquet lawn, something associated with violence, cruelty, evil across the way. One began to believe in heaven because one believed in hell.[33]

This primitive religious sense was to remain shapeless, "without dogma" for a long time. Anglicanism, as Greene knew it, failed to provide symbols vigorous enough to match the intensity of his own private vision. "The Anglican Church had almost relinquished Hell," Greene has written, "it smoked and burned on Sundays only in obscure provincial pulpits."[34] And having suffered what he thought of as hellish torments every weekday as a schoolboy, he must have found the Sunday sermons in the Berkhamsted chapel extremely unrealistic.

As we know, it was literature, not religion, that first gave Greene some support for his innate religious sense. He writes that *The Viper of Milan* "had given me my pattern —religion might later explain it to me in other terms, but the pattern was already there—perfect evil walking the world where perfect good can never walk again. . . ."[35] We have seen how Marjorie Bowen's gothic pessimism far more than the kindly practical morality of home or chapel (or the blandishments of traditional melodrama) helped to "explain the terrible living world of the stone stairs and the never quiet dormitory."[36] And now we can make the interesting connection between those first stirrings of religious sensitivity, however vague and tentative, and his first desire to write: "It was as if I had been supplied once and for all with a subject."[37]

It is also important to note that, as far as Greene was concerned, Anglicanism not only failed to take into account the reality of evil, but, as a corollary, failed to represent the good strongly enough to kindle his imagination. "The Anglican Church could not supply . . . intimate symbols for heaven," he writes. "Only a big brass eagle, an organ voluntary Lord Dismiss Us With Thy Blessing . . . ," and he extends the list to include other gentle but ineffective images associated with his home, "the quiet croquet lawn where one had no business, the rabbit, and the distant music."[38]

Nine years later, at twenty-two, he found in Catholicism a theological pattern and the shaping dogma that could at the same time realistically accommodate his intuitive sense of evil and effectively counterbalance it with powerful symbols for the good. "One began slowly, painfully, reluctantly to populate Heaven. The Mother of God took the place of the brass eagle; one began to have a dim conception of the appalling mysteries of love moving through a ravaged world—the Curé d'Ars admitting to his mind all the impurity of a province. Péguy challenging God in the cause of the damned. It remained," Greene writes, "something one associated with misery, violence, evil."[39]

In the light of these revelations Greene's assertion that he is "a Catholic with an intellectual if not an emotional belief in Catholic dogma" deserves some reinterpretation. It does not mean, as certain critics and the statement itself seem to imply, an impersonal assent to the articles of the Roman faith. It suggests rather that in Catholic dogma Greene found a logical explanation and affirmation of some of his earliest private perceptions. His conversion to Catholicism may not have coincided with any emotional experience—that took place long before—but it came as the consolidation of an attitude which was at the very basis of his vocation as a novelist. It is in this sense that one should interpret Greene's confession in *Journey Without Maps*:

"I had never experienced a conversion. . . . I had not been converted to a religious faith. I had been convinced by specific arguments in the probability of a creed."[40] As far as his work as a creative writer was concerned, the important fact was not the conversion, but the fact that his responses to religion were to begin with, and were to remain, fundamental and personal ones.

The only other reference that Greene has made in his books to his conversion is to state, again in *Journey Without Maps*, that it left him with an impression that he had "taken up the thread of life from very far back, from so far back as innocence,"[41] and in his Mexican travel book he speaks of the atmosphere of the border as giving the same illusion of "starting over again."[42] In the long run, however, the idea of conversion as change remains illusion for Greene. "Conversions don't last," he writes, "or if they last at all it is only as a little sediment at the bottom of the brain."[43] But he allows that perhaps the sediment has some value, and certainly the idea of the possibility of change remained a necessary one for him. It was one which he experienced at the beginning of each of his trips, to Africa, Mexico and elsewhere, and undoubtedly he felt the same sensation of hope and excitement at the outset of his adventure into faith. In Ronald Matthews' book, *Mon ami Graham Greene,* speaking of his conversion Greene remembers "a slight feeling of fear. One had started out on a new road and one had covered a certain distance. And one felt the question stirring in oneself 'Where is this going to lead me?' "[44]

The border mentality is characteristic of all Greene's early heroes. Andrews is caught between the romantic heaven represented by Carlyon or his mother, and the realistic hell of life at school or on board his father's smuggling ship. Oliver Chant is a "Happy Man," and by that token is not religious by nature. But by the end of the novel, through a series of disillusionments, he has been led up to the borderland of unhappiness. In *Rumour at Nightfall* the balance of interest swings uneasily between Crane and Chase representing the two countries of heart and mind. This much at least of these early novels is closely linked to the obsessive personal experience which was at the same time essentially religious in character and very fertile ground for the novelist's imagination. This much is true, just as in *Young Man in Chains* the feeling of imprisonment, if not the final release, is the true part of the novel, stemming from the deepest source of Mauriac's sensitivity.

But now one must pose an interesting and awkward question: Does Andrews' salvation through Elizabeth, or Crane's through Eulelia, correspond to as fundamental a level of experience as the disquieting sense of divided loyalties, uncertainty, and fear of betrayal (as well as the excitement) which characterizes a border existence? Or is it simply, like Jean-Paul Johanet's conversion, a well-intentioned contrivance to illustrate the letter of the author's belief? One must inevitably doubt the sincerity of Greene's endings. The conversions of his heroes are as unconvincing as the misty characterizations of his heroines, and it is enough to point to the fact that he is only able to sustain Andrews and Crane in the converted state for the briefest moment before dispatching them to a violent end.

Tracing the process of their enlightenment back several steps, however, one may ask what characteristics in these heroes permit Greene to envisage a conversion for them, even if it is not convincingly realized in the novel. Here we touch solid ground again and some of those prepossessing personal themes which are at the root of his inspiration. In the chapter on childhood experiences the theme of betrayal was singled out as one of these obsessions. It is now interesting to observe further that Greene's typical hero is not only betrayed but betrayer, as Carlyon says of Andrews, "He's a sort of Judas." The same could be said of Chant, Chase and Crane: these and many later heroes are unwillingly but inevitably failures in faithfulness. This characteristic of inevitable weakness is the one that sets Greene's hero apart from the traditional hero of melodrama, for not only do circumstances run against him, but he betrays himself by not living up to the romantic ideal of heroic steadfastness. Consider a character like Andrews in a religious context and one cannot fail to see in him an embodiment of the Christian concept of fallen man. Moreover, Andrews' oppressive awareness of his own shortcomings is another trait which situates him in a Christian framework. In short, what Allott calls the theme of the divided mind,[45] in this and other early novels, is simply a literary term which embraces the psychology of the sinner.

In this light it does not much matter that Andrews' conversion under Elizabeth's guidance is unconvincing. It is interesting but not essential to note that Greene provides a fictional structure for him to achieve a state of Grace ("confession" of his cowardice to Elizabeth, "penance accepted" in performing several dangerous acts on her instigation, and finally the realization of a kind of inner peace or "absolution"). What is important is that Greene, who once defined the only distinguishing marks of a Christian civilization as "the divided mind, the uneasy conscience, the sense of personal failure,"[46] conceives him to be, in this sense, a Christian hero—a sinner, but, to quote Péguy whom Greene quotes in *Brighton Rock* and *The Heart of the Matter,* "the sinner is at the very heart of Christianity."

Many of Andrews' other obsessions besides betrayal—fear, flight, and a frustrated sense of justice—can be related to this basic sense of sinfulness. Unlike Mauriac who works within a narrower ethical frame, Greene does not usually consider sexual promiscuity a sufficient symbol of evil. But after his night with Lucy, Andrews is stricken by a sense of "a terror of life, of going on soiling himself and repenting and soiling himself again," and elsewhere in the early work there is a suggestion of a certain queasiness before the animal appetites. But the "terror of life" has other roots than this, and it is again associated with the idea of betrayal and self-betrayal. What really disturbs Andrews is not so much having given in to his lust for Lucy as having betrayed Elizabeth. Referring to the physical passions which bedevil his own fallen heroes, Mauriac speaks in several places of "the sin we cannot not commit."[47] One might parallel this sentiment by describing Greene's heroes as living in a constant terror of infidelity as the temptation to which they inevitably submit.

Similarly the pattern of fear and flight in *The Man Within*, although successfully exteriorized in action, operates on an internal level and, as I have suggested, Andrews' flight from Carlyon through the fog is in reality a flight from himself, as oppressing and as futile as the sinner's attempt to evade his guilty conscience.

Finally, the idea of justice is characteristically complex in this novel. We are asked to sympathize with a Judas figure and no simple code of conventional justice will allow us to understand him. In all his novels Greene willfully complicates the issues, the allegiances, the calls on his hero's better nature, and a more intricate and more paradoxical solution than that of the "poetic justice" of conventional melodrama is necessary to resolve his perplexities. In the end Greene appeals beyond a humanitarian sense of justice to a Christian one.

The choice of a fallen hero persecuted by a deep-seated sense of sin is also a constant one in Mauriac's fiction, and we have traced its origin to his own Jansenistic background. Greene's borderland is Mauriac's prison. In place of Greene's sense of betrayal in deed, which is related to the adventure novel, Mauriac uses the classical conflict of French fiction—betrayal of the spirit by the flesh. Greene's hero is tried in terms of physical action, Mauriac's in terms of passion, but beneath these traditional differences both are recognizably the same type, sharing a sense of insufficiency, a terror of life, a haunting preoccupation with death; they are complex, tormented figures who cannot be simply catalogued and judged if they are to be fully understood.

This fundamentally Christian and Catholic view of man is the starting point and guide for Greene's and Mauriac's characterization. In fact, in their middle, pre-Catholic novels they scarcely leave the ground of fallen nature, indicating only by intimation the presence and counterbalancing action of Grace. The general subject of Mauriac's novels of the twenties might be described in a phrase of Pascal's that Mauriac has often used: "La misère de l'homme sans Dieu"[48] and Kenneth Allott chooses "The Fallen World"[49] as title for his discussion of Greene's novels of the thirties. In mid-career both novelists turned sharply away from the religious speculation of their early novels, from any attempt to solve their heroes' difficulties in last chapter conversions, and restrained themselves to describing "a world in revolt against the tribunal of conscience, a miserable world emptied of Grace."[50] In the closing lines of The Enemy Mauriac writes: "Where is the artist who may dare to imagine the processes and shifts of the great protagonist—Grace? It is the mark of our slavery and of our wretchedness that we can, without lying, paint a faithful portrait only of the passions."

Behind this sense of limitation lay Mauriac's desire to break with the past and associate himself more closely with the prevailing literary powers of the N.R.F. One has only to compare two interviews given at ten years' interval, the first while he was writing Young Man in Chains in 1912,[51] the second just after the publication of A Kiss for the Leper[52] to measure the change in his ambitions. The first is full of hopes for a Catholic renaissance in literature and praise of contemporary writers who show the way; the second is a caustic disclaimer of any strong literary or religious influence on his work and an assertion of his own artistic independence. But if Mauriac was to sever ties with his Catholic youth, his work, nonetheless, reposed on a Catholic foundation. In a score of places in his critical writings of the twenties he tried to rationalize his apparent desertion of Catholic themes by stating that it was "impossible to reproduce the modern world as it is without showing God's laws violated,"[53] and by claiming that in this way his work was an indirect apology for Christianity. He sincerely felt that he could best combat the influence of Gide, Proust and Freud in a world in full crisis of dechristianization by meeting them on their own ground. He did not deny their influence, but insisted on what he felt to be a grave shortcoming in their outlook. Of Gide he wrote: "His internal disarray becomes the matter of his art . . . that is the most noble use that man without God can make of his own misery."[54] His reserves about Proust's art centered in the assertion that "God is terribly absent from the works of Marcel Proust."[55] And his criticism of Freud's influence is implied in this statement: "The thing that is common to all literary and philosophical extremes in vogue today . . . is that they are mystiques divorced from God."[56] Although his own novels often rivaled those of his non-Christian contemporaries in cynicism and pessimism, and described the absence of God more forcefully than the presence of Grace, the awareness of this absence marked all his work with an essentially Christian stamp.

If one now reconsiders the triple bondage of Mauriac's heroes in the novels of the twenties, what one might call his "negative Catholicism" comes into focus. The sense of incommunicability and solitude which haunts his tragic figures is answered, not by a contrived fictional release but by the operation of the communion of saints. The failure of human love in his novels is not a condemnation of passion but points to another kind of love. This other love, in turn, is the only force which can alter the fatality which governs the destinies of his characters.

To illustrate Mauriac's Christian response to the triple

bondage of his characters, one must briefly review the major novels examined in the last chapter, and one may begin with the question of the characters' imprisoning sense of solitude. In *The River of Fire* a minor character buried in the background of the novel, Marie Ransinangue, a young peasant girl who had first excited Daniel Trassis' sexual appetite, lingers in the limbo of his memory and expiates for his life of debauchery by her life in a Carmelite convent. Lucile de Villeron is likewise, but in a much more open fashion, charged with Gisèle's salvation; yet Mauriac has the realism not to present her as a plaster saint, but enters fully into the doubts and fears and suspicions of her own hypocrisy which plague her while she tries to rescue Gisèle. A similar theme runs through *The Enemy* where the hero's mother, despite her narrow Catholicism which as much as anything has estranged her son from her, assumes the one part she can in the drama of his degradation—suffers for him and offers her suffering on his behalf. In the later novels where the isolation weighs more heavily and extends to include all the characters, as for example in *The Desert of Love,* no one figure, major or minor, is singled out as the expiatory victim. But the continuous operation of this supernatural communion is suggested when, for example, Thérèse identifies her loneliness with the loneliness of the priest: "He too had chosen the way of tragedy. To the solitude within he had added that desert which the soutane creates around those who wear it." And the whole idea of the interaction of human destinies through suffering and sacrifice is thrown into a Catholic perspective in this thought of Pierre Gornac's in *Lines of Life:* "He saw, with the eyes of the spirit, God fastened there with three nails, motionless upon the cross, incapable of doing anything for man save shed His blood. Thus must His true disciples do: intervening only by way of sacrifice and blood-offering. One can change nothing in human beings. . . . All one can do is bleed and obliterate oneself for them."

Such passages are rare enough in these dark novels, but they do situate suffering and isolation in a Catholic context. And although he was unwilling to go further than to suggest the Catholic answer without applying it, there can be no doubt that in Mauriac's mind only this belief makes the desolation tolerable.

Probing deeper in this direction to include the second aspect of the characters' bondage, the failure of human love, one must alter the previous statement that there is no expiatory victim in these novels; there is none, one should have said, whose role is purely expiatory, for Mauriac's heroes and heroines, no matter how warped or thwarted their passions, are at the same time the hunters and the hunted, tormentors and tormented. "One of two things she must be," a stranger thinks on seeing Thérèse for the first time, "either criminal or victim." But he hesitates to choose, and it is obviously Mauriac's intent that we, too, should reserve judgment. Through his long line of heroines condemned to passion but never granted its fulfillment, Mauriac suggests that there is a close analogy between insatiable sexual appetite and spiritual love. "Only some mystical experience could offer a haven for that drifting and dismasted heart," the narrator in *Questions of Precedence* says of his sister Florence. Augustin, who had been Florence's victim in love but who had accepted his misery in a spirit of Christian sacrifice, draws a parallel between his life and hers. Speaking of "the doctrine which sets an infinite value on suffering," he says: "Perhaps lives which, by the standards of this world, have been a failure, will, by those of the absolute, show as the only true successes." In the novel, although Florence is not saved, her potentiality for salvation, and even more, is thus indicated. Similarly, in *The River of Fire,* although Gisèle succumbs to her passion, the theme of the novel might be stated in these words of Lucile de Villeron: "Was not that passion for self-destruction which can be found in passion at its most intense, that utter surrender to sin, sometimes the sign of a vocation?" Maria Cross is another of these heroines whose life by worldly standards is a failure, but who is caught up in a mystique of passion from which some striking analogies are drawn to a religious vocation. At one point the doctor observes that she "speaks of sexual pleasure precisely as Pascal has spoken of the faith." She dreams of "someone with whom we might make contact, someone we might possess—but not in the flesh—by whom we might be possessed," and her passion for Raymond partakes of this desire to make a pure contact with another being. Just as Florence is drawn irresistibly to the young Augustin, Maria is fascinated by what she takes to be the secret of Raymond's innocence and in his face she sees "the outward and visible sign of a soul I longed to possess." She is disillusioned but, as the doctor says, there are in Maria Cross "the makings of a saint." In the same fashion Thérèse, by her passionate nature, her curiosity about the souls of others, her suffering, her martyrdom of solitude, experiencing " a sense of complete detachment which seemed to have cut her off from the rest of the world, and even from herself," bears the marks of a dark, unrealized sanctity. Jean Azévédo, detecting in her "a hunger and thirst after sincerity," tells her: "Accepting ourselves for what we are forces each of us to come to grips with his real nature, to see it clearly and engage it in mortal combat." Thérèse lacks the heroic virtue to do this, but she does have the lucidity which Mauriac says is a prerequisite of sanctity. She briefly envisages release in the form of faith; once in a dream she sees herself performing miracles; but finally she remains one of those whose vocation it is to experience with passionate intensity the longing for an absolute fulfillment without ever finding the means of satisfying it. And, as in the case of all Mauriac's outcast heroines, her drama is heightened by the fact that she is surrounded on all sides by the hostility and indifference of those who are not passionate by nature, that "blind, implacable race of simple souls" who are dead in spirit.

The third imprisoning element, which encompasses the other two, is the characters' sense of being controlled by an inescapable destiny. "We can paint, without lying, only the passions." This is what Mauriac called "the servitude" of the novelist at a time when, from the evidence of *Souf-frances du chrétien,* he felt with particular vividness the tyranny of the flesh and the misery of man's fallen state. His acute sense of his own limitations led him to portray a corrupt world, one in which solitude is the overwhelming reality and love is turned from its true source. This was man's fatality. But just as Grace moves behind the isolation in the mystical operation of the communion of saints, and love, though thwarted and deformed, echoes a greater love (the original title of *Genetrix* was *Il n'est qu'un seul amour*),[57] so the sense of predestination which shackles his characters to their unhappy fates, while it is presented with disconcerting intensity, calls forth an answer from its opposite. "There is only one force in the world which offsets the rules of the game, which breaks fatality to create a new fatality," Mauriac wrote in an essay contemporary with these novels. "It is only Grace that can sometimes surmount nature."[58] Among other reasons, because he had not then experienced the renovating power of Grace in his own life, it did not make a strong appearance in the novels of the twenties. But it was there all the same, moving like a hidden presence behind the tragic lives of his characters.

Greene's main concern, like Mauriac's, in the novels which followed his juvenilia was to perfect his technique and to suppress those personal obsessions, religious in character, which had obtruded in the early novels. This search for a new objectivity was not, in his case, complicated by religious scruples of any kind. He had never officially declared his religious affiliations as Mauriac had done, nor was he writing for a Catholic public. He had rather overstated his ideas about Catholicism in *Rumour at Nightfall* (as he had overstated nearly everything else), and it was a natural move in the general sense of his new efforts at self-discipline that he should strictly curtail references to religion in the fiction that followed.

A few characters in the novels of the early thirties cling to a remnant of belief. Czinner in *Stamboul Train* feels a vague nostalgia for the Catholic faith of his childhood. Minty in *England Made Me* is an Anglo-Catholic, but all that his religion gives him is a little twisted aesthetic pleasure, and perhaps a sense of his own futility. Jules Briton, the Soho waiter in *It's a Battlefield* takes some reassurance in the notion of sin. But these are incidental points and have little bearing on the general development of these three novels which describe a world where religion plays an insignificant part.

If the world that they described was irreligious, however, Greene was not. He was keenly aware of his predicament as a Christian writer in an apathetic society, and although at this time he did not express his concern directly in stories with Catholic heroes and themes, his work, like Mauriac's in the twenties, was tacitly critical of *"la misère de l'homme sans Dieu."* The novels from 1932 to 1936 were Catholic by omission, and it would not be difficult to find in them parallels to Mauriac's themes of solitude, frustrated love, and an overriding sense of fatality, as well as variants on Greene's own obsessive and inherently religious themes. Instead of reviewing them all in this light, however, I would like to concentrate on one in particular which I have not yet examined, *A Gun for Sale* (1936). As the last novel in this series, in many respects it foreshadows *Brighton Rock*, his first openly Catholic novel. But it is also typical of the preceding novels where an unstated religious view infiltrates and colors the narrative, as brief references back to these will show.

With Andrews, and with Conrad Drover in *It's a Battlefield*, Greene had already experimented with a criminal hero. With Raven in *A Gun for Sale* he investigated the basic type, the professional gangster, and for the first time used the criminal underworld as a metaphor for the fallen world. It is a world characterized by violence, treachery and brutality, a world on the verge of war where petty crime and crooked international politics overlap. As part of his job—"Murder didn't mean much to Raven"—the gangster hero has killed the War Minister of a small foreign state without knowing that, in the interests of the munition makers, this assassination is calculated to touch off an international conflict.

Opposed to this anarchy and evil is the system of organized justice whose representative is a police officer, Detective-Sergeant Mather. Like the Assistant Commissioner in *It's a Battlefield*, Mather is motivated by a dogged sense of duty and does not speculate on the nature of the criminal world to which he is opposed. He is simply "part of an organization." "He liked to feel that he was one of thousands more or less equal working for a concrete end . . . to do away with crime which meant uncertainty. He liked to feel certain. . . ."

Already realism is on Raven's side for he does not delude himself with hopes of certainty but is an inmate of Greene's hell, and we are led to take his point of view throughout most of the novel. Almost immediately he is associated even more intimately with Greene's private vision and forced into a borderland between good and evil, for he is betrayed by the lawless when he is paid off for his killing in counterfeit notes. Stung by an unusual sense of injustice, he moves to settle scores with his betrayers and, since he is wanted by the police as carrier of the counterfeit notes, he finds himself in the complex double role of hunter and hunted.

Most of Greene's obsessive themes are present in the story as set: pursuit, betrayal, life on the border, a frustrated sense of justice. They are entirely objectified in the rapid action of the novel and might well be passed over as having no connection with religious questions, if Greene did not follow up his story on a deeper level. *A Gun for Sale* would lose all its significance except as entertainment if it were simply the account of Raven's revenge. As much as anything else, however, it is a study of conscience. A study of awakening conscience, one should say, for what interests Greene even beyond the excitement of the double chase is the painful thawing out of Raven's icy heart.

At first Raven is just an instrument for murder, a weapon "formed by hatred." But he is driven by betrayal, by the unaccustomed "sense of injustice" to act independently. In the course of his hunt he becomes involved with Anne Crowder, a chorus girl very much like Coral Musker in *Stamboul Train*. He uses her as a cover and, although she is frightened, she is plucky and open with him and does not betray him to the police despite the fact that she is Detective-Sergeant Mather's girl. Trust, too, is an unaccustomed emotion for Raven, but he grows to trust Anne. Alone with her in a deserted coal shed, gratefully feeling "her sympathy move silently towards him in the dark," he confides in her, tries to tell her in his inarticulate way something of his past, and feels "a low passionate urge towards confession." When Anne discovers that he is the murderer of the old War Minister, however, revulsion replaces her sympathy. In the end she, too, betrays Raven and he is left bitterly to reflect: "There was no one outside your own brain you could trust: not a doctor, not a priest, not a woman." But having been able to call Anne his friend has nonetheless changed him, and he has felt "the ice melt at his heart with a sense of pain and strangeness as if he were passing the customs of a land he had never entered before and would never be able to leave."

Raven's revenge is successful, and before he is shot himself he is able to track down and kill the men who had betrayed him and who had planned the political assassination. This satisfies an elementary sense of justice, the poetic justice of conventional melodrama. But Greene transforms his melodramatic material and transcends poetic justice by letting religious overtones invade and color the conclusion. Because our sympathy has been stirred for Raven, his final betrayal and death leave a sense of unfulfillment which is reflected in Anne's mind at the end of the novel. Although she has helped to prevent a war, she is haunted by Raven's ghost and by a sense of failure in her responsibility towards him, by the feeling that she has betrayed a friend. And she briefly feels a need to atone by suffering. This is a lightweight novel, and something that can be construed as a happy ending is required to round it off. So Anne's sentiment of failure fades beside the glow of happiness that she feels in the prospect of marriage to Mather, the man she loves. But for an entertainment, the novel carries a great deal of meaning between the lines. Greene intimates that the "safety" which Anne feels in Mather's love is really illusory and speaks ironically of "feeling safe, like feeling in love without the passion, the uncertainty, the pain." (One remembers his description of a Christian civilization as characterized by "the divided mind, the uneasy conscience, the sense of personal failure.") Although war may have been temporarily averted, its shadow hangs over the end of the novel. Although criminals may have been brought to justice, we have been led to see a continuation of the underworld in the shoddy suburbia of Nottingham and London, a wasteland of tired, corrupt little lives. And finally, throughout the novel the betrayal of Raven is counterpointed by references to another betrayal: It is Christmas time and Raven sees a crib scene in a religious shop by the Cathedral:

He stood there with his face against the glass staring at the swaddled child with a horrified tenderness, "the little bastard," because he was educated and knew what the child was in for, the damned Jews and the double-crossing Judas and only one man to draw a knife on his side when the soldiers came for him in the garden.

Greene offers no solution, he does not even suggest, as Mauriac does, the means by which Grace may enter into this fallen world. Yet "the passion, the uncertainty, the pain," and the sense of failure and betrayal experienced in varying degrees by the major figures in this novel, as well as in *Stamboul Train, It's a Battlefield,* and *England Made Me,* are not only a vestigial sign of Christian conscience but, in opposition to the apathy and hostility of the irreligious world, a positive footing for a religious attitude.

This attitude was declared openly and forcefully in the next novel. Greene has spoken of *A Gun for Sale* as a dry run for *Brighton Rock* (1938) and of Raven as a sketch for Pinkie.[59] The principal difference between this first Catholic novel and the preceding novels is that an implicitly religious vision now becomes explicit, and themes formerly scored in a minor key are now set in a major one. The gangster hero is given a Catholic conscience. The underworld setting is now unmistakably "ravaged and disputed territory between two eternities." Greene now deals with murder in terms of mortal sin and states that the theme of the novel is "the incommensurable consequences of any single act."[60] Pinkie's crimes in the novel are not measured by the standards of moral right and wrong but are considered in terms of the absolutes of good and evil. "He had started something . . . which had no end. Death wasn't an end; the censer swung and the priest raised the Host. . . . He had no doubt whatever that this was mortal sin and he was

filled with a kind of gloomy hilarity and pride. He saw himself now as a full grown man for whom the angels wept."

But the novel does not just deal with damnation. "One
wanted to make a character," Greene says of Pinkie, "who
everyone would have said was destined to be damned, and
yet leave the reader wondering if he couldn't be saved after
all."[61] However diabolical Pinkie's pride, he remains a sinner within reach of salvation. In their Catholic novels
Greene and Mauriac continue to prefer the prodigal, the
social outcast, the abnormal character, to force home the
principle that Christ came to save "that which was lost,"
or, to use the words which Greene gives the old priest at
the end of *Brighton Rock,* to illustrate "the ... appalling ...
strangeness of the mercy of God."

To make this central character more sympathetic, he is
usually surrounded by narrow-mindedness, ignorance and
pharisaism. Mauriac writes that in his Catholic novels one
of his aims was to convince a certain race of religious bigots
"that by their mediocrity, avarice, injustice, and above all
by their intellectual dishonesty, they create a vacuum
around the Son of Man 'who came to seek out and save that
which was lost.' ... This monopolization of Christ by those
who are not of His spirit is the essential theme of *The Knot
of Vipers.*"[62] It is typical that Mauriac attacks hypocrisy
and lack of charity in his fellow Catholics, while Greene
tends to oppose to Catholic heroes engaged in a spiritual
struggle the materialistic bias and lack of understanding of
an atheistic world. But Mauriac, too, is sharply critical of
modern substitutes for religion. Irène de Blénauge in *That
Which Was Lost* (1930), for example, is driven towards suicide not only by the callousness of her husband and the arid
piety of her Catholic mother-in-law, but also by her reading
of Nietzsche, the writer whom Mauriac holds chiefly responsible for the modern decay of faith. And in this novel,
as in all Mauriac's work, the frenetic pursuit of pleasure is
condemned as the sign of a rootless and irreligious society.

For his part, as he grew more familiar with Catholic characters and themes, Greene turned to Mauriac's perspective. After *Brighton Rock* with its rather overstated contrast between pagan Ida Arnold and Catholic Rose and Pinkie, he began to introduce internal criticism. *The Power and the Glory* (1940) contains both: opposition between the agnostic police lieutenant and the priest, and criticism of the self-righteousness of the pious Catholic woman in the prison cell. In Louise Scobie in *The Heart of the Matter* (1948) Greene again satirizes narrow piety; his play *The Living Room* (1953) contains a bitter attack against those who are Catholic in the letter but not in the spirit of their belief, and the religious bigot is epitomized in the person of Rycker in *A Burnt-Out Case* (1961).

Taking the defense of the criminal against the police, of the outlaw against society, favoring the prodigal to the eldest son, the Publican to the Pharisee, Greene and Mauriac give all their novels a Christian orientation. But not satisfied with an appeal beyond conventional justice to the abstract principle of divine mercy, in their Catholic novels they went further to embody Grace in different forms. Usually it appears as some kind of innocence. Louis, the old miser in *The Knot of Vipers* (1932) is made sensitive to Grace by the purity of childhood in his daughter, Marie, and of youth in his nephew, Luc. "Your parade of high principles, your hints, your expression of distaste, your pursed lips," he writes to his pious wife, "these things never made me so truly aware of evil as did that boy. . . . I felt myself in comparison with him, deformed. . . . In him I seemed to see Marie again: or, rather, what I felt was that the same fresh spring, which had bubbled up in her and then gone underground again, was once more gushing at my feet." Scobie cherishes the memory of his dead daughter in the same way, and the priest in *The Power and the Glory* is also brought into touch with innocence condemned to death. "Why, after all, should we expect God to punish the innocent with more life?" is his bitter thought when he sees the dead Indian child. But the force of his love for his own daughter makes him realize at one and the same time the quality of love demanded of him as a priest and his own inadequacy. "One must love every soul as if it were one's own child. The passion to protect must extend itself over a world. But he felt it tethered and aching like a hobbled animal to the tree trunk."

In these novels Grace is also apparent in the priesthood. The Abbé Ardouin is another source of purity in Louis's experience in *The Knot of Vipers,* and Mauriac's two other Catholic novels, *That Which Was Lost* and *The Dark Angels* (1936), deal with the vocation of young Alain Forcas. The Mexican priest in *The Power and the Glory,* through his humility and his faith, is a recipient of Grace but, characteristically, he is at the same time not a heroic figure but weak and faltering in his ministry. The novel illustrates, as Mauriac says in his preface to the French edition of the book, "that mysterious love which seizes a man in the depths of his ridiculous misery and absurd shame to make him into a saint and a martyr."[63]

When Alain Forcas first speaks to his sister Tota about his vocation, she misinterprets his words and thinks he is telling her that he is in love. The relationship between these two loves had already intrigued both authors, and I have referred to it in connection with Mauriac's heroines in the novels of the twenties. The priest's affection for his daughter in *The Power and the Glory,* the mixture of love and pity which governs Scobie's life in *The Heart of the Matter,* Rose's love for Pinkie in *Brighton Rock,* in each case leads the character to make a Péguy-like sacrifice of his own salvation for the sake of those he loves. Scobie speaks for them and their author when he says, "against all the teaching of the Church, one has the conviction that love—any kind of love—deserves a bit of mercy." As much as Mauriac's tormented heroines these characters belong to the race of the passionate—passionate and passion's victims at the same time—and although they may misdirect their love, they are at least alive in the spiritual sense and know love's power. The most daring examination of this theme comes in *The End of the Affair* where the total abandonment and gift of herself in pleasure is the quality which leads Sarah Miles into sanctity. "Aren't lovers nearly always innocent?" Greene asks in this novel.

The insistence on the ties between sacred and profane love is another theme common to both authors in their Catholic novels because it permits them to emphasize the meeting of nature and Grace in the human medium. Of Gabriel Gradère, the corrupt hero of *The Dark Angels,* Mauriac writes that despite his multiple crimes "he still belongs to the realm of the spirit. He is no stranger to the priest Alain Forcas but a citizen of the same invisible city. . . . He communicates with the supernatural from below."[64] And the reverse is as true, that Alain, despite his purity, knows better than any the depths of Gradère's degradation. "*The Dark Angels,*" writes Mauriac, "illustrates the idea that in the worst criminal there still subsists some of the element of the saint he could have become, while, on the contrary, the life of the purest being holds terrible potentialities."[65] This novel and *Brighton Rock* are two variations on one theme that might be stated in the words that Greene gives the priest at the end of his novel: "Corruptio optimi est pessima," or in these from *The Dark Angels*: "Those who seem dedicated to evil may, perhaps, be chosen above their fellows: the very depth of their fall gives a measure of the vocation they have betrayed. None would be blessed had they not been given power to damn themselves. Perhaps, only those are damned who might have become saints." The complex identification of sin and sanctity is further illustrated when Mauriac writes of this novel, which, finally, is the story of Gradère's salvation through Alain's purity: "This is the most carnal of my novels, the most deeply rooted in human filth."[66] It is in the same spirit that the Mexican priest tells his miserable people, "Heaven is here: this is part of heaven just as pain is part of pleasure. . . . The police watching you, the soldiers gathering taxes, the beating you always get from the jefe because you are too poor to pay, smallpox and fever, hunger . . . that is all part of heaven—the preparation." And in *The River of Fire* Lucile de Villeron states: "Nobody is absolutely pure: apart from sinners there are only the purified."

Good and evil not only resemble each other in spiritual potential in the Catholic novels but also constantly interact. Mauriac calls the novels dealing with Alain Forcas "novels of the reversibility of merits as well as novels of vocation. Alain is one of the chosen, called from the midst of this fallen world to suffer and atone for all my miserable heroes."[67] Pinkie and Rose, the Mexican priest and his betrayer, Sarah and Bendrix are linked in the same way. "What was most evil in him needed her: it couldn't get along without goodness," Greene writes of Pinkie. Alain experiences "almost a physical sense of the co-inherence of souls, of that mysterious union in which we are all of us involved alike by sin and Grace." And writing of *The Power and the Glory,* Mauriac describes its theme as "the use made of sin by Grace."[68]

What is particular to both Mauriac's and Greene's portrayal of the action of Grace is that they choose to describe it working, not in hygienic splendor, but through what is most corrupt in humanity. This dictates their treatment of themes showing the interaction of good and evil; it also decides the point of view adopted in their novels. Greene is certainly indebted to Mauriac for the form of *The End of the Affair.* The first person narrative technique and the complex shifting back and forth in time is that of *The Knot of Vipers.* More important, in each of these two novels the narrator considers himself to be an enemy of religion, cut off from Grace by the knowledge of his own moral ugliness. The hatred and avarice of Louis, the narrator in *The Knot of Vipers,* is matched by the hatred and jealousy of

Bendrix in *The End of the Affair*. But in the end this self-knowledge leads Louis towards God. He passes through his avarice, like Gradère through his degradation, and reaches the supernatural from below. He so frees himself that his grand-daughter speaks of him as "the only truly religious person I have ever met." In the same way Bendrix's "record of hate" is really a love story, and not only of his passion for Sarah but of his involvement in her love for God. At the end Bendrix is not immune from that other love himself, and his bitterness is a gauge of his commitment. At the end he feels "less hate than fear. For if this God exists, I thought, and if even you—with your lusts and your adulteries and the timid lies you used to tell—can change like this, we could all be saints by leaping as you leapt, by shutting the eyes and leaping once and for all: if *you* are a saint, it's not so difficult to be a saint." In these novels Greene and Mauriac choose to write of their faith from a hostile point of view, not so much in a concern to persuade non-believers, as to show that the truth of their religion has a universal reach and conforms to human realities of the harshest kind.

These are the predominant themes of the Catholic novels. They develop naturally and inevitably out of the imaginative vision which shaped the novels that went before. Moreover, in each case the Catholic novels belong to a cycle which, for all its importance, comes to an apparent end. After these several experiments in Catholic fiction, religious themes go underground again and both novelists revert to their earlier style and subject. So if one attributes this overt treatment of Catholicism to some kind of "conversion," one must also account for the following "relapse." It is much more to the point to stress the consistency of the artistic vision, and this becomes even more striking when one considers these Catholic themes, not just as subjects for the two novelists, but as principles that profoundly influence their whole creative attitude.

NOTES TO CHAPTER 7

1. "Préface," *Oeuvres Complètes*, III, ii. (*Oeuvres Complètes* is hereafter cited as *O.C.*)
2. "Préface," *O.C.*, VII, i.
3. *Supplément au "Traité de la concupiscence" de Bossuet* (Paris, 1928), p. 121.
4. "Souffrances et bonheur du chrétien," *O.C.*, VII, 226.
5. "La Vie de Jean Racine," *O.C.*, VIII, 101.
6. "Dieu et Mammon," *O.C.*, VII, 307.
7. *Ibid.*, p. 331.
8. Robert J. North, *Le catholicisme dans l'oeuvre de François Mauriac* (Paris, 1950), p. 63.
9. "Souffrances et bonheur du chrétien," *O.C.*, VII, 251.
10. "Dieu et Mammon," *O.C.*, VII, 331.
11. North, *op. cit.*, p. 73.
12. "Souffrances et bonheur du chrétien," *O.C.*, VII, 263.
13. "A Spoiled Priest," *The Spectator*, CLV (December 6, 1935), 956.
14. "Three Travellers," *ibid.*, CLXIII (December 8, 1939), 838.
15. *Journey Without Maps*, p. 312.
16. Ronald Matthews, *Mon ami Graham Greene* (Paris, 1957), p. 113.
17. "The Job of the Writer," *The Observer* (September 15, 1957), p. 3.
18. T. S. Eliot, *Essays Ancient and Modern* (London, 1934), p. 93.
19. "The Art of Fiction," *Paris Review*, No. 3 (Autumn, 1953), p. 38.
20. "Edwardian Inferno," *The Lost Childhood*, p. 92.
21. *Ibid.*, p. 93.
22. "Henry James: The Religious Aspect," *The Lost Childhood*, p. 38.
23. "La Civilization chrétienne est-elle en péril?" *Essais Catholiques*, pp. 17-18.
24. *Ibid.*, p. 18.
25. "Dieu et Mammon," *O.C.*, VII, 286.
26. *Ibid.*, p. 287.
27. *Ibid.*, p. 289.
28. Matthews, *op. cit.*, p. 112.
29. *Journey Without Maps*, p. 4.
30. "The Art of Fiction," *The Paris Review*, No. 3 (Autumn, 1953), p. 38.
31. *The Lawless Roads*, p. 234.
32. *Ibid.*, pp. 29-30.
33. *Ibid.*, pp. 4-5.
34. "Henry James: The Religious Aspect," *The Lost Childhood*, p. 36.

35. "The Lost Childhood," *ibid.*, pp. 16-17.

36. *Ibid.*, p. 16.

37. *Ibid.*

38. *The Lawless Roads*, p. 5.

39. *Ibid.*, pp. 5-6.

40. *Journey Without Maps*, p. 263.

41. *Ibid.*, p. 116.

42. *The Lawless Roads*, p. 15.

43. *Journey Without Maps*, p. 263.

44. Matthews, *op. cit.*, p. 113.

45. Kenneth and Miriam Allott, *The Art of Graham Greene*, Chap. II, "The Divided Mind."

46. "La Civilization chrétienne est-elle en péril?" *Essais Catholiques*, p. 21.

47. The phrase is originally Gide's. Mauriac quoted it in *Supplément au "Traité de la Concupiscence" de Bossuet* (p. 85), but omitted it from *Souffrance et bonheur du chrétien*.

48. "Le Roman," *O.C.*, VIII, 268; "Préface," A. Gide, *Lafcadio*, p. 9; "Le Romancier et ses personnages," *O.C.*, VIII, 299.

49. Allott, *op. cit.*, Chaps. III and IV.

50. "Préface," *Trois Récits* (Paris, 1929), p. xiv.

51. "Enquête sur la jeunesse littéraire," *Revue Hebdomadaire*, IV (April 6, 1912), 59-72.

52. "Les Maîtres de la jeunesse littéraire," *Revue Hebdomadaire*, XII (November 25, 1922), 441-4.

53. "Préface," *Trois Récits*, p. xiv.

54. "Préface," A. Gide, *Lafcadio*, p. 9.

55. "Le Roman," *O.C.*, VIII, 281.

56. *Paroles en Espagne*, p. 21.

57. S. S. de Sacy, *L'Oeuvre de François Mauriac* (Paris, 1927), p. 75.

58. "La vie de Jean Racine," *O.C.*, VIII, 143.

59. Matthews, *op. cit.*, p. 179.

60. *Ibid.*, p. 214.

61. *Ibid.*, p. 197.

62. "Préface," *O.C.*, III, iv.

63. "Mes grands hommes," *O.C.*, VIII, 430. This article appeared originally as a preface to *La Puissance et la gloire* (Paris, 1948).

64. "Préface," *O.C.*, III, ii.

65. *Ibid.*

66. *Ibid.*

67. *Ibid.*

68. "Mes grands hommes," *O.C.*, VIII, 430.

8

THE CATHOLIC NOVELIST
AND CREATION

What is known in French criticism as "the problem of the Catholic novelist" declared itself early for François Mauriac. Stated in its simplest terms it consisted in the apparent contradiction between his vocation as an imaginative writer and his vocation as a Christian. The one constrained him to deal honestly and objectively with the unedifying matter of his art—corrupt humanity and the play of the passions—the other demanded that he should bear witness to the revealed truth of his Catholic faith. Mauriac describes this conflict as a clash between "the disinterestedness of the artist" and "the sense of utility of the apostles."[1]

Under constant critical pressure from both sides, on religious as well as on artistic grounds, Mauriac tried to define and defend his intermediary position in a series of apologetic essays which run the length of his career and provide an interesting record of different stages in his internal debate. Also the same basic problem came readily to mind when, as critic himself, he turned to examine the work of other writers. Thus, in 1924, in the preface to an early version of *Les Caves du Vatican,* we find him writing a paradoxical defense of Gide's utility to the Christian cause: "Any writer who adds to our knowledge of ourselves prepares the way for the influx of Grace."[2] In another mood, assailed by doubts as to the compatibility of the two vocations, he disengages in a study of Jacques Rivière (1926) "his inclination to discover contradictory vocations in himself,"[3] and writes: "Perhaps it was the artist in him that resisted blindly to the work of Grace . . . but what writer, albeit he believes in the supernatural, could turn an indifferent ear to this prayer, which a reading of Saint Thérèse inspired in him: 'Oh God, lead me not into the temptation of sanctity.' "[4]

In his own work Mauriac's artistic conscience led him to fight shy of "a certain type of edifying literature" which falsified life. "The transcendence of Christianity," he wrote in 1924, "is strikingly revealed in its fidelity to life as it is. There is no need to tamper with reality. To describe modern man in all his misery is to reveal the chaos left in this world by the absence of God."[5] Or so he rationalized, prompted by a deep conviction that he must at all costs remain faithful to his artistic vision. But with another side of himself he was aware of the despairing quality of such a work, of the danger he incurred himself in working so close to the passions, and of the risk of endangering the belief of his readers. The problem, which was ever present to him in his creative work, was how to introduce Grace into his fallen fictional universe without quitting reality.

One solution was to approach this problem on the theoretical level and to try frankly to illustrate certain Catholic themes in his fiction, and we have seen his various experiments in this direction. But there was another way to assure the presence of Grace in his work which applied for all his fiction, "Catholic" novels or not, and as this method is intrinsically linked, in a practical way, with some of the most basic creative problems a novelist has to face, it deserves the closest attention.

In several key essays written at the peak of his career, *Le Roman* (1928), *Dieu et Mammon* (1929), *Le Romancier et ses Personnages* (1932), Mauriac examines in an absorbing, personal way the technical problems of his craft. Situating modern French fiction in a historical perspective, in *Le Roman* he recognizes the psychological novel—*Adolphe, La Princesse de Clèves*—in which "the human being is in some sort designed and ordered as nature is at Versailles,"[6] as being the traditional expression of French genius. But however much this type of novel is the French heritage, Mauriac denounces in the novels of Balzac and Bourget and in the critical theory of Taine, an abuse of logic in art, and especially in the creation of character, and in *Le Roman* he states that his contemporaries have much to learn from Dostoevski.

The Russian novelist, Mauriac states, did not treat his characters as types, but as individuals. His main concern was "to leave untouched the tangled skein of human personality. He refused to introduce either preconceived order or logic into the psychology of his characters, created them without beforehand passing any judgment on their intellectual or moral value. . . . They are creatures of flesh and blood, burdened with heredity and moral flaws, susceptible to disease, capable of almost anything, for good as for evil, and in whom one can expect everything, fear everything, hope everything."[7] Admitting that he has been profoundly influenced by Dostoevski himself, Mauriac poses as the challenge for the modern French writer "to disown nothing of the tradition of the French novel, and yet to enrich it with the help of foreign masters, both Anglo-Saxon and Russian, and in particular to profit from the example of Dostoevski. The problem," he concludes, "is to leave to our heroes the illogicality, the indeterminateness, the complexity of living beings, and yet to continue to construct and order as befits the genius of our race."[8]

And immediately Mauriac introduces an interesting theological parallel to clarify this double obligation. Suggesting that, under certain important reserves, one can compare the relations between the novelist and his characters to those between God and His creatures, he points out that the chief problem, in theology as well as in literature, is one of reconciling the liberty of the creature with the liberty of the creator. "The heroes of our novels must be free," he writes, "in the sense that the theologian says that man is free. The novelist must not intervene arbitrarily in their destinies. . . . The French novelist who follows the plan he has conceived, changing nothing, and with a rigorous logic, who austerely and inflexibly directs the characters of his novels in the direction he has chosen for them, closely resembles the God of Jansenius."[9]

To illustrate, on the contrary, the situation where the novelist's character liberates himself from his author's control and exercises free will, Mauriac cites his own experience as a novelist:

When one of my characters moves obediently in the direction I have assigned him, when he develops through all the stages I had predetermined and fulfils every gesture I expected of him, I begin to worry. This submission to my design proves that he has no life of his own, that he has not detached himself from me, in short, that he remains only an essence, an abstraction. I am not content with my work unless my character resists me, unless he rebels against the things that I had decided to make him do. Perhaps this accounts for the fact that all creators prefer the recalcitrant child, the prodigal son to the wise one. I am never so reassured about the value of my work as when my hero obliges me to change the direction of my novel, as when he pushes and drags me towards horizons which I had not at first envisaged. This personal experience may help to emphasize the obligation we all have, each according to his capacity, not only to follow the French tradition and order the psychology of our protagonists, but also to give our confidence to these beings who have issued from us and into whom we have breathed life. We should respect their oddities, their contradictions, their extravagances, and take into account everything in them which appears unforeseen and unexpected, for that is the very beating of the heart of flesh and blood that we have given them.[10]

Before following up some of the implications of this parallel between creator and Creator, it is interesting to notice that Greene observes the same phenomenon with regard to the invention of character. Less prone to theorize about his art than Mauriac, he does not speak in his own person but in the character of Bendrix, the novelist-hero of *The End of the Affair*, but he has confirmed that the experience described here is essentially his own.[11] "Always I find when I begin to write," says Bendrix, "there is one character who obstinately will not come alive. There is nothing psychologically false about him, but he sticks, he has to be pushed around, words have to be found for him, all the technical skill I have acquired through the laborious years has to be employed in making him appear alive to my readers. . . . The saints, one would suppose, in a sense create themselves. They come alive. They are capable of the surprising act or word. They stand outside the plot, unconditioned by it . . . [but] he never surprises me, he never takes charge. Every other character helps, he only hinders." And Bendrix, who is something of a Jansenist by nature, sees himself as one of these inert characters: "We have to be pushed around," he writes glumly. "We have the obstinacy of nonexistence. We are inextricably bound to the plot, and wearily God forces us here and there according to His intentions, characters without poetry, without free will, whose only importance is that somewhere, at some time, we help to furnish the scene in which a living character moves and speaks, providing perhaps the saints with opportunities for their free will."

It is necessary to read these observations in the context of the novel, for Bendrix, who plays opposite a living character and a saint, Sarah Miles in the novel, is jealously obsessed by the notion that he is being "pushed around" by a God who has intervened arbitrarily in his relationship with his mistress. But judging, not from this bias, but from Bendrix's general experience as a novelist, which one can equate with Greene's own, his description of the creative process and of the habitual liberty exercised by his characters tallies with Mauriac's statement in Le Roman.

There are two sides to the proposition however. If one grants that the novelist's creatures must be free if they are to come alive, must be free to resist their author's will and capable of the surprising act or word, "on the other hand," Mauriac writes, "God also must be free, infinitely free to act upon His creatures, and the novelist must enjoy the absolute liberty of the artist over his work."[12] This part of the proposition is certainly easier to accept. Although it would not be difficult to assemble a large body of evidence in support of Greene's and Mauriac's assertions that their characters usually enjoy a certain amount of liberty, most novelists and critics would undoubtedly prefer to restrict themselves to dealing with the artist's liberty to control his material. In our case, however, since both Greene and Mauriac insist on the importance of a dialectic between the freedom of creature and creator, the question becomes not whether the artist controls his material, but how he is to intervene and act in his fictional universe. And when the artist's themes are religious, and the matter he deals with is, on another level, the intervention of the supernatural in the natural world, the problem becomes doubly acute.

How shall the Catholic artist show the movements of Grace through the fallen world? Both Mauriac and Greene have been absorbed by this problem which combines theological and artistic considerations in a fascinating way. Each has tried to solve it in his own manner, but finally their solutions meet and are mutually illuminating. For Mauriac, the temptation to intervene in the destinies of his characters presented itself most frequently in straightforward religious terms. The means were provided in the Catholic themes of conversion, vocation, the reversibility of merits, and the communion of saints, themes which sometimes decided the development of the plot, and at others remained in the background to be drawn into prominence by the occasional author's aside to direct the reader's interpretation of the drama. The temptation of edification, in short, of bearing witness to his faith, was a constant hazard to Mauriac as an artist. Referring to a short story, *"Le Visiteur Nocturne,"* (1920) Mauriac calls it "an attempt, often renewed during my career, to be edifying. . . . Nothing shows better than this little story how entangled I become in the idea of edification once I give in to it."[13]

Aware, then, of the danger to his art of an abuse of his liberty as creator, how did he resolve the problem, in religious terms of showing the presence of Grace without violating nature, in artistic terms of acting on his characters without restricting their essential liberty. The first requirement was to leave character entire, that is, to let it grow according to its own interior logic so that it did not simply develop to illustrate a preconceived pattern of events, but determined them, as it were, out of its own nature. Mauriac's close knowledge of the country, climate and society of his own province, and the exceptionally close ties of his characters to these external elements contribute to this kind of natural, not to say spontaneous generation. With the same aim of respecting his characters' individuality, Mauriac took care, as we have seen, not to dissipate the central mystery of their personality. That sense of the uncommunicable, which has been linked to his obsession with the essential solitude of every human being, operates on the creative level as a sentiment of humility (and of frustration) before the secret complexity of his characters which invites clarification, but not, finally, violation. Writing of certain of his characters who seem to him to be more alive than others, Mauriac says, "the portion of mystery, of the uncertain, of the possible is greater in them than in other characters."[14] One might say that Mauriac's respect for the individuality and mystery of his characters gives them a spiritual dimension, gives them, in Greene's phrase, "the importance of men with souls to save or lose."[15]

Only when his characters have been so conceived and are to this extent independent does he feel free to act upon them. And even so, he characteristically expresses his power over them in terms of their power to resist him. Referring to the Catholic novels, and in particular to *The Knot of Vipers,* he writes in *Le Romancier et ses personnages* of "struggling against his characters." "As they possess, in general, powers of resistance and defend themselves tooth and nail, the novelist can, without risk of deforming them or of making them less vital, manage to transform them. He can breathe a soul into them, or, more properly speaking, can oblige them to discover their own souls, without danger of destroying them."[16]

The emphasis that Mauriac lays on the power of his characters to resist his will corresponds in his interpretation of Catholic themes to his belief that the novelist's domain is the flesh and the passions, or at the very most, that intermediate area of conscience where the struggle between the flesh and the spirit is waged; that the novelist cannot venture with indemnity into the realm of Grace. "In the world of reality you do not find beautiful souls in the pure state," he writes in *Dieu et Mammon.*

These are only found in novels, and bad novels at that. What we call a beautiful character has become beautiful at the cost of a struggle against itself, and this struggle should not stop until the bitter end. The evil which the beautiful character has to overcome in itself and from which it has to sever itself, is a reality which the novelist must account for. If there is a reason for the existence of the novelist on earth it is this: to show the element which holds out against God in the highest and noblest characters—the innermost evils and dissimulations; and also to light up the secret source of purity in creatures who seem irreparably fallen. . . . The reason why most novelists have failed in their portrayal of saints may be due to the fact that they have drawn creatures who are sublime and angelic but not human, whereas their sole chance of success would have lain in concentrating on whatever sanctity allows to subsist of what is most miserably human in human nature. And this is the special realm of the novelist.[17]

This is the substance of Mauriac's artistic credo, and it is everywhere related to his Catholic view of man as a sinner, a fallen creature. As a novelist he resigns himself to describing "what is most miserably human in human nature." "God is inimitable, He escapes the novelist's grasp," he writes in *Dieu et Mammon*. "Nothing is more elusive in human life than the finger of God. It is not that it is not visible, but its imprint is so delicate that it disappears as soon as we try to capture it." And he speaks of the inevitable impression of "arbitrariness and misrepresentation"[18] which results when the novelist tries to recreate the way of Grace. And yet, reality is not all on the side of nature, and the dialectic between nature and Grace must be felt in the character's life if the characterization is to be true. The creature must be free to follow the downward slope of his own nature; the creator must be free to struggle against him to check his fall.

It may be objected that Mauriac's characters tend to exercise their liberty only in the direction of evil, and that they are rarely inclined to the good. Apart from the evidence that this *is* the natural inclination (and that sanctity, as Mauriac says, is surmounting nature),[19] the limitations of the novelist himself function here to decide the character of his creatures. The parallel between the human and divine creator is accurate only up to a point. "Of all men, the novelist is most like God," Mauriac writes, but adds, "he apes God,"[20] and the liberty that he dispenses is, finally, a partial liberty. In his parody of Creation, fallen himself, he is better equipped in imagination to provide his creatures freedom to fall than freedom to save themselves. In short, the characters which he draws out of his own substance and into whom he breathes life are created in his own imperfect image and reincarnate his own temptations and failings more accurately and vigorously than his limited experience of Grace. "The absolute liberty of the artist over his work" is not absolute after all, but very relative. "Our judges come down on us as though our work were entirely dependent on our free will," says Mauriac in *Dieu et Mammon*, "as if we made a deliberate decision to write a good or a bad book, tell an edifying story or a scandalous one. They do not seem to have the remotest idea of the mysterious, unforeseeable and inevitable elements in all creative novel-writing. . . . Just as there is a close bond between a man's character and what happens to him during his life, so there is a similar relationship between a novelist's character and the creatures and events brought into being by his imagination. But this is not to say that he is any more the absolute master of these creatures and events than he is of the course of his own fate."[21]

We must return to this question of the limitations to the novelist's creative power later on, but first we should try to follow through Mauriac's thought in search of a means to resolve the apparently conflicting obligations to present character as true to nature and yet susceptible to be acted on by Grace. The key is provided not in his criticism but in his novels, and once more it is closely related to his Catholic belief.

The *romans noirs* stated Mauriac's obsessive vision of man's natural bondage—solitude, rendered insupportable by a desire for contact, which is, however, predetermined to failure. In the natural order it was next to impossible to alter another destiny, or one's own. His imprisoned characters victimized one another without being able to control or gratify their passions.

But as we have seen, even in these dark novels the order of Grace stood behind the order of nature, and, without violating it, sometimes acted through nature to transform it: through the communion of saints to transform the solitude, through Christian love to transform passion, through Grace to break the natural fatality. There was only one way, but there was one, in which man could act to surmount nature in himself or to intervene in other destinies, and that was to situate himself at the center of the Christian mystery as Pierre Gornac had done at the end of *Lines of Life*, to accept his human bondage and limitations in its transforming light. In a passage already quoted in part, Pierre Gornac gives the essence of the Christian solution:

He saw, with the eyes of the spirit, God fastened with three nails, motionless upon the cross, incapable of doing anything for men save shed His blood. Thus must His true disciples do: intervening only by the way of sacrifice and blood-offering. One can change nothing in human-beings, nor can human-beings change themselves unless it be by the Creator's will operating in each one of them. They must be ransomed as they are, with all their load of propensities and vices: they must be taken, ravished, saved, with all their sins still on them. All one can do is bleed and obliterate oneself for them.

For "Creator" read "novelist" and the method by which he can act on his fictional universe without distorting it through edifying intervention is revealed in this passage. It is nothing short of adopting a Christian, that is to say, a Christ-like attitude towards these creatures of his imagination. Mauriac himself has never pursued this aspect of the analogy between theology and art, but one of his critics, Henri Clouard, writing about his *Life of Jesus* says:

If one considers this "biography" as a novel, one can justly say, so far reaching is Mauriac's sympathy for his characters, so great is his effort of comprehension, so fully does he assume their suffering, that he is not only the God Creator of his characters, but also that he is the Christ of his characters.[22]

When questioned about the aptness of this statement, while he was too modest to claim that such an attitude was his particular creative prerogative, Mauriac did assert that it described one of the central tenets of his belief. "My faith is deeply influenced by Christology," he said. "I believe that we are each the Christ for one another. Insofar as we are wronged by others, know their weaknesses, sins, evil, and accept them, we are the Christ for them. And they, in the measure of their awareness and acceptance, for us."[23] There is not the least doubt that this attitude is carried over into Mauriac's creative work. In the following pages I will be examining several aspects of his fiction on this premise, and in each case it illuminates the particular quality of his art. But even before the detailed analysis, when one considers the breadth of vision and depth of compassion that has gone into the characterization of Jean Péloueyre, Thérèse, Louis of *The Knot of Vipers*, or Brigitte Pian, *la pharisienne*, one can claim for Mauriac, if he will not claim it for himself, that even though his imitation of Christ is necessarily imperfect, this is the means by which he has fulfilled the role of Grace in his novels and has assured his characters a maximum of liberty.

It has already been said that Greene is even more reticent, more reluctant to generalize than Mauriac, yet in his criticism, in the few essays he has written on the art of fiction, and in his novels themselves, there is much evidence to show that he shares Mauriac's basic approach to the creation of character; and examining his work from this angle we can gain further insight into the functioning of this type of creative mind. First, one must note his admiration for the very thing we have been discussing, Mauriac's power in creating character. His characters exist, Greene maintains, independent of plot, with a kind of self-sustained reality. "Wipe out the whole progression of events," he writes of Mauriac's novels, "and we would be still left with the characters in a way that I can compare with no other novelist. Take away Mrs. Dalloway's capability of self-expression and there is not merely no novel but no Mrs. Dalloway: take away plot from Dickens and the characters who have lived so vividly from event to event would dissolve. [But take away the particular actions and experiences from Mauriac's novels] and the characters, we feel, would have continued to exist in identically the same way."[24]

So much for Mauriac's success in freeing his characters from their fatality, from their author's will expressed in terms of plot. In the same essay Greene touches on the secret behind this liberation when he writes that Mauriac's "moral and religious insight is the reverse of the obvious" and praises his characterization of *la pharisienne* who "under her layer of destructive egotism and false pity is disclosed sympathetically to the religious core." The key word is "sympathetically" by which Greene refers to Mauriac's capacity for assuming the character of his heroine. She is a hypocrite and Mauriac paints her true to nature, but he does not arrest his analysis here, and carried on by the sympathetic faculty does not judge her but shows how she learns through hypocrisy, shows, in Greene's words, that "the hypocrite cannot live insulated forever against the beliefs that she professes."[25] By the projection of himself into his character Mauriac is able to struggle against her propensities and vices and, without directly intervening to save her, but also without denaturing her, can oblige her "to discover her own soul." In this way he avoids the double hazard of edification (making her better than she is) or of caricature (making her less than she is capable of becoming). As vicious as she is, Brigitte Pian remains a potentially tragic figure because she has the importance of someone with a soul to save or damn, and this is what Greene implies when he writes that "there is irony but no satire in M. Mauriac's work."[26]

I am aware of introducing several new and overlapping terms in this description of Mauriac's art of characterization, but they will be clarified in pursuing our examination of Greene's views on the creative process a little further. In several novels he suggests that the act of imagination is intimately associated with the outgoing creative impulse that we have been discussing. A good place to observe this first is in *A Gun for Sale*, for here we can see imagination at work in a very primitive state as it stirs painfully to life in Raven's mind. "Made by hatred" into an instrument for destruction, he is at first totally deficient in the imaginative faculty. "Raven could never realize other people; they didn't seem to live in the same way as he lived; and though he bore a grudge against Mr. Cholmondely, hated him enough to kill him, he couldn't imagine Mr. Cholmondely's own fears and motives. He was the greyhound and Mr. Cholmondely only the mechanical hare. . . ."[27] But events in the novel are designed to make Raven see another's point of view. Thrown off balance by the unfamiliar sense of injustice, he is first astonished to "realise" a crippled slattern from his boarding house: " 'You don't need to talk to me about justice,' she said. 'Driving me like I was in prison. Hitting me when you feel like it. Spilling ash all over the floor. I've got enough to do with your slops. Milk in the soap dish. Don't talk to me about justice.' Pressed against him in the tiny dark box she suddenly came alive to him." Later, when Anne dashes a cup of hot coffee in his face, the pain makes him realize the pain of others: "This was pain. This was what the old War Minister had felt, the woman secretary, his father when the trap sprang and the neck took the weight." These brief flashes become concentrated as his trust and feeling of friendship for Anne grow. When she disappears, "for the first time since his mother died he was afraid for someone else." He tracks her to a seedy rooming house and there, "his brain stirring with another's agony," he becomes keenly aware of his own inadequacy: "Oh to know, to know. He felt the painful weakness of a man who had always depended on his gun." But his imagination rises to the occasion, and because he is led on by a "sense of someone's terror" he discovers where they have hidden the girl, stuffed upright in a chimney. As the thawing of Raven's icy heart continues, his powers of imagination increase. He begins to see the War Minister he had killed as a human being. He dreams of him as an innocent old man coming towards him saying, "Shoot me in the eyes. . . . Shoot, dear child. We'll go home together. Shoot." A sense of guilt and the "passionate urge towards confession" accompany this humanization of Raven and also the desire for pardon and understanding. "Perhaps if we knew all there was to know, the kind of breaks the fellow had had, we'd see his point of view," he says hopefully to Anne.

Raven, however, is not saved by his imagination. His destiny is to be an instrument to the end; his mechanical efficiency as a killer is only faulted a little by the stirring of this dormant faculty. But one cannot help sympathizing with him, because Greene has, through *his* imagination, shown us "the kind of breaks the fellow had had," and has led us to see his point of view. The novel is, after all, based on the gamble of understanding this killer. Few of the characters who come into contact with him do. "Old age had killed the imagination," Greene writes of Sir Marcus. Mather, the policeman, at one point "realises" Raven: "the thin limping shadow became a human being who knew the girl he loved," but most of the time duty and routine dull his sensitivity, and one of his colleagues summarizes his habitual attitude towards the criminal in the line of poetry: " 'He must be wicked to deserve such pain.' It was a comforting line, he thought; those who followed his profession couldn't be taught a better." Even Anne, who comes closest to understanding him, is finally repelled by the brutality of his acts: "She felt no pity at all. He was just a wild animal who had to be dealt with carefully and then destroyed." In the end her imagination fails and she, too, betrays him. This study of imagination in the novel is, of course, full of religious implications. To bear down on one of the more obvious points, it will be remembered that, in contrast to the insensitivity of other characters to his plight, Raven feels a "horrified tenderness" for the betrayed Christ. It is not too fanciful to see another religious image behind the story and another Christ-figure in the person of Raven's innocent victim, the old War Minister, who in the dream pardons Raven, as Christ pardoned the good thief.

This, in fact, is the quality and degree of imagination that Greene invokes for the understanding of his criminal hero. It is exactly the same sort of challenge that Mauriac has set himself and his readers in his creation of Thérèse Desqueyroux. He, too, opposes to his criminal protagonist characters who do not understand. Thérèse yearns for a sign of compassion and forgiveness from her husband, Bernard. "All through the journey she had been busy, quite unconsciously, creating a Bernard who might be capable of understanding, of trying to understand. But she had only to see him, even for a moment, to remember what he was really like—a man who had never once put himself in another person's shoes. . . ." Yet although he does not at first feel the slightest pity for Thérèse, at the end the reward of Thérèse's suffering is that "unknown to herself she had troubled Bernard's peace of mind. She had tangled him in a maze of uncertainty, so that he had been forced to question her, like a man who cannot see his way clear before him, but gropes and hesitates. He was no longer the simple creature he had been: consequently, he was no longer implacable." He gives way "to a sudden desire to understand" and loses "the advantage of that attitude of contempt" by which he had dominated her, and they know a moment's intimacy before he once more becomes a stranger, one of that "blind implacable race of simple souls ... who are incapable of love."

In these two novels the authors do not intervene directly to save their criminal heroes, but they solicit the kind of attitude that is potent to save them, and their own effort of understanding and compassion corresponds to Grace working to redeem their fallen characters.

Like Mauriac, Greene lays no direct claim to this method of creating character and introducing Grace into his novels. He is content to write about the technical problems of his craft. But whether it is modesty that prevents him from publicly examining this aspect of creation, a general dislike of theory, or whether such concerns do not rise to the level of consciousness, they are, nonetheless, everywhere present in his criticism and in his own creative work. And they crop up conspicuously whenever he writes about the artistic problems that hold him most at heart.

As we have seen, one of Greene's obsessional themes is the idea of justice. In nearly every novel there is the same opposition between Greene's criminal hero and a character or group of characters who aspire to certainty, justice, and social order. In most cases, to suit convention, the criminal is "brought to justice." But this kind of reckoning is not enough for the serious novelist. "It is in the final justice of his pity," Greene writes of Henry James, "in the completeness of an analysis which enables him to pity the most shabby, the most corrupt of his human actors, that he ranks with the greatest of creative writers."[28] And it is this same "pity" which motivates Greene's creative act, that encourages him, like James, to render "even evil 'the highest kind of justice.' "[29]

In creating Pinkie in *Brighton Rock*, for instance, Greene rejected the melodramatic device of "poetic justice" and set out to apply the creative justice of James, which was poetic in the far different sense that " 'the poetry is in the pity.' "[30] He did not judge Pinkie as a criminal, as Ida Arnold did

(" 'I'm like everyone else. I want justice,' the woman cheer-
fully remarked as if she was ordering a pound of tea"). He
described but did not condone her simple ideas of right and
wrong and her simple mission of vengeance, of "seeing that
evil suffered." In contrast, Greene treated Pinkie as a sinner, not simply judged by the right and wrong of society,
but haunted by his Catholic knowledge of good and evil.
What he showed in this novel was not crime punished by
justice, but sin redeemable by love, for despite the horror of
Pinkie's deeds and the gravity of his mortal sin, Rose expiates for him; we are not satisfied by his death as finality,
and beyond the reach of justice lies "the appalling strangeness of the mercy of God." This is the Catholic theme of
the novel. But in the creative act, which is also the novel,
Greene, as author, fulfills the role of mercy. He suspends
judgment and invites his reader to do the same. Of Pinkie
he might say, like one of Henry James's characters: "He
was no horror, I had accepted him."[31]

The Power and the Glory is an even more straightforward
case of the author suspending judgment, refusing to over-
simplify, and compassionately identifying himself with his
characters. It is more straightforward because in the story
itself the novelist's attitude is embodied, as it is not in
Brighton Rock, in the character of the central figure, the out-
lawed priest. Although he is judged, by the state as a criminal, by certain of his fellow Catholics as unworthy of his
ministry (as the Reverend Dr. Hyde judged Father Damien),
he does not judge his persecutors. Confronted in the prison
cell by the complacency of the pious woman, he becomes
painfully aware of his own habits of complacency—"it
seemed to him that he was another of the same kind"—and
far from condemning her, he thinks: "When you visualize a
man or a woman carefully, you could always begin to feel
pity . . . that was a quality God's image carried with it . . .
when you saw the corners of the eyes, the shape of the
mouth, how the hair grew, it was impossible to hate. Hate

was just a failure of imagination." The same compassionate attitude operates earlier when the priest reveals his identity to the gold-fanged mestizo, the Judas figure. "At the center of his own faith there always stood the convincing mystery—that we were made in God's image—God was the parent, but He was also the policeman, the criminal, the priest, the maniac and the judge . . ." and he sees God's image in his betrayer. These passages might be compared to Mauriac's view of man in *Le Roman* as "the creature who carries everywhere in himself, in his noble face, in his body, in his desires, and in his love, the imprint of the all-powerful God. Even the most debased human creature," writes Mauriac, "resembles Veronica's veil, and it is the artist's role, even through him, to make visible to all eyes the image of that exhausted face."[32]

The priest in Greene's novel loves his fellows because his imagination allows him to see God's image even in the most corrupt of them. He loves them through Christ, and like Christ sacrifices himself for them. But it is not just in his heroic martyrdom that he resembles Christ; indeed, Greene is at pains to show the unheroic side of his death. Rather, his Christianity shows in the commonplace action of Christian love which determines his conduct throughout the novel, and which is constantly revealed in his attitude towards others. He sees their weaknesses and vices in himself and identifies himself with them. He does not judge them. And one is reminded of what Greene wrote of Stevenson's defense of Father Damien: "The novelist has this in common with the priest, that he studies mankind only after having plumbed the depths of his own heart and soul. If only to defend himself, he must defend others. He dare not over-simplify."[33]

The time has come to clear up a misnomer. The creative pity that Greene defines as the poetry of James's fiction, and the pity that the priest feels for the occupants of the prison cell when he sees them created in God's image, is not pity in the conventional sense. If justice is not enough for the creative writer, neither is pity, understood as a condescending or indulgent attitude towards those who are less blessed than oneself. In an essay entitled *Why Do I Write* (1948) Greene opposes to this partial pity, the sympathy required of the novelist, who must be free "to draw his own likeness to any human being, the guilty as much as the innocent." It is the "genuine duty" of the novelist, Greene writes, "to awaken sympathetic comprehension in our readers, not only for our most evil characters, but for our smug, complacent, successful characters." The creative writer must be free to transcend allegiances to any restricting group morality, Greene asserts, and he defines "the virtue of disloyalty" as the virtue of prime importance to the novelist. "Loyalty confines us to accepted opinions, loyalty forbids us to comprehend sympathetically our dissident fellows; but disloyalty encourages us to roam experimentally through any human mind: it gives to the novelist the extra dimension of sympathy."[34]

The identification between priest and novelist permits us to link this artistic sympathy to its theological counterpart, Christian love. In fact, the attitude which Greene and Mauriac try to adopt towards their characters is, in many respects, a close parallel to the virtue of charity. Charity does not discriminate but is extended freely to all, to the guilty as well as to the innocent, to the smug and complacent as well as to the guilty. Charity is not condescending; it is not handed down to the unfortunate, but operates from the level of misfortune. It does not pretend to remove evil or grief by simply removing the apparent causes, but tries to enter into the other's suffering by assuming part of the misery.

The virtue of charity is the God-like virtue. Practiced, or at least paralleled in the novelist's art, it becomes the Christ-like identification of the author with his characters. The novelist's charity operates to complicate any simple inclination towards judgment. "The most horrible thing in the world," writes Mauriac, "is justice separated from charity,"[35] and in the realm of art, justice working alone produces caricature rather than character. Moreover, the exercise of true charity in the creative act prevents the opposite abuse—the benevolent intervention of the author in the destinies of his characters. That, after all, is another way of regulating justice. This vulgarization of charity into simple pity is related to the temptation of edification, and "literature," says Greene, "has nothing to do with edification."[36] If, on the other hand, the author is guided by charity, he will try to follow Christ's example in his relations with his own creatures. The true disciple, Mauriac writes, does not presume to change the destinies, even of those he loves, but imitates Christ, "intervening only by the way of sacrifice and blood-offering." The compassionate author likewise does not intervene except by assuming the total nature of the characters he creates "with all their load of propensities and vices . . . with all their sins still on them." His artistic freedom is expressed as his freedom "to draw his own likeness to any human being." The creative artist, Greene writes, is "damned . . . to sympathy,"[37] and he states that the attitude of the novelist before his characters should be: "There, and may God forgive me, goes myself."[38] The power of this compassionate attitude, of this creative love, resolves the paradox of the contradictory claims of the essential liberty of the artist over his work and the equally necessary liberty of his characters. The work of charity in the creative act assures the freedom of creator and creatures alike.

Perhaps in trying to clarify this mystery—and it still remains a mystery—I have made it sound too easy. Compassion cannot simply be turned on, put into practice at will, learned. To borrow the testimony of another French Catholic novelist, Georges Bernanos writes: "One does not learn man like a table of Greek verbs, but by a violent effort of sympathy in the etymological sense of the word."[39] The root meaning of "sympathy" is "to suffer with." "Compassion" has the same root; "comprehend" is close in origin; and, if one can trust to the wisdom in words themselves, perhaps even "understand," whose derivation is obscure, springs from the same source. But one cannot simply decide to suffer with or to comprehend one's characters without that "violent effort" that Bernanos speaks of. The difficulty in application of this creative attitude is paralleled by the enormous difficulty in practice and the immense simplicity in concept of the idea of Christian love.

The difficulty becomes immediately apparent on the theoretical level. Although one can compare God and the novelist as creators—and one may even suggest that if God created man in His image, one of the principal faculties with which He endowed His creature was the faculty for creation[40]—still the artist is in an intermediary role, fulfilling a double function as creator, but at the same time, as creature. He is concerned to dispense liberty to his own creatures, his characters, but does not know perfect liberty himself. He wishes, let us say, to extend a God-like compassion over his fictional universe, but knows only too well the limitations of his own charity. And behind characters created with all the disinterested love he can muster, and freed as completely as possible from his imprisoning will, he is all too conscious of the grimace of his own imperfect image reflected in the creatures he has made.

These theoretical difficulties might not have much weight if they remained theoretical. But they manifest themselves in countless ways in the practical problems of the novelist. One of the dangers is that the compassionate attitude may get out of hand. In an early review Greene accused Hugh Walpole of "a misuse of the author's personality, of an incomplete parturition. His characters never have independent life. On them Mr. Walpole fathers his own generous, if rather indiscriminate, enthusiasms."[41] But although he condemned Walpole's "chatty asides" and his abuse of the artist's liberty, he was quite aware that the mood of the story should be "enclosed, as it were, by the artist's temperament"; that it was not enough that characters should be observed truthfully and objectively, but that they should "have time to be matured in the author's mind and to emerge as personal as well as general symbols."[42] And the same year he wrote of a volume of short stories: "Mrs. Whitaker's stories . . . are quite without a common mental background to stamp them as Whitaker. One doesn't, Heaven forbid—want any outpouring of cheap pity in Miss Mansfield's manner; compassion is a quality that can be overworked . . . but there is nothing here to hold the stories together."[43]

The problem of striking a balance between impersonal objectivity and incomplete parturition, of knowing how to admit that "enclosing" temperament without its stifling the liberty of the characters, is a technical problem which has bothered both Greene and Mauriac and has given rise, in the latter's case, to some interesting criticism. The most famous is Sartre's attack on Mauriac's second novel about Thérèse, *The End of the Night* (1935); the most telling is contained in a long essay by Claude-Edmonde Magny in her *Histoire du roman français depuis 1918.* "Few novelists," writes Mlle. Magny, "seem to be so implicated in the stories they tell, so impregnated with them, so fully participant. One would say that Mauriac cannot cut the umbilical cord which ties him to his creatures." And she writes that the fascination which he exerts on his readers springs from the fact that he communicates to them "the anguish of the creator before these creatures who are still part of his flesh, united to him by still living bonds which he finds impossible to break."[44] This aptly describes the sympathetic union between the author and his characters which we have been examining; and the complicity, not so much in particular sins, but in the general sinfulness of his characters, which Mlle. Magny says Mauriac conveys with unusual force, corresponds point for point with his belief in original sin, in the corrupt nature of fallen man.

But here Mlle. Magny's criticism quits literary matters to join Sartre's philosophical objections to Mauriac's work. "The absence of liberty in the character of Thérèse," she writes, "is the direct consequence of the attachment which her spiritual father feels for her," and she goes on to claim that Mauriac, like Thérèse in this novel, dreams of "holding the creature that he loves in absolute dependence to himself . . . an atrocious dream," she calls it, "of love like a prison, a goal, a concentration camp."[45] She concludes that Mauriac's characters remain passive victims of sin and of their sinful destinies because their creator tends to take a quietistic, not to say Jansenistic attitude towards sin in his own philosophy.

I think that the problem is correctly stated, but that Mlle. Magny's criticism, like Sartre's, overlooks Mauriac's own perfect awareness of it and his repeated attempts to struggle against this tendency. It is fair to say that he does not succeed in solving the problem in *The End of the Night,* for example (both she and Sartre deal almost exclusively with this novel which Mauriac himself admits to be imperfect), but it is not fair to suggest that he was not conscious of the problem, nor to overlook his expression of intent in the preface to this novel which runs exactly counter to her accusations. Referring to Thérèse, Mauriac writes: "She took form in my mind as an example of that power, granted to all human beings—however much they may seem to be slaves of a hostile fate—of saying 'No' to the law which beats them down."[46] It is evident that Mauriac has a more rigorous concept of destiny than Mlle. Magny, but necessary to add that he is just as concerned to accord liberty to his creatures within the framework of his belief as she is when she judges his characters on her own philosophical premises.

And here is the root of her criticism. She does not conceive a creator who remains attached by bonds of love to his creatures, who remains solicitous for them, who offers them the freedom of his love, but, when it is spurned, continues to act through his sacrifice and suffering for them. The love of the creator as Mauriac conceives it, is, in effect, inescapable. One can sympathize with Mlle. Magny's wish that the characters should experience "a love which consists in loving creatures in their liberty and in their happiness,"[47] but when, as a Christian, one believes that true happiness comes from loving a loving God and unhappiness invariably follows one's rejection of Him, one must at least grant that Mauriac's action as creator in his fictional world is consistent with his belief.

The same basic disagreement shapes Sartre's criticism. In one of his earliest essays Sartre fastened on a stylistic trick of Mauriac's whereby the author comments on his characters *in propra persona* during the course of the action. In this way, Sartre maintains, Mauriac, like the God of the Jansenists, weighted the scales for or against his characters, controlled their destinies, and deprived them of freedom. Accusing Mauriac of the sin of pride he wrote: "He has chosen to ignore . . . that the theory of relativity applies intrinsically to the novelist's universe and that in a true novel there is no more place for a privileged observer than in the world of Einstein . . . M. Mauriac has preferred himself. He has chosen divine omniscience and omnipotence. But a novel is written by a man for men. In the sight of God, who penetrates appearances without coming to rest in them, there is no novel, there is no art, since art lives by appearances. God is not an artist; neither is M. Mauriac."[48]

In objecting to the convention of the omniscient author, Sartre was, of course, attacking a well-worked tradition and was simply using Mauriac as whipping-boy. In its place, he proposed that the novelist should create the illusion that the characters, enjoying a kind of existentialist freedom, acted independently of their creator. Technically speaking, the convention of the disappearing, or "absent" author is as valid as the older convention of the story teller, and Sartre was right in maintaining that one should not mix the two genres as he found, with some reason, that Mauriac did in *The End of the Night*. But in the end he was defending a technique of illusion, an artifice, as though it were on the side of reality, and as if the older, franker device, which acknowledged the presence of the author behind the work, were estranged from reality.

Without knowing Sartre's criticism, Greene instinctively took Mauriac's part on this question. "The novelist is not in the position of a chairman at a debate," he wrote in an early piece of criticism, "it is not his business to be impartial, but to present life as he sees it."[49] In a later essay on *A Woman of the Pharisees*, commenting on the presence of the author's I behind the "I" of the narrator, he claimed that Mauriac asserted "the traditional and essential right of a novelist, to comment, to express his views. . . . How tired we have become of the dogmatically 'pure' novel," he wrote. "The exclusion of the author can go too far. Even the author, poor devil, has a right to exist, and M. Mauriac reaffirms that right."[50] And after quoting two examples from Mauriac's novel, he concludes: "In such passages one is aware, as in Shakespeare's plays, of a sudden tensing, a hush seems to fall on the spirit—this is something more important than the king, Lear, or the general, Othello, something which is unconfined and unconditioned by plot. 'I' has ceased to speak, I is speaking."[51]

In terms of the religious analogy which we have used and which Mauriac had elaborated to explain some of these artistic difficulties long before Sartre undertook to draw his attention to them, Greene recognizes in his criticism Mauriac's right to exercise his liberty as creator over his fictional universe—the necessary counterpart of assuring the liberty of the creature. Sartre deals convincingly with half the proposition, and one can be grateful for the additional emphasis he gives to the idea—difficult enough to conceive in terms of art—that the characters must be free. His total view of the creative process, however, is less complex than Mauriac's for, unrealistically, it does not take into account the paradox of the coexistent freedom of the creator. To suggest that the novelist can totally absent himself from his work is a piece of sophistry. It does imply, however, in terms of the religious analogy, that God can, and probably does absent Himself completely from His creation, and one cannot help thinking that this was exactly what Sartre had in mind in his criticism of Mauriac's Christian esthetic of the novelist-God.

However that may be, Mauriac was profoundly aware of the fact that, as Sartre said, "the novel is written by a man for men," and consequently that in his role as creator the novelist could only "ape God" in His creative role. He knew and accepted his human limitations and, however helpful the analogy between God and the novelist might be in illuminating some of the mysteries of creation, he realized that he could not accept the glib identification between himself and God that Sartre had wished on him. He recognized that just as the most well-intentioned Christian can give only an imperfect imitation of Christ, so every parallel drawn in the analogy between God's creative function and his own must take account of the same deformation. Thus he accepted that the novelist's omniscience would be more prescriptive; that the image he stamped on his creatures would tend to bear heavily the traits of his own limited personality; that the liberty that he dispensed would necessarily be less full, and that the action of his grace in his fictional universe would be more artificial and arbitrary.

Still, a goal had been set, and even if he fell short of it, knowing the conditions of his creative act gave direction and purpose to his work. The central problem remained how to reconcile in artistic terms "the eternal contradiction . . . between man's liberty and divine prescience,"[52] and we may now consider how this problem presents itself in terms of certain specific technical difficulties: in the relationship between plot and character, in the dangers of different sorts of intervention, in the limitations of characterization and in other related questions.

The use of author's asides and the exercise of the right to comment on the thoughts and actions of one's characters is a device that is fairly innocuous in itself, but one which takes on symbolic importance because it represents the greater control that the author exercises over his characters in terms of plot. Here the eternal contradiction makes itself felt most keenly, for how, in a practical sense, in the simplest sense, can one shape the story without one's foreknowledge of the events interfering with the freedom of the characters? For Greene and Mauriac this remained a problem that arose anew with each successive novel, and that had to be solved, for better or for worse, in each case with a different set of circumstances. But certain general principles do evolve from a study of the interplay of plot and character in their fiction. First, their novels are usually character-centered. Greene has described the art of fiction as "the creation of character through narrative,"[53] and borrowing a metaphor from Eliot has spoken of the function of plot as "the meat a burglar gives a watchdog to keep him quiet."[54] In this connection we remember his opinion that Mauriac's characters dominate the particular events in their stories and that the events "disappear from the mind, leaving in our memories only characters whom we have known so intimately that the events at one period in their lives chosen by the novelist can be forgotten without forgetting them."[55] Given vital characters then, the plot dictates itself, as it were, developing on a principle which Mauriac holds that "one's character is one's destiny."[56]

But, as we have seen from Bendrix's testimony in *The End of the Affair*, not all characters act of their own free will; some "have to be pushed around," some "have the obstinacy of non-existence." In his own case Greene cites the journalist Conder in *It's a Battlefield*, Krogh in *England Made Me*, Ida Arnold in *Brighton Rock*, Wilson in *The Heart of the Matter*, and Smythe in *The End of the Affair* as examples of wooden characters who had to be animated by technical virtuosity. He calls them characters "one didn't believe in."[57] Also, in any novel, no matter how independent the characters, it is obvious that to a certain extent the author must consciously order material that has gratuitously been provided by his subconscious. In his conversations with Ronald Matthews, Greene reveals that only one novel, *The Confidential Agent* (1939), which he considers a bad one, was written "blind," without his knowing from one day to the next what was going to happen. "Ordinarily," Greene explains,

from the beginning I know the main outlines of my story and, more or less, how it will end. But, naturally, during the writing the story can take another turning, if, for example, a character to whom one had not given much importance begins to come alive. When that happens one may find that a character introduced incidentally in chapter three, by chapter thirteen is giving his own colour to the story, not perhaps dictating the principal episodes, but showing the particular fashion in which events are going to evolve.[58]

And he gives as an example of a minor character who came alive and conditioned the development of a novel, Minty in *England Made Me*.

It is typical of Greene that a discussion of how the author controls his story should end in his giving yet another instance of partial loss of control. The author's preference for this type of creative experience is revealed in another remark of Greene's: "One of the reasons why the short story is so much less interesting than the novel is that in a short story one doesn't have a chance to abandon oneself to one's spontaneity. The plan of a short story must be completely established from the first and there is no room to develop the incidental characters."[59] And in a lighter vein, speaking of the element of inevitability in the development of a novel, he states: "Writing a book is like feeling pregnant. The thing kicks and goes on kicking until you have it. Situations and characters insist on being born."[60]

In *The End of the Affair* novelist Bendrix speaks of "the passion . . . the excitement of remembering what one had never consciously known," and further on describes the phenomenon of creation in these terms: "We remember the details of our story, we do not invent them." This observation is exactly echoed in Mauriac's statement, "I do not invent, I rediscover."[61] Such remarks suggest the inner necessity which, under ideal conditions, governs the development of plot when it grows out of character; they describe that favored situation where the prescience of the author and the independence of the characters are in perfect harmony. Such affirmations also put one in mind of the classical analogy for explaining the coexistence of God's foreknowledge and man's free will, which maintains that God foresees the future as though He were remembering the past. This may not be much help in plumbing the mystery, but it does suggest the suspension of active control in shaping destiny, or plot, and it emphasizes the importance of memory in the creative act. Referring to the work of memory on a practical level Greene observes: "If one wants a description to move a reader, especially when the scene is foreign, comparisons must be found for it from a memory that is important to the author,"[62] and he attributes a growing difficulty in conveying sense of scene in his novels to the fact that he has begun to exhaust the influence of his childhood. This statement is matched by Mauriac's admission that "everything I write that is prompted by

present experience miscarries unless it finds a correspondent reality in the Bordeaux of my memory,"[63] or by his
description of his novels as "composed from detail provided by recollection, fixed by memory."[64]

On a deeper level memory works in a more complex way.
To explain the experience of dealing with characters who
"come alive," Greene says that he is not so much surprised
by their unexpected actions in regard to the development of
the plot, as in discovering the memories of such characters[65] which are full of unexpected details. Mauriac's
choice, for some of his best novels, of a first person narrator who directs the development of the story by reviewing
his own past, seems to be in keeping with this experience,
and one might describe the reflective, first person narrative
as being the form which most naturally accommodates the
dual liberty of creature and creator for this kind of novelist.

How to regulate the balance between plot and character
is just one of the problems which the novelist constantly
confronts. The dialectic between control and abandonment,
between plan and spontaneity, between conscious and unconscious elements in creation, never ceases. There are
other related problems which are just as permanent and
just as difficult. One of the most pressing of them we have
already touched on: the danger that compassion, the sympathetic attitude of the author, may degenerate into mere pity;
not that the characters remain wooden and have to be
articulated by the author's ingenuity, but that they may
make too insistent demands on the author's compassion because of their very vitality and lead him to intervene arbitrarily in their destinies, to act through pity on their behalf.
"One must love one's characters," says Greene, "but one
can love them too much."[66]

We know the power that Thérèse exerted on her author's
imagination; how she demanded life, developing out of
earlier heroines, and, even after her own novel, continued
to exist with such immediacy in Mauriac's mind that he

wrote several other stories for her and finally another complete novel, *The End of the Night*. In the preface to this book Mauriac admits that he wanted to invent a Christian end for Thérèse. Characteristically, he adds, "though I had no idea how this particular night *would* end."[67] But although Mauriac resisted the temptation of "saving" Thérèse, the whole of the novel was, in a sense, an act of indulgence on the part of the author towards this irresistible character. In one of his prefaces to *Oeuvres Complètes* Mauriac describes *The End of the Night* as "a book in which I surrendered to the fascination exerted on me by one of my creatures about whom everything had already been said."[68]

Although he expressed it in different terms, Greene knew the same problem. He was well aware that "compassion . . . can be overworked," that "serious understanding and sympathy" could degenerate into "patronage or whimsicality"[69] on the one hand, or into "the terrible and terrifying emotion of pity"[70] on the other. The experience of his own early novels had taught him the penalties of "a lack of detachment,"[71] and for a time in his middle novels, he became chiefly concerned to perfect the illusion of objectivity in his work. Nevertheless he recognized that objectivity was an illusion, and he remained convinced that the author could not absolutely detach himself from his characters, that the whole problem lay in how to discipline his attitude towards them. So engrossing was this problem that once he had begun to master it in the practice of his craft, he returned to examine it as a theme in his fiction.

In two entertainments, *The Confidential Agent* (1939) and *The Ministry of Fear* (1943), and in one major novel, *The Heart of the Matter* (1948), the central characters experience in their relations with others difficulties of the same order as those that the novelist incurs in his relations with his characters. D., the spy-hero of the first of these novels, acts at the opening of the book out of a dull sense of duty.

His attitude towards others is neutral, it is one of professional detachment. But half-way through the novel, his mechanism of protective indifference, much as in Raven's case, is thrown out of kilter by a sense of injustice when Else, an innocent girl who had helped him, is cruelly murdered. Pity stirs, and with it a desire for vengeance, a desire, one might say, actively to take in hand in the plot of his own adventure and to regulate justice. This motive leads D. on a wild and melodramatic chase after Else's murderers which is only partly successful. But more important than the success or failure of his vendetta is the fact that out of his reluctantly awakened sense of pity he rediscovers an unsuspected capacity for love. It is not an easy emotion. He realizes that his love for Rose Cullen may bring only "fear, jealousy and suffering," but his attitude towards the world has been changed by it from one of weary indifference, through the intermediary stage of pity—of indignation at injustice—to a slowly developing sense of love and trust: "He suddenly felt a tremendous gratitude that there was somebody in the warring, crooked, uncertain world that he could trust besides himself. It was like finding in the awful solitude of the desert a companion."

The three stages of D.'s developing attitude (note that he is taken one stage beyond Raven), can roughly be compared to the two extremes of detachment and partisanship, and a final attitude of sympathetic tolerance on the part of the author towards the events and characters in his novel. These three stages are explored again in the next novel, *The Ministry of Fear*. In place of D.'s hardened protective indifference we are presented with Arthur Rowe's adolescent romanticism and his belief that the world is serious and beautiful and that good and evil are clear-cut issues. Rowe the optimist is the obverse of D. the pessimist, but Indifferent Man or "Happy Man" their initial attitude is equally unstable and unrealistic. The two heroes' experiences coincide in the second phase of "The Unhappy Man." The sense

of injustice which sends D. on his mission of personal vengeance is matched by Rowe's sense of pity which drives
him to the "mercy" killing of his wife because he cannot
bear to see another's suffering. As much as D.'s vendetta,
Rowe's act is motivated by a desire to regulate justice, to
intervene in the destiny of another. But by the end of the
novel Rowe knows the danger of pity—"Pity is cruel, pity
destroys, love isn't safe when pity's prowling round"—and
he learns to accept those things which he revolted against
—suffering, unhappiness, the apparent absurdity of life.
His future with Anne Hilfe is to be based on deception, but
he accepts that: "It isn't being happy together, he thought
as though it were a new discovery, that makes one love, it's
being unhappy together. . . . It seemed to him after all that
one could exaggerate the value of happiness."

"The horrible and horrifying emotion of pity" is as destructive to the creative attitude as it is to love. It drives the
author to prefer justice to compassion; to take sides for and
against his characters; to solicit sympathy for those he considers innocent at the expense of those he considers guilty.
It leads him to substitute melodrama for tragic realism.

These terms accurately describe Scobie's failings in the
next novel, *The Heart of the Matter*, where the same problem is explored even more searchingly. He has, to begin
with, many of the qualities of the compassionate author.
He shares the gift of being able to draw his own likeness to
any human being: "Inexorably the other's point of view
rose on the path like a murdered innocent." In his professional duty he is, compared to Greene's other police officers
(most of whom are good men), an example of compassion.
"A policeman must be the most forgiving person in the
world if he gets the facts right," he thinks, and he is not
scandalized by the corruption he has to deal with on the
African post: "Here you could love human beings almost as
God loved them, knowing the worst." "We'd forgive most
things if we knew the facts," he says (as if in answer to

Raven's plea for understanding in *A Gun for Sale*), and later: "If one knew the facts would one have to feel pity even for the planets, if one reached the heart of the matter?"

Despite these proofs of love, however, Scobie does not get the facts right and does not reach the heart of the matter, and the novel describes again the prepossessing theme of the degeneration of love into destructive pity. There are similarities with the preceding entertainments. Scobie is worn by life like D., but instead of being left indifferent he is cursed by pity: "He knew from experience how passion died and how love went but pity always stayed, nothing diminished pity." Pity declares itself in the same way for Scobie as for Arthur Rowe—he cannot bear to see others suffer, least of all to make others suffer. Pity corrupts him. First it leads him to criminal negligence for his wife's sake, then to adultery when, out of pity, he takes Helen Rolt as his mistress. Finally, because he cannot bear to think of the suffering that his rapidly compounding sins and crimes cause God, pity leads him to self-destruction. "I can't give her pain, or the other pain, and I can't go on giving you pain. Oh God, if You love me as I know You do," prays Scobie, "help me to leave You. Dear God, forget me." The essential difference between Scobie and either Rowe or D. is that, although he tries to regulate justice as they do, he himself is the victim of that justice. The destructive power of pity is turned inward and the result is not vendetta or mercy killing, but suicide.

Quite apart from the religious injunctions against it, suicide, the destruction of the individual by his own last despairing act of free will, is one of the most horrible and tragic ends that the creative artist, as defender of the individual, can envisage. And this story of Scobie's lack of self-understanding, and of the brutal judgment he passes on himself, is meant to inspire horror in us. We are meant to see the distinction between pity and love in this novel and how pity spoils a great capacity for love in this man. We are meant to see how "Scobie the Just" succumbs to the temptation of melodrama when, motivated by pity, not charity, he relies on his own justice, not on God's mercy.

On the other hand, although this is a story about pity, it is told with compassion. Greene's attitude towards Scobie is neither condemning nor condescending, and the novel is not a moral tale. Scobie (like Pinkie and the whiskey priest) judges himself damned, but we are invited, not to judge him, but to sympathize with him in the root sense of the word. At the end of the novel Greene lets Father Rank speak for the compassionate author when he counters Louise Scobie's readiness to judge her husband with: "For goodness sake, Mrs. Scobie, don't imagine that you—or I —know a thing about God's mercy." It is another case of Greene's leaving as final arbiter, not justice, but "the appalling strangeness of the mercy of God."

So complex are the relations between love and pity in Scobie's case that we must push our inquiry one step further and ask whether Greene's compassion has not been tried in another way in the creation of this character; whether he has not been tempted, not so much to condemn Scobie's weakness, as to condone it; whether, in short, he has not fallen into Scobie's own error. To be sure, the novel ends indeterminately like The End of the Night and Greene, like Mauriac, avoids the gross temptation of intervening to save his hero in extremis. But there are several indications (apart from the fact that he had treated the same theme in these three novels), that Greene is particularly susceptible to the pull of pity, and that Scobie's temptation embodies a difficulty which stands at the center of his own belief and creative act. For one thing, he is now inclined to take a rather doctrinaire view of the novel, insisting on Scobie's flaw much more than his treatment of it in the novel warrants, which betrays, one feels, misgivings that he had gone too far in the direction of indulgence in the novel itself. He has referred to Scobie (as Mauriac to

Thérèse) as an example of a character "that one had loved too much."[72] Furthermore, his desire to pardon runs, in general, very close to an inclination to condone. Asked by Ronald Matthews if his sense of sympathy could stretch to pardon everyone—Nazi executioners, torturers of children, he replied:

How often does the criminal see his crime as others see it? Isn't it true that he is so locked up in a prison of egotism (a place as full of misery as any other place of captivity), that he thinks of himself as someone to be pitied rather than detested. Our disgust at the thought of him is understandable, but we haven't the right to call that disgust Christian.

It is certain that if we knew everything about him, as far back as his childhood, and beyond, to the point where the blood of a great-grandfather and a great-grandmother filled him with certain obsessions and terrors, that we would find it impossible to condemn him radically.[73]

In the same conversation Greene admitted that he found it hard to believe in the reality of damnation and speculated that perhaps even Satan might be pardoned at the last. "I find it very difficult to believe in sin," he said in another interview. "Personally I have very little sense of it."[74] And one is reminded of his statement: "Mauriac's sinners sin against God. Mine, try as they may, never quite manage to."

One may prefer the apparent rigor of Mauriac's belief, contained in his reply to this statement of Greene's: "We all sin against God. Any sin is a sin against God." But it should be added that Mauriac closed these remarks by saying, "We all sin against God. But there is the mercy of God which is greater than all that."[75] And although, from his own background and point of view Mauriac finds that there is "a secret complaisance" in Greene's treatment of sin and Grace, and finds, on the one hand, that the idea of sin seems to reassure Greene, and that, on the other, he makes himself too readily the accomplice of Grace, "What counts," Mauriac continues, is the presence of Grace. What counts is the evidence that there is "something else" than this flesh and this blood, and that He who made men of flesh and blood in His image has, from all eternity, consented to all the profanations that this resemblance implies. We rediscover the Christian faith through his work; his responses to the idea of Grace and salvation escape the rigid classifications of our theologians and casuists. From our point of view he gives God a liberty which is at the same time terrible and reassuring because, finally, God is love, and if nothing is possible to man, everything is possible to eternal love.[76]

On the artistic side Mauriac has been as conscious as Greene of the difficulty of maintaining a balance between indulgence and judgment. "You cannot depict fallen creatures from above," he writes in Le Roman. "They must be stronger than their creator to live. He does not lead them; it is they who set the pace. If there is no complicity, there will be judgment and the work will be spoilt."[77] And so he accepts as his material "what is most miserably human in human nature," just as Greene resigns himself (the difference in accent is again apparent) to write about "dull shabby human mediocrity."[78]

The point of view for treating this subject—the point of balance between complicity and judgment in the attitude of Christian sympathy and love—is extremely difficult to strike. And Mauriac knows as much as Greene how delicate the equilibrium is, and how difficult, how supernaturally difficult, to maintain. The artist's own human limitations make each book a new challenge, make Mauriac write: "I have never begun a novel without hoping that it would be the one that would make it unnecessary for me to write another. I have had to start again from scratch with each one. . . ."[79] and lead Greene, in the same spirit of humility, to speak of each new novel as "a different kind of failure."[80]

We have been examining some of the obstacles that stand permanently in the way of the application of charity in the creative act. To belittle them would invalidate the first principle. Perhaps the most discouraging limitation which the novelist has to accept is not that his manipulation of plot interferes with his characters' liberty, nor that his intervention as Grace in his fictional universe is so often arbitrary and artificial, but the fact that he invariably creates his characters in his own image. No matter how wide or varied his range of models and experience, or how skilled he is in creative extraversion—in moving out of himself to put himself in their place—he cannot avoid impressing upon these creatures the cast of his own features, the limitations of his own character. The principle of selfless love is one thing; the practice is another, and Mauriac writes with eloquent humility in *Le Romancier et ses personnages* about what he calls "the irremediable misery of the novelist's art."[81]

An extraordinary power of deformation and gross magnification is an essential part of our art. . . . The novelist not only amplifies out of all proportion, and creates monsters out of almost nothing, he also isolates and disengages thoughts and feelings which in reality are enclosed, enveloped, softened and countered by other, opposing sentiments. . . . One might say of this art, so highly esteemed and honoured, that if it achieved its object, which is to represent the complexity of a human life, that it would be incomparably closer to the divine than anything else in the world. The promise of the serpent of old would be fulfilled, and we would be as gods. But, alas, how far we are from that! . . . The individual as the novelist studies him is a fiction. . . . In the individual he isolates a passion, and in the group he isolates an individual. And in so doing, this painter of living subjects represents the contrary of real life: the art of the novelist is a failure.[82]

These limitations are incumbent on the creator who remains a creature himself. He cannot escape them any more than he can escape his own humanity. But he can accept them as a frame of reference, and in his creative work, as in his religious life, he can aspire, with the help of Grace, to surpass his own nature. "The novelist," writes Mauriac, "must resign himself to the conventions and lies of his art." But he allows that he may "approach truth by refraction,"[83] and adds: "Doubtless our *raison d'être*, the thing that gives validity to our absurd and strange profession, is the creation of a fictional world through which real men may see more clearly into their own hearts, and may feel towards one another more comprehension and pity."[84] In the sense of this charitable attitude which underlies the creative act, the two vocations, religious and artistic, are inextricably interwoven, and, as Greene writes: "The creative act seems to remain a function of the religious mind."[85]

NOTES TO CHAPTER 8

1. "Dieu et Mammon," *Oeuvres Complètes*, VII, 291. (*Oeuvres Complètes* is hereafter cited as O.C.)
2. "Préface," A. Gide, *Lafcadio*, p. 11.
3. *Le Tourment de Jacques Rivière*, see "Du Côté de Chez Proust," O.C., IV, 300.
4. *Ibid.*, p. 304.
5. "La Vie et la mort d'un poète," O.C., IV, 393.
6. "Le Roman," O.C., VIII, 276.
7. *Ibid.*, pp. 274-5.
8. *Ibid.*, p. 276.
9. *Ibid.*, p. 278.
10. *Ibid.*, p. 278-9.
11. Personal interview with Graham Greene, January, 1962.
12. "Le Roman," O.C., VIII, 278.
13. "Préface," O.C., X, iii.
14. "Le Romancier et ses personnages," O.C., VIII, 297.
15. "François Mauriac," *The Lost Childhood*, p. 70.
16. "Le Romancier et ses personnages," O.C., VIII, 299.
17. "Dieu et Mammon," O.C., VII, 315-17.
18. *Ibid.*, p. 316.
19. "La Vie de Jean Racine," O.C., VIII, 143.
20. "Le Roman," O.C., VIII, 263.
21. "Dieu et Mammon," O.C., VII, 318.
22. H. Clouard, *Histoire de la littérature française du symbolisme à nos jours*, II, 283.
23. Philip Stratford, "One Meeting with Mauriac," *The Kenyon Review*, XXI (Autumn, 1959), 619.

24. "François Mauriac," *The Lost Childhood*, p. 72.

25. *Ibid.*

26. *Ibid.*

27. When we first meet Pinkie he is described in the same terms: "The imagination hadn't awakened. That was his strength. He couldn't see through other people's eyes, or feel with their nerves. . . ."

28. "Henry James: The Private Universe," *The Lost Childhood*, p. 30.

29. *Ibid.*, p. 21.

30. *Ibid.*, p. 29.

31. *Ibid.*, p. 30.

32. "Le Roman," *O.C.*, VIII, 283.

33. "Les Paradoxes du christianisme," *Essais Catholiques*, p. 46.

34. *Why Do I Write?* (London, 1948), p. 47.

35. *L'Affaire Favre-Bulle* (Paris, 1931), p. 45.

36. *Why Do I Write?*, p. 32.

37. *The Confidential Agent*, Uniform Edition (London, 1961), p. 168.

38. *Why Do I Write?*, p. 47.

39. Georges Bernanos, "A propos de Mont Cinère," *Les Nouvelles Littéraires* (August 26, 1926), p. 1.

40. *cf.* Dorothy Sayers, *The Mind of the Maker* (New York, 1956).

41. "Fiction," *The Spectator*, CLIII (September 21, 1934), 412.

42. "Fiction," *ibid.*, CLIII (September 7, 1934), 336.

43. "Short Stories," *ibid.*, CLIII (November 23, 1934), Book Supplement, p. 28.

44. Claude-Edmonde Magny, *Histoire du roman français depuis 1918* (Paris, 1950), p. 130.

45. *Ibid.*, p. 133.

46. Preface to "The End of the Night," *Thérèse* (London, 1947), p. 163.

47. Magny, *op. cit.*, p. 141.

48. Jean-Paul Sartre, "M. François Mauriac et la liberté," *La Nouvelle Revue Française*, No. 305 (February 1, 1939), p. 226.

49. "Fiction," *The Spectator*, CLIII (July 27, 1934), 144.

50. "François Mauriac," *The Lost Childhood*, p. 70.

51. *Ibid.*, p. 71.

52. "Souffrances et bonheur du chrétien," *O.C.*, VII, 241.

53. "Fiction," *The Spectator*, CLI (December 1, 1933), 820.

54. "Short Stories," *ibid.*, CLVII (November 20, 1936), Book Supplement, p. 32.

55. "François Mauriac," *The Lost Childhood*, p. 71.

56. "Dieu et Mammon," *O.C.*, VII, 318.

57. Ronald Matthews, *Mon ami Graham Greene* (Paris, 1957), p. 173.

58. *Ibid.*, p. 185.

59. *Ibid.*, pp. 185-6.

60. Jenny Nicholson, "Graham Greene: A 'Third Man' in Real Life," *Picture Post* (August 14, 1954), p. 18.

61. "Vue sur mes romans," *Le Figaro* (November 15, 1952), p. 1.

62. Matthews, *op. cit.*, p. 41.

63. "Bordeaux ou l'adolescence," *O.C.*, IV, 173.

64. "Postscript," *The Loved and the Unloved* (London, 1953), p. 141.

65. Personal interview with Graham Greene, January, 1962. The same phenomenon is illustrated in Greene's interest in the dreams of his characters. See *In Search of a Character*, p. 75 n.

66. Personal interview with Graham Greene, January, 1962.

67. *Thérèse* (London, 1947), p. 163.

68. "Préface," *O.C.*, II, iv.

69. "Three Travellers," *The Spectator*, CLXIII (December 8, 1939), 838.

70. *The Ministry of Fear*, Uniform Edition (London, 1950), p. 73.

71. "Thunder in the Air," *The Spectator*, CLIX (August 6, 1937), 252.

72. Personal interview with Graham Greene, January, 1962.

73. Matthews, *op. cit.*, p. 253.

74. "The Job of the Writer," *The Observer* (September 15, 1957), p. 3.

75. Philip Stratford, "One Meeting with Mauriac," *The Kenyon Review*, XXI (Autumn, 1959), 618.

76. "Préface," V. de Pange, *Graham Greene* (Paris, 1953), p. 10.

77. "Le Roman," *O.C.*, VIII, 283.

78. *The Ministry of Fear*, p. 31.

79. "François Mauriac," *Writers at Work* (New York, 1959), p. 44.

80. Personal interview with Graham Greene, January, 1962.

81. "Le Romancier et ses personnages," *O.C.*, VIII, 294.

82. *Ibid.*, pp. 293-6.

83. *Ibid.*, p. 307.

84. *Ibid.*, p. 308.

85. "Mr. Maugham's Pattern," *The Spectator*, CLX (January 14, 1938), 59.

9

THE NOVELIST AS PLAYWRIGHT

It is Martin Turnell's contention, as well as the opinion of several French critics, that Mauriac's imaginative gifts began to fail in the early thirties and that *The Knot of Vipers* (1932) is "the first work of his decline."[1] To hold this view one must discount such a masterpiece as *A Woman of the Pharisees* (1941) and undervalue the two short late novels *The Little Misery* (1951) and *The Loved and the Unloved* (1952). But it is true that Mauriac's novels of this period reflect a changing, unsettled attitude towards fiction, which is paralleled by a growing interest in the theater. And since a similar development of interest in the drama characterizes Greene's work in the fifties, this chapter will be principally devoted to examining the relationship between fictional and dramatic genres in these two authors' experience. What specific factors brought about this change in creative emphasis? What connection did their experiments in the drama have with their earlier fiction? And what was the influence of this experience on their later novels?

A certain restlessness declares itself in Mauriac's novels of the early thirties—a growing impatience with the narrow mold of the fictional form he had made his own in the twenties, and a desire for expansion and renewal. This first becomes evident in the contrast between *The Knot of Vipers* and *The Frontenac Mystery* (1933). The former is dry, bitter, dramatic in the old style, and one of the most concentrated and skillfully manipulated of Mauriac's novels from a technical point of view. The latter is diffuse and gentle, a lyrical evocation of childhood and adolescence in the Guyenne countryside. Instead of focusing on a crisis in the life of a central protagonist, *The Frontenac Mystery* traces the slow and relatively uneventful growth of a family of three brothers and two sisters, watched over by their devoted mother. The narrative line which carries them from childhood to maturity is simple, relaxed and chronological. And dealing, as it does, chiefly with the ambiguities of adolescence, the novel relies far less for its effects on dramatic tensions than on the creation of a tenuous and translucent mood, on capturing what Mauriac calls "the vegetal atmosphere of my childhood."[2]

The fact that these two novels stand in such marked contrast is no coincidence. Mauriac intended *The Frontenac Mystery* as an antidote to the previous novel. His concern to redeem vipers by doves[3] was in part prompted by a serious illness. Early in 1932 he had undergone an operation for cancer, and uncertain of its outcome, he wished to leave as possibly the last item in his literary legacy a book that would be less offensive to his next of kin. In this, the most autobiographical of his novels, he set out to celebrate family life and family solidarity in an attempt to counterbalance that one-sided picture of avarice and self-interest in the family circle that he had painted in *The Knot of Vipers.*

These are the immediate and personal reasons for the change in manner. But underlying them is a more profound and lasting concern for renewal through experiment in technique. With its decentralization of character and the attenuation of dramatic elements, *The Frontenac Mystery* is the first evidence of the need that Mauriac felt at this time "to enlarge the scope"[4] of his fiction. He named the form he had tried in this novel *mémoires imaginaires*[5] after Duhamel. In succeeding novels he turned elsewhere for models and inspiration. Both *The Dark Angels* (1936) and *The Unknown Sea* (1939) came under the influence of the English novel. In them Mauriac attempted to capture the essence of "those leisurely stories, very long and very slow, in which time itself makes up the thread of plot, and which I have always preferred as a reader," he states, "to stories drawn up according to the formula classical French tragedy; *'des caractères, un catastrophe.'* "[6] Of *The Unknown Sea* he writes: "Here is clear evidence of my ambition to multiply the number of characters and let them carve out their own solitary paths, at their own speed—the sense of the novel resulting from the crossings and recrossings of these separate solitudes."[7] In *The Dark Angels* Mauriac also incorporated elements from another fictional type, the crime novel, and, surprised at his own facility in this genre, writes: "*The Dark Angels* revealed unexpected possibilities to me. I might have succeeded as well as another in Simenon's line—and perhaps if I had known Graham Greene earlier. . . ."[8]

Against this background of experiment in varied fictional forms, Mauriac's shift of interest to the drama, while it partakes of his general concern for renewal, appears as a reversion to his earlier style. On the surface, his decision to try a play seems to have been determined by external circumstance. A friend of his from Bordeaux, Edouard Bourdet, just named administrator of the *Comédie Française*, commissioned his first play in 1937. But temperamentally Mauriac had always felt that he had some natural affinities for the stage. He writes of "the temptation of the theater" as being common to all novelists, yet goes on to specify, "perhaps it was less difficult for the author of *Genetrix, Thérèse Desqueyroux,* and *A Woman of the Pharisees* to write a play than for many of my colleagues, since my novels belong to that school which developed out of classical French theater, and in particular from the tragedy of Racine. The shadow of Phèdre falls over almost all my fiction and it was not difficult for me to create for the stage a dominant figure whose passion is the motivating force behind the whole action."[9] All his drama was indeed in the Racinean tradition, and was closely allied to his fiction, particularly to that of the twenties.

He found the new genre quite congenial. It allowed him to treat familiar material, but it also provided the technical challenge which seems to have been necessary for him at this time. Bending his invention to conform to the strict requirements of the new medium, he was not obliged to force his talent, but could devote all his energies to bringing one of his characteristically intense and mordant stories to the stage. The true line of Mauriac's development seems to run through successive renunciations rather than through exfoliation. In the late twenties he had found an answer to spiritual anxiety by returning to "purify the source" of his religious sensibility. In a parallel way, the solution to a period of artistic unrest was found, finally, not in breaking new frontiers, but in refusing the temptation of escape and in returning, in an even severer discipline, to his source material. It is in this sense that his drama, more than the experimental fiction of the period, continues the direct line of development which, in Greene's words ,"gives to a shelf of novels the unity of a system."[10]

Greene's introduction to theater was by way of cinema. Like Mauriac, he had had some experience as a drama critic (for eight months in 1941 he was drama critic for the *Spectator*), and in 1942 he wrote a brief history of English theater entitled *British Dramatists*. But this critical contact with the stage was completely overshadowed by his familiarity with the cinema. From 1935 to 1940, with only a few interruptions, he was regular weekly film reviewer for

The Spectator, and in 1937 he was part-editor and film critic of *Night and Day,* a short-lived satirical weekly designed as a Londoner's *New Yorker.* Besides his experience as a critic, Greene learned the craft of cinema in more practical ways. The first of his novels to be filmed was *Stamboul Train* in 1933. It was an artistic failure and Greene panned it himself in his travel book *Journey Without Maps.* During the war several more novels were made into American films. He had no hand in adapting them but had already done some writing for the screen, providing the original script for a film called *The Green Cockatoo* in 1938, and an adaptation of Galsworthy's *The First and the Last* (retitled *Twenty-one Days*) in 1939-40. Immediately after the war, beginning with a scenario for *Brighton Rock* in 1946, he engaged in a period of intense activity in the creative side of cinema which reached its peak in two films made with Carol Reed, *The Fallen Idol* (1948) and *The Third Man* (1949). In the fifties still more novels were adapted, and Greene became known as the most-filmed British novelist. But despite the fact that he continued to produce stories and scripts, and acted as associate producer for several films, his interest in cinema now began to wane. And it is at this point that he took up the theater.

In contrasting the talents of the two novelists, it has already been suggested that Mauriac's is basically theatrical, while Greene's is cinematic, and before examining the reasons for Greene's switch to drama, it is appropriate to say a little more about the relationship between his novels and the art of the film. This can best be done by referring to his *Spectator* reviews. Greene's critic's mask was one of a sophisticated acidity. He had no patience with Hollywood "ballyhoo" and deplored the taste of an age "whose popular art is on the level of *The Bride of Frankenstein.*"[11] But his criticism was far from negative. He attacked the abuse of the form and sided with those "who believe that an art may yet emerge from a popular industry."[12] And he devoted considerable space to describing his hopes for what he called "poetic cinema."[13]

In 1937, for example, he wrote that the great advantage of cinema over the contemporary stage or novel was that it satisfied, in Thomas Mann's phrase, "the gnawing surreptitious hankering for the bliss of the commonplace."[14] Dismissing the genteel popularity of such writers as Walpole, Priestley and Coward, he claimed that the cinema could provide "a genuinely vulgar art,"[15] "as popular and unsubtle as a dance tune,"[16] and that it should "dive below the polite level to something nearer common life."[17] "The novelist may write for a few thousand readers," he pointed out, "but the film artist *must* work for millions. It should be his distinction and his pride that he has a public whose needs have never been met since the closing of the theatres by Cromwell."[18]

Here, and in *British Dramatists,* he developed the same thesis with specific reference to the theater, maintaining that "the decline from Webster to Tennyson is not a mere decline in poetic merit . . . but a decline in popularity" and insisting that "the Elizabethan stage provided action which could arouse as communal a response as bear-baiting. . . ."[19] "And when we have attained the more popular drama," he wrote,

even if it is in the simplest terms of blood on a garage floor ("There lay Duncan laced in his golden blood"), the scream of cars in flight, all the old excitements at their simplest and most sure-fire, then we can begin—secretly with low cunning—to develop our poetic drama ("The power to suggest human values"). Our characters can develop from the level of *The Spanish Tragedy* towards a subtler, more thoughtful level.[20]

It is obvious that Greene's pronouncements on popular poetic cinema and drama coincided closely with his own current ambitions in fiction. *A Gun for Sale, Brighton Rock, The Confidential Agent,* and the other novels of this period were all attempts to rehabilitate a brand of popular melo-drama and to re-endow it with Webster-like intensity. It is more difficult to account for the fact that when Greene himself turned to the stage fifteen years later, most of these popular elements were subdued, disguised or missing, and it becomes apparent that his growing interest in legitimate theater corresponds to a gradual change in the character of his fiction.

One can begin to trace this change from *The Heart of the Matter* on. Although this novel relied on a tropical setting for atmosphere like *The Power and the Glory*, it was much more closely fashioned, with fewer characters and less ac-tion; the pattern of pursuit remained but was turned from exterior to interior; the cental problem no longer had social or political overtones but remained firmly psychological. Greene treated the theme of pity again as he had in *The Confidential Agent* and *The Ministry of Fear*, but he es-chewed many of his familiar melodramatic devices, and although the war figures in both novels, in *The Heart of the Matter* it is subdued and distant.

In all these respects there is further development in the same direction with the next novel, *The End of the Affair*. There is a narrowing compass of action and a tightening of situation—technically this was Greene's most complex novel, but also the most unified, written entirely from the first person viewpoint. There is less dependence on set-ting—not Africa but London, and not the seedy squalor of earlier London novels but suburban propriety. And as in the following dramas, there is an ever more penetrating analysis of conduct in a domestic situation.

From the evidence of these novels alone, one could pre-dict that the dramatic form stood in the direct line of his development. The limiting of action, the deepening of in-sight into character, the domestication of setting and at-mosphere, the increase in quantity and flexibility of dia-logue all point to the challenge of the three unities, to an action single and complete and of a certain magnitude, and to the author alive only in his characters.

Certain factors are circumstantial to this change in emphasis. Without questioning Greene's sincerity one can say that in 1937, as a young novelist eager to make his mark, he knew the value of an outspoken opinion and had no fear of overstatement, and one can hardly bind him to the letter of his critical views at that date. But by the early fifties, half a dozen novels later, he had sufficiently proved himself, and maturity and success had somewhat blunted the edge of his enthusiasm for popular art. The war, too, which Greene saw as an almost apocalyptic outbreak of universal violence, had somewhat slaked his craving for fictional excitement. And finally, after 1945, what interest he retained in popular melodrama had been largely diverted into his work for the cinema.

But even here Greene's growing impatience with film work is symptomatic of his shift in interest towards the drama. He has spoken of script-writing slightingly as simply a means of livelihood, and in a sarcastic mood calls it "the novelist's Irish sweep: money for no thought, for the banal situation and the inhuman romance: money for forgetting how people live."[21] "Film-making can be a pretty distressing business," he says, "for, when all is said and done, a writer's part in making a film is relatively small."[22] He resents losing control over his story, dislikes the impersonality of the studio, has frequently announced that he would write no more scenarios, and after work on a film speaks of returning with relief to the novel. In contrast he has written glowingly of his "very happy" introduction to the theater:

I had not anticipated the warmth, the amusement and the comradeship, the delight of working with players interested not only in their own parts but with the play as a whole (a film actor is hardly aware of what happens when he is not on the set), nearly a dozen lively informed intelligences criticizing and suggesting.

... Above all I had not realized that the act of creation, as with the novel, would continue so long after the first draft of the play was completed, that it would extend through rehearsals and through the preview week. It is for the act of creation that one lives. . . .[23]

There is one other major reason for the interest which Greene began to show in drama in the early fifties. Like Mauriac, he found creative stimulus in the new form during a slack period. With *The End of the Affair* he felt he had reached the end of a cycle in his fiction. *The New Statesman* had slated this novel as "the last . . . that a non-specialist will be able to review,"[24] and Greene, who now spoke of having got over his "fixation" with characters like Pinkie and Scobie, decided that his next novel would "not deal explicitly with Catholic themes at all."[25] But *The Quiet American* was still several years away, and in the interim he welcomed the thought of experiment in a new genre. Reviewing Leon Edel's edition of *The Plays of Henry James* in 1950, Greene suggested that James's primary motives for trying the new form were fame and money (not to be overlooked as motives for himself), but he added that James was "challenged as any artist by a new method of expression. The pride and interest of attempting the new possessed him."[26] More modestly and more whimsically he has excused his own experiments in drama with the phrase "One must try every drink once."[27] But clearly it was the technical challenge which in his maturity tempted him to the most objective and exigent of literary forms.

Greene's introduction to the theater was an obvious first step and also a failure. In 1950 he adapted *The Heart of the Matter,* for the stage. The play, backed by Rogers and Hammerstein and produced by Basil Dean, closed quietly in Boston before ever reaching Broadway. A French adaptation of *The Power and the Glory* by Pierre Bost in 1953 was more successful, and Greene worked on an English version of the script prior to its London opening several years later.

But questions of adaptation aside, his first original drama, *The Living Room* (1953), also owed a great deal to his fiction. Like Mauriac, he found challenge enough in accommodating his novelist's skill to the new medium without venturing to treat new material. So although he had decided to abandon Catholic themes in his new novel, he reverted to the old "fixation" in his first play. *The Living Room* deals with a love affair tragically complicated by religion as in *The Heart of the Matter* or *The End of the Affair*. Its bitter lover, unappealing wife, long-suffering young mistress and ineffectual priest are stock Greene types whose roles have been newly apportioned and whose situation has been transposed to the stage. The outcome of the play is also typical: another provocative suicide, the salvation of the Catholic heroine hanging in the balance between justice and mercy.

It is easy to pick up these echoes of earlier novels, but it is far more interesting to ask what Greene's work in the new vehicle represented to him, and what he learned from it. Of immediate concern were many technical problems relating to what Greene has peevishly called, with reference to film work, "those apparently interminable transformations from one treatment to another."[28] In developing his ideas for *The Third Man*, for example, he had found it necessary to begin with a familiar form, and had written out his story in full before he and Carol Reed began work on the scenario. "One cannot make the first act of creation in script form," he said at this time. "Even a film depends on more than plot, on a certain measure of characterization, on mood and atmosphere; and these seem to me almost impossible to capture for the first time in the dull shorthand of a script."[29]

This points up the central difficulty that the novelist encounters in writing in the dramatic form. Even more than in the film scenario he finds his creative freedom curtailed and disciplined. He must forego his habitual prerogative to comment, to interpret in the margin of the action. The spoken word must carry the full weight of his characters' thoughts and feelings. Their opportunities for self-revelation must be managed within the limits of a credible series of encounters within one or two static sets. And the novelist's license to create mood and atmosphere is reduced to a few terse stage directions. In short, the whole development of the story depends on characterization, and characterization on dialogue.

If he had been able to strike a compromise of working from narrative to scenario in writing *The Third Man,* drama allowed no such gradations but demanded uncompromisingly that he should learn to depend absolutely on "the dull shorthand of a script." Conscious of this challenge and stimulated by it, Greene wrote *The Living Room* directly in script form, and speaks of his intent as being "to fuse everything and put it into dialogue."[30]

What exactly is implied in this new emphasis on dialogue, beyond purely technical considerations? In an early article Greene had referred to the importance of language in drama as a means of transforming melodramatic material. "But we have almost given up hope," he wrote in 1936, "of hearing on the contemporary stage words with a vivid enough imagery to convey the climate of the play. Only one such transformation on the modern stage comes to my mind: the opening scene with the two prostitutes in Eliot's *Sweeney Agonistes.*"[31] In *British Dramatists,* he drew further examples from the drama of the past. He prized in Webster "the keen, economical, pointed oddity of the dialogue,"[32] in Shakespeare "the verbal power which continually puts a scene before our eyes far more vividly than the later scene-painters could do it."[33] He even praised "the magnificent voluptuousness"[34] of Browning's dramatic verse. But when Greene turned to drama himself, he did not attempt to exactly reduplicate these effects. Admittedly, one could argue with Peter Glenville, that "the writings of Graham Greene

appear to have the detailed salty immediacy of actual everyday life, but in fact it is everyday life brilliantly transformed
by Mr. Greene's special imagination and personality."[35] But
one would also have to acknowledge that this description
is truer of Greene's novels than of his plays, and that it fits
his use of language as narrator better than the dialogue of
his characters. In the plays the ascendant element is actuality not imagery, and in them what Evelyn Waugh calls "the
rich idiosyncrasy of phrase"[36] in Greene's fiction is almost
entirely absent.

How did Greene treat dialogue in his plays, then, to transform and explain melodrama, for we must pause briefly
here to state that despite the chastening of style and domestication of setting which led through the preceding
novels towards the dramatic form, the plays themselves deal
with deliberately grotesque situations. Peter Glenville who
first directed The Living Room describes it as "a dilemma
pushed to its farthest limit," which, he continues, "is a necessary condition of any good play, be it tragedy or farce."[37]
Rose Pemberton in this tragedy becomes the mistress of a
married man on the night of her mother's funeral and is
torn between her love for Michael and the pain his wife's
jealousy and suffering cause her. Her dilemma is heightened by the fact that she lives it out under the disapprov-
ing eye of the Church represented by her two pietistical
great-aunts and their brother, an invalid priest. The Potting
Shed (1957), a mystery not a tragedy, is still built around
an extreme situation. The secret concealed in the potting
shed is nothing less than the suicide and resurrection from
death of the hero, James Callifer, a traumatic childhood experience which resulted in partial amnesia. His agnostic
family had hidden the facts from him, and it is only at the
death of his father that he begins to reassemble fragments
of the past and finally discovers that it was the prayer of
his uncle, a young Catholic priest, that brought him miraculously back to life. In Greene's farce, The Complaisant

Lover (1959), the stock comic situation of the cuckold husband is given one grotesque twist by making him complaisant, and another by forcing his rival to become complaisant
too, and enter into a comic *ménage à trois* with the woman
he has seduced and the man he has deceived. In short, an
unconventional and often violent situation seems to be a
prerequisite for the exercise of Greene's imagination in
drama as in fiction, and his problem remained how to control and draw significance from the given melodramatic
material.

As suggested, the prime means was the handling of language. Greene's dialogue, though it is not poetic in the sense
of striking phrase and wide use of imagery, might be called
poetic in terms of precision of statement. Writing of Shakespeare, Greene had said:

In the plays the poetry is rightness—that is nearly all: the *exact*
expression of a mental state: the *exact* description of a scene.
Shakespeare's poetry is not poetry in any usually accepted meaning of the word—it is simply the right phrase at the right moment, a mathematical accuracy as if this astonishing man could
measure his words against our nature in a balance sensitive to a
fraction of a milligramme.[38]

And Greene set as his own ideal the art of exactitude which,
as he rightly said, was a poetic standard.

Secondly, to give density to dialogue, behind the func-
tional give-and-take of conversation he set a background
of serious dialectic. Over one-third of *The Living Room* is
concerned with a close—though dramatic—discussion of
the Catholic attitude towards sin. A good half of this discussion is carried in the sharp thrust of debate between
Father Browne as Catholic priest, and Michael Dennis as a
skeptical professional psychologist. *The Potting Shed* does
not make as rigorous demands on intellect, but the same
polarity of opposing views underlies the dialogue, for
James Callifer's father is a noted agnostic, and the antago-

nism between his father and his uncle, William Callifer, a Catholic priest, is the crux of the mystery, and explains James's own attempted suicide and the veil of secrecy that was drawn about his strange recovery. There are no theological implications in *The Complaisant Lover,* but there is a fundamental opposition between two moralities, between that of Victor Rhodes, the husband, and that of Clive Root, the lover, resolved in the end by the paradoxical morality of complaisancy.

"The theatre," wrote Greene, "is an art of discussion, a fact which Dryden's plays illustrate as well as Shaw's,"[39] and his own dramas, whether comedies or tragedies, are not simply exploitations of grotesque situations, but are conducted in terms of challenging intellectual argument.

In this regard it is necessary to state that Greene's dialectic does not make for oversimplification but rather for complexity. Father Browne does not speak only as a priest, nor Michael only in his capacity as a professional psychologist. Both are too deeply and personally involved in the debate as individuals. Despite his training, Father Browne fails to find the right words to save Rose in her dilemma. His religion is as powerless as Michael's psychology. As though to guard against the pat solution, Greene actually dismembers his priest (he has lost his legs in an automobile accident and is confined to a wheel chair) and isolates him by many years of inactivity from the fruitful practice of his ministry and, ironically, psychologist Michael is burdened with a neurotic wife. Father William Callifer is handicapped the same way: he has been sent to an obscure parish, has taken to drink and has lost his faith. Similarly in *The Complaisant Lover* neither husband Rhodes nor lover Root is entirely likeable or capable. Intense and provocative discussion is common to all Greene's drama, but not from theoretical heights. The discussion devolves at the level of human suffering and even when solutions are offered, as in the comedy, they are tentative and equivocal.

To state this in another way, one might say that Greene held in his dramas to that other definition of poetry which he had borrowed from Ford Madox Ford as a standard for his fiction, intending that it should be poetic in its "power to suggest human values." In *British Dramatists* he had described the morality play as "the bones without the flesh," and had deplored the fact that "so often in twentieth-century drama we have the flesh without the bones."[40] In his own terms, he tried to correct the balance and to approach what he felt Shakespeare had achieved—a dialectical tension between the morality and the play of character.[41]

What are the bones of Greene's plays? All of them deal directly with questions of life and death. Rose's suicide is matched by James Callifer's hanging, and midway in *The Potting Shed* by a renewed threat of suicide. Even *The Complaisant Lover* has its moment of horror when Victor Rhodes shuts himself in the garage and turns the car's engine on, only to be saved by his sense of the ridiculous because "the district is wrong for tragedy." Whether an actual death is in question or not, the old aunts in *The Living Room* are haunted by fear of it, as are the elder Callifers, and the taint of mortality embitters Greene's comedy. The fear of death, in fact, not only motivates the sterile superstitions of the Brownes and the Callifers, but drives them into intransigent defensive positions at opposite ends of the scale of belief, into narrow Catholicism on the one hand, and categorical agnosticism on the other.

Set against the fear of death and its resultant emotional and moral sclerosis is the rebellious, irrational force of love. It is personified in Greene's heroines. Rose, and Mary Rhodes in *The Complaisant Lover,* on the simplest level only want freedom to be happy with the men they love. Rose prays: "Dear God, give us more love. Give us a life together." Mary, who loves both her husband and her lover, wants to keep them both, wants "to have her cake and eat it too." In the tragedy Rose's love is thwarted; in the comedy Mary's extravagant wish is satisfied. But the dogged naïvete which, in the name of love, confronts the intolerance of convention and the cruelty of circumstance is the same in both plays. The childlike quality is stressed in each case, and in *The Potting Shed,* the mystery is solved by Anne Callifer, James's niece, a teenage girl who operates as a detective on the simple faith that "Everything is possible."

As one might expect, romantic love is linked to religious love in these plays, particularly in *The Living Room.* "What's the difference between this sort of love and any other?" Rose challenges her Aunt Helen. And when Aunt Helen warns Rose that she will die in mortal sin if she continues her affair with Michael, "God's got more sense," Rose replies. "And mercy." Though Rose's defiant faith is contrasted to her aunt's narrow fear, finally she too fails in her trust of God. "You have free will and you don't trust Him," James admonishes her. "He suffers for that too. Because He would make things so much easier for you if you would shut your eyes and leave it to Him." But Rose cannot shut her eyes; she has been forced to think; she has lost some of her innocence through her unhappy experience, and some of her childlike faith in love. Still, like all Greene's sinners she is not condemned. And the final appeal is made, as usual, through the priest. "Mercy is what I believe in," James tells his sister, and through Rose's suicide the old aunts do conquer their fear of death.

There is nothing very new here in terms of theme. These problems had been aired before. But it is important to see that Greene's drama has as solid a bone structure as his Catholic novels. And if we pursue our examination of the plays in terms of the author's creative attitude, more insight, the nerve structure, as it were, is disclosed. To begin with, Rose and Mary Rhodes, and to some extent Anne in *The Potting Shed,* represent not only the force of love but also, in their childlike anarchy of outlook, the essential individualism of the creative artist. Moreover, Rose is like the novelist in that "she cannot remain indifferent to another's suffering." Like the creative writer, she is damned to sympathy. Michael's wife, Marion Dennis, becomes a reality for her in the same way that an author's character takes on independent life. "She was just a name, that's all," Rose breaks out at the climax, "and then she comes here and beats her fists on the table and cries in the chair. . . . It was only like something in a book, but now I've seen them together. I've seen him touch her arm. Uncle, what am I to do? Tell me what to do Father!"

That cry for help, picked up by Rose from Marion Dennis, transmitted to Father James and thence to the audience, is echoed in various circumstances by nearly every other character in the play, not excluding Aunt Helen, who is first described as being able to "steer straight through other people's lives without noticing." That universal cry for help symbolizes the demands made by the characters on an author like Greene. And it is particularly interesting that in this play, through the person of Father James, Greene gives a much more extended reply than he usually permits the priests in his fiction. Characteristically, but quite in keeping with the artist's concern to preserve the liberty of his creatures, Father James is not allowed to save Rose, he is not even allowed an effective formula for salvation. When Rose tells him that she cannot push her claim and go away with Michael because she cannot bear his wife's pain, "You're such a child," he says. "You expect too much. In a case like yours we always have to choose between suffering our own pain or suffering other people's. We can't not suffer." Rose, like Scobie and other Greene heroes, chooses to suffer her own pain. But Father Browne is left, like the compassionate author, to suffer for others. As suggested, Greene has imposed on him a kind of saving physical impotence by making him legless. He is spiritually impotent too. "Last night God gave me my chance," he tells

Michael Dennis after Rose's suicide. "He flung this child here, at my knees, asking for help, asking for hope. . . . I said to God, 'Put words into my mouth,' but He's given me twenty years in this chair with nothing to do but prepare for such a moment, so why should He interfere?" It is the author's test, too, not to interfere but to create the climate of sympathy that answers the cry for help.

This kind of impotence, of course, is the very opposite of indifference. Greene relates it to prayer. "You can pray," is the only advice that Father Browne is able to give Rose, and later, thinking of his insufficiency, he adds: "If I'd ever really known what prayer was, I would only have had to touch her to give her peace." The total understanding implicit in that remark is, of course, Godlike, and for Father James, as for Greene, understanding of this kind is inevitably tied to mercy. God's justice "has nothing to do with a judge," Father James tells Michael. "It's a mathematical term. We talk of a just line, don't we? God's exact, that's all. He's not a judge. An absolute knowledge of every factor —the conscious and the unconscious—yes, even heredity, all your Freudian urges. That's why He's merciful."

Of course, neither artist nor priest can do more than aspire to that kind of knowledge. But "why shouldn't you love God just because you don't understand Him?" Father James asks Rose. And relating understanding and love in another context, "You love Michael now," he says, "but in ten years you'll have understood him to the last word and thought and gesture. It needs a terrible lot of love to survive understanding." This difficult understanding, sanctified by love, is the vocation of the Christian and the writer. It is exercised through faith, faith in something which by nature outstrips human understanding. "You make things so complicated," says Rose to her uncle. "You simplify too much," he replies. "I don't understand," says James Callifer referring to what happened to him in the potting shed.

"But I couldn't believe in a god so simple that I could understand him."

Faith, finally, is not so much a creed held as an attitude of mind, not so much acquisition as desire. And although the goal may be as distant, uncertain and unknowable as God often seems to be in Greene's novels and plays, the means of reaching towards this goal is certain and invariable. As we have seen, it is characterized by that "violent effort of sympathy in the etymological sense of the word," that Bernanos speaks of. This act of creative sympathy is strikingly dramatized in the second of Greene's plays, The Potting Shed, in Father William Callifer's memory of the prayer he made over the body of his dead nephew:

I prayed. I was a model priest, you see, with all the beliefs and conventions. Besides I loved you. Yes I remember now, how I loved you. I couldn't have a child and I suppose you took his place . . . when I had you on my knees I remember a terrible pain —here. So terrible I don't think I could go through it again. It was just as though I was the one who was strangled—I could feel the cord round my neck. I couldn't breathe, I couldn't speak, I had to pray in my mind, and then your breath came back, and it was just as though I had died instead. So I went away to bury myself in rooms like this.

Prayer, love, compassion (alarmingly physical identification in this case) come together in this act of faith. The price that James's uncle pays for this concentrated effort is complete emotional and spiritual evacuation. For thirty years afterwards he exists emptied of belief. He does not want to remember his act, shirks the responsibility of the pain of remembrance. In this play, as in The Living Room, the importance of remembering is stressed in various ways. It is as important as the recognition of guilt, or as accepting people as individuals, and the psychologist who helps restore James Callifer's memory (his name, Dr. Kreuzer, is significant) fills the role of priest in The Potting Shed. Like his uncle, James too has been emptied of feeling and belief: ("You're not alive . . . you never felt pain," his wife Sara accuses him.) But the twin destinies of uncle and nephew meet again when, under the stimulus of Anne Callifer's curiosity ("You can't be certain of anything can you?") and Dr. Kreuzer's treatment, James is forced to remember. He in turn forces his uncle to recall the details of his prayer. The resurrection of the past restores the priest's faith, and James leaves him praying after thirty years' aridity. James too, experiences a rebirth of faith. It is not demonstrative, overt or comforting, but it is coincident with a return of love and feeling; he is alive again.

As far as belief in God is concerned, all he can say is, "I've seen the mark of His footsteps going away." It is a paradoxical proof of God's presence, this sense of His absence, but the sentiment is echoed by other characters in the play. "I don't believe in this miracle," says James's mother, "but I'm not sure any longer . . . when you aren't sure you are alive." And the most provocative statement of faith is given to Dr. Kreuzer who says: "No I don't believe. Sometimes I doubt my disbelief." It is such tenuous faith, or, on the other hand, such an irreducible core of faith which resists almost universal hostility, that seems to stimulate Greene's creation. The state of uncertainty inspires him for it makes the greatest demand on his powers of mercy and sympathy. " 'The poetry is in the pity,' " Greene had written of James's novels. And his own plays are poetic in the same basic sense, for in situation, dialogue, dialectic and structure they are designed to exercise and to solicit this creative pity.

Tragedy, and even mystery-drama, are forms which are well suited to handle the extreme opposition between mercy and judgment, between love and experience, which is as central to Greene's plays as to his fiction (*The Living Room* approximates the Catholic novels, *The Potting Shed* the entertainments). But one might object that this inherent polarity is inimicable to comedy, which is characterized by compromise not tension, by resolution not dilemma. Not only do there seem to be fewer opportunities for sympathy in comedy, but also, to effect the comic dénouement, the author is called much more strongly to intervene in the destinies of his characters. The question now arises, how does Greene meet these requirements in his comedy, *The Complaisant Lover,* and does this change in genre correspond to a change in outlook?

One should point out immediately that many characteristic overtones run through this comedy, and that several times it threatens to collapse into tragedy. "We aren't allowed a tragedy nowadays without a banana skin to slip on and make it funny," the lover, Clive Root, says bitterly and, as mentioned earlier, Victor narrowly skirts suicide, his only comment: "It's unfair isn't it, that we're only dressed for comedy." Greene's comedies are, as he says himself, "sadly funny," a mixed genre.

Other apparent innovations lose something of their novelty when exposed to close examination. Greene's choice of hero for *The Complaisant Lover* is significant. The dentist-husband, Victor Rhodes, represents an extreme form of humor. As a confirmed practical joker he is a comic grotesque and is at first presented unsympathetically. Dribbling glass, musical cushion, plastic rat, the tiresome anecdote and the tired joke, and the slightly ridiculous aura of his profession are, in one sense, the paraphernalia that make him a suitable victim for cuckoldry. In the first scene we are emphatically on the side of Mary Rhodes and her lover, whose affair carries the promise of adventure and escape. But Greene (who is a practiced practical joker himself) has a special sympathy for Victor and, in the end, lets his brand of humor triumph. Our own liking for him grows when, in the middle of the play, unexpected and unsuspecting, he blunders in and interrupts the "serious" affair between his wife and her lover and turns their romance,

Clive feels, into a "cheap farce." In the last act, when their deception has finally become known to him, he fights back against conquering lover Clive Root with the only weapon he has, his sense of humor, which now shows itself allied to a sense of humility and to the generosity of his love for Mary. This love is contrasted to Clive's possessive passion, just as Rose's love for Michael was contrasted to Marion Dennis' jealous need of him in *The Living Room*. "I'd forgive him anything. Would you?" Marion fiercely challenges Rose in the earlier play. "No. Because I love him." Rose replies, "I wouldn't want to hold him prisoner with forgiveness. I wouldn't want to hold him a minute if he wanted to be somewhere else." This love which risks the freedom of the beloved is the same kind as Victor's in the comedy. Here the problem is complicated because Mary wants both kinds of love. "She wants to have her cake and eat it," Clive says indignantly. "That's exactly what she said," Victor replies. "Don't you love her enough to try to give her that kind of cake? A child's cake with silver balls and mauve icing and a layer of marzipan."

In the comedy Greene dissolves the perplexity of choice and lets his childlike characters have their cake and eat it too. The cry of "help" which ran unanswered through *The Living Room* is replaced by the phrase "I'm sorry," which occurs six times in the last ten pages of *The Complaisant Lover*. Greene hears the repentance of his characters and dispenses absolution. At the final curtain the stress of the conventional triangle is dissipated, Clive no longer opposes but becomes a reluctant third party in the farcical solution; all three are complaisant, the joke is complete. One might say that in this comedy Greene exercises the compassionate faculty, first by identifying throughout with the clown and underdog, Victor, and second by becoming himself an accomplice in the rigged conclusion of complaisancy, which leaves him, as author, in the position of practical joker *vis-à-vis* his victim, the audience.

This leads one to consider what special interpretation Greene gives to the comic attitude towards life in general, and in particular to his own grotesque variant of humor, the practical joke. And this examination reveals at once the element of consistency in Greene's vision, whether expressed in comic or in tragic terms, and further, a slightly new emphasis to his creative outlook.

In *The Complaisant Lover* Greene comments through Clive Root on the possible significance of the practical joke. Having just fallen victim to one of Victor's tricks, Clive says wryly, "Jokes like this must be a compensation for something. When we are children we're powerless, and these jokes make us feel superior to our dictators. But now we're grown up, there are no dictators. . . ."

The answer is, of course, that in Greene's view, and in a metaphysical sense, we are still powerless, and the child-like response is still as valid as any. The dictators remain as the incalculable and often absurd forces of circumstance which control particular destinies, and the practical joke is a means of challenging the absurd and of asserting individuality. In an early review Greene approvingly quoted the French psychologist Dugas' definition of laughter as "*l'expression de l'individualité . . . la réaction de l'individu contre l'ordre des choses établies qui l'écrase.*"[42] Elsewhere he has written of hoaxes as being performed by "men who sympathize with the defeated and despise the conqueror and dare do nothing but trivial mischief to assert their independence."[43] It is an interpretation which corresponds closely to Greene's own views on the function of the creative writer whose job is "to engage people's sympathy for characters who are outside the official range of sympathy,"[44] whose role is "to be a piece of grit in the state machinery."[45]

In this sense Greene's work is consistent, whether the mode is comic or tragic, and the potential for this kind of humor was always latent in the work of an author who could write: "The truth is seldom tragic, for human beings are not made in that grand way. The truth may be sad but it is nearly always grotesque as well."[46] The correlation between tragedy and comedy is underlined again in a quotation like the following: "As Chaplin learnt long ago, the man who falls downstairs must suffer if we are to laugh; the waiter who breaks a plate must be in danger of dismissal. Human nature demands humiliation, the ignoble pain and the grotesque tear. . . ."[47] And Greene again touched the link between the two genres in writing of Chekov: "He had no critical sympathy for the realists who confined themselves to the present, or for the escapists who confined themselves to dreams of an impossible happiness. His genius was tagged to the absurd, the shameful, the grotesque fact; but in every play that he wrote he allowed the aching heart to speak its criticisms through wild hopes."[48]

There is a considerable margin, however, between these statements, and Greene's attitude as displayed in *The Complaisant Lover*. When he turned to the comic genre himself, Greene subdued the aching heart and no longer rebelled so violently against the grotesque fact as he had in his tragic novels. Suffering is still present in the comedy, but it is attenuated by a new tolerance in outlook which lets the humorous side of the grotesque assert itself while its nightmare aspect goes into decline. Despite the challenging ending, there is in Greene's comedy an internal balance. He has tempered his habitual appeal to mercy with justice.

This new quality is not conspicuous or melodramatic; it is not justice in the narrow sense of rewards and punishments. It has more to do with comprehensiveness of vision, as suggested in *The Living Room* in Father James's equation of God's justice to the mathematical exactness of His knowledge of human beings, or as indicated in Greene's description of the poetic quality in Shakespeare as lying in the "mathematical accuracy" of his expression. Reviewing G. H.

Hardy's *A Mathematician's Apology* in 1940, Greene had been impressed by similar parallels between poetry and mathematics. The qualities which Professor Hardy required for mathematical beauty—*generality, depth,* "a very high degree of *unexpectedness* combined with *inevitability* and *economy*"[49]—corresponded closely to a definition he himself had given in 1934 of a really fine style as being "no more than a neatness, an economy, a completeness of expression."[50] Greene was now particularly impressed by the possibilities of a creative parallel. Hardy's book revealed mathematics to be "a creative and not a contemplative art." "I know no writing," Greene states, "except perhaps Henry James's introductory essays which conveys so clearly and with such an absence of fuss the excitement of the creative artist."

It was this kind of mathematical discipline which Greene attempted to apply to his own creative work in the fifties. As will be seen in the next chapter, this change in emphasis bore fruit in the late novels. But it became first and most clearly evident in his experiments in drama where the austerity of the form acted as a controlling agent and the requirements of the comic genre in particular led to a greater tolerance, balance, and justice in Greene's general creative view.

Drama played a similar role in Mauriac's experience but with different results. He turned to "the narrow technique of the theater,"[51] in hopes of renewal, not in range, but in depth. "A novelist is often accused of not renewing himself," he wrote at the time of his first play. "I believe on the contrary that his first duty is to remain himself, to accept his limitations. The effort towards renewal must be made in terms of the mode of expression. It is excellent for a novelist to submit himself to constraints hitherto unknown to him."[52]

Though he took a characteristically firm stand on the question of renewal, it was a vexacious subject. In *Le Ro-*

mancier et ses personnages he revealed that he had discovered, after writing *The Knot of Vipers*, that its hero Louis, recalled trait for trait, Fernand, hero of *Genetrix*.[53] Then there was the more embarrassing example of his second novel on Thérèse which had left him feeling that he had given in to his fascination with a character "about whom everything had already been said." His limitations were making themselves felt. He hoped that by frankly accepting them and by translating his material into an even stricter form, he might escape "the temptation which we all know of publishing a book which is entirely unlike anything we have done before."[54] He hoped that he might free himself from the influence of his type characters, not by abandoning them and seeking new ones, but by recreating them in a more objective discipline in which "deeper reaches of their beings"[55] would reveal themselves.

All four of Mauriac's plays, in consequence, are made out of the stuff of his novels. The setting is the familiar one of the isolated country house belonging to the landed Guyenne bourgeoisie. Imprisoned by the summer's heat inside the house and inside the tight circle of the family, the characters in each case are lured into hope of escape by the intrusion of an outsider. But after the links of the various kinds of love which bind the family have been twisted and tested by this experience, in each case the play ends, the chain unbroken, the despair sharpened, the characters locked in their separate suffering and left with nothing but a bitter memory of "that one minute, the only one perhaps, when the door of the cell stood open and there was no one waiting in the corridor."[56]

The particular details in which this general theme is developed are also taken direct from the *romans noirs* of the twenties. Drawing examples from one play alone and the least typical of the four, *Passage du Malin*, will illustrate just how dependent Mauriac was on his former creation. This drama is the only one not set in Les Landes although the seaside villa is reminiscent of scenes from *Questions of Precedence*. One of the main springs of the action is the dominating passion of Irma Tavernas, a reincarnation of the mother-monster in *Genetrix*. The son she smothers with her love is again called Fernand, and his first wife, now dead, is called Mathilde like that earlier victim of maternal jealousy. The outsider in the play, *le malin,* is a woman-runner, an older version of Daniel Trassis from *The River of Fire*. The Gisèle whom he pursues (Agnès Lorcat in the play) is protected by Bernand Tavernas' present wife, Émilie, who is a somewhat more complex Lucile de Villeron. As a major figure Émilie is one of Mauriac's passionate heroines, and although she differs in background and character from Maria Cross, she exerts the same fascination over others, experiences the same mystique of passion, and is loved by and drawn to her husband's eighteen-year-old son by a first marriage, whose name, Raymond, recalls the young hero of *The Desert of Love*. These echoes, though more than incidental, are not singled out to condemn Mauriac but to illustrate that his dramas remain, in theme, character, and setting, entirely within the narrow borders of his fictional province.

But one can also observe an intensification of certain major themes when they are disengaged from the familiar narrative fabric. The most striking difference between novels and plays is the increased darkness of the latter. True, Mauriac's novels had always dealt with frustration, defeat and despair, but this had always been relieved by a little light, and not only in the Catholic novels. But now, accentuating familiar themes for the stage, Mauriac developed them all in the lower ranges of his palette. Religion plays no part in his dramas: the only priest represented (in *Le Feu sur la Terre*) is a worried functionary trying to extract school fees from the impoverished local gentry. The permutations of love in the plays are exceptionally sterile and are never clearly related to that unknown which gives each equation a transcendent value. A brief summary of the four plays will demonstrate their unrelieved gloom.

In *Le Feu sur la Terre* (1950) Mauriac describes the fiercely possessive love of Laure de la Sesque for her brother, Maurice. This incestuous passion almost breaks his marriage; Maurice almost abandons his wife, Andrée, and their child, to follow his infatuation for a young neighbor, Caroline, whose destiny Laure controls; when her plans fail, Laure almost commits suicide; and the play ends in an atmosphere of stifling irresolution.

In *Les Mal Aimés* (1945) the childhood affection of Élizabeth de Virelade and a neighbor's son, Alain, has grown into love only to be cruelly forbidden by Élizabeth's tyrannical father who, as a widower, jealously wants to keep his daughter with him. To be near Élizabeth, Alain marries her younger sister Marianne, and only once at the play's climax realizes the possibility of flight with Élizabeth from the insufferable situation. But the couple let the chance slip, and the play ends with these lines:

M. de Virelade: You were ready to abandon me. You were with him in the car, and it wasn't for love of me that you came back. When will you have done tormenting me Élizabeth?

Élizabeth: How does one lay down a burden? Mine is fixed to my shoulders, nailed there.

Marianne: I too know what it is to be crushed under an intolerable weight, and it is you, Élizabeth who have laden me with it. . . .

Élizabeth: And yet, we love each other.

In *Asmodée* (1938), the *pièce rose* of Mauriac's *pièces noires* if one can call it that, a young couple, Emmanuele de Barthas and an English visitor, Harry Fanning, do find happiness, though it is qualified by Emmanuele's question: "Will there ever be a time when we will say: 'Here it is, we have it at last. This is happiness,'" which expressed "with an ardour in which you feel all her future suffering."

But the main subject of the play is the mute rivalry of Emmanuele's widowed mother, Marcelle, for Harry's love. Tracing back the chain of unhappy passion, Marcelle is loved by the spoiled priest Blaise Coutûre, her son's tutor, while he in turn is hopelessly loved by Mademoiselle, the younger children's governess. With the departure of the young lovers the house settles back into unhappiness and unfulfillment, Marcelle closeted with her sinister confidant and jailer, M. Coutûre.

Passage du Malin (1947) again treats a doomed love. Trying to protect her charge, Agnès Lorcat, from the pursuit of Bernard Lecêtre, Émilie Tavernas becomes his victim for a night. Carried away by passion she makes ready to give up her post as directress of a school and to live with Bernard. But faced with the final decision she is saved, rather unconvincingly, by conscience, "that sickness of which we are never cured." And to Bernard's last plea: "The day that you call me back I will leave everything and come," she replies, "I will not call again. One does not escape twice from the prison to which I am returning."

As illustrated in this brief survey, Mauriac fastened on some of his most abiding obsessions to exploit in the new medium: the broken family; the gulf between parents and children crossed only by the one-way thrust of possessive passion; the contrast between the normal lines of love and perversions of them; the almost universal failure of normal love to rival the perverted passions; and, finally, the suggestion that pure affection only exists in childhood, and that the only way of love for his beleaguered heroines is bleak renunciation and barren suffering.

Comparing Mauriac's plays with Greene's, and keeping in mind the dual interpretation of Greene's drama, some interesting contrasts are revealed. In so far as Greene's plays represent a consistent artistic outlook, they stress the melodramatic quality of his imagination as opposed to Mauriac's essential realism. Greene forces every situation to its extreme: to suicide in his tragedy, in a lighter mood to the detection of a supernatural mystery, or to the improbable solution of complaisancy in his comedy. Mauriac's dramas are played out in a much narrower range and are marked by lack of resolution, by a return to prison after the briefest vision of escape. Marianne and Laure contemplate suicide but draw back before the act; Émilie, Élizabeth and Marcelle envisage happiness through sexual fulfillment, but are frustrated of a solution. The heat has gone from passion in Mauriac's plays. The chilling atmosphere created and controlled by M. Coutûre in *Asmodée* foredooms any real outburst. The same kind of totalitarian control, exerted by Virelade in *Les Mal Aimés* and by Laure in *Le Feu sur la Terre*, ensures that the fire will not break out but only smoulder, and destroys the hope of any competing passion. There is no opportunity in Mauriac's plays for a defiant act of love, either in terms of violence, or as a rebellious practical joke. His lovers are disarmed and vanquished from the start. Mauriac's dramas are blocked out in various shades of black, in contrast to which the melodramatic qualities of Greene's dramas stand out flamboyantly.

The contrast is heightened because Mauriac's plays are so much starker than his novels. The typical conflict in his fiction has already been described as being based on an opposition between the flesh and the spirit, between nature and Grace, which even by Mauriac's standards is a somewhat melodramatic struggle. In the plays this quality is all but dissolved, and its extreme limits are severely curtailed. The dynamic stress is reduced, the illusion of escape denied, bodily passion and spiritual suffering become one and become Mauriac's mature, pessimistic expression of the human situation. The French title of *The Unknown Sea* (1939) was *Les Chemins de la mer*. The subtitle of his last play, written ten years later, is *Le Pays sans chemin*. Mauriac describes Blaise Coutûre in *Asmodée* as "what is left of a human being when an immense Grace has withdrawn from his life."[57] In his plays he apparently left the borderland of nature and Grace to explore the lives of those for whom "the road of life is a dead-end, leading nowhere."[58] He left the temptations of the flesh to examine the temptations of despair, as expressed in these terms by Marianne in *Les Mal Aimés*: "I remember at the Lycée writing my name in chalk on the blackboard, and then I would rub out the letters one by one until nothing was left but black."

Mauriac's plays contain then, as Greene's do, a concentrated restatement of basic themes, but also a change in emphasis. We saw that Greene's work in drama, and particularly in the comic genre, contributed to this new emphasis. Can the increased severity of Mauriac's artistic point of view be attributed, in like manner, to the change to the dramatic form? The main difference between novel and play is, of course, the absence of the author as regulator of time sequence, as creator of atmosphere, as spokesman for his characters' inmost thoughts, and as interpreter of the action. One can catch the novelist's sense of constraint in such shorthand stage directions as: "A fine October afternoon. One must feel, despite the sunlight, the atmosphere of the first wood fires," or "The beginning of a sweltering afternoon. All the shutters are closed. An arrow of sunlight on the hardwood floor."[59] One remembers what Mauriac made of such settings in his novels, and one realizes what a challenge the dramatic form is, for it deprives him of one of his main assets—his descriptive poetic style.

He had also lost considerable control over characterization, for his habitual method alternated between description of his characters' feelings and a subtler, omniscient commentary on them. He was, of course, as aware as Greene was of the need "to fuse everything and put it into dialogue." "The great difficulty in writing for the stage," Mauriac declared in preface to the volume of plays in his *Oeuvres Complètes*, "especially for the novelist, lies in the apparent facility of writing dialogue." And he pointed out that to combat this deceptive facility the novelist-turned-playwright must guard against the relatively lax practice of the novel—"where there is really no serious risk in getting sidetracked a little"[60]—and concentrate on intensity and economy. In his own work he aspired to a Chekov-like simplicity, to "a psychological drama stripped of all the accessories and trappings of show business,"[61] and to "a style spare and direct, but pure, a conversational style but one which, when read carries with it the quality of the written word."[62]

The necessary emphasis on dialogue meant new concentration on character. In his first play, *Asmodée*, Mauriac had been concerned to transpose the atmosphere of his novels to the stage. But seeing that the play succeeded not because of the atmosphere but because of the characters, in his next play, *Les Mal Aimés*, he decided to "conform to the aim of Racine as he expressed it in *Britannicus*, to restrict myself to 'an action which, developing methodically towards its end, is carried entirely by the interests, feelings and passions of the characters.'" Mauriac further expressed his aims in these terms: "I wished to prove to my critics and to myself that my characters exist in themselves, that they have enough density to do without everything that a novelist surrounds them with, and that dramatic poetry is, in a sense, nothing more than the emanation of those feelings by which the characters are possessed."[63]

This statement of Mauriac's attitude towards his characters provokes a consideration of how, in his plays, he fulfills the role of compassionate author. Obviously he is as vitally concerned as ever to guarantee the liberty of his characters, now not only on general creative grounds, but doubly so, because the success of the dramatic form itself depends on a new objectivity, and requires that the author shall remain, much more than in the novel, out of the picture, speaking only through his characters. The harshness of Mauriac's drama can in part be explained by the fact that, denied the usual means of exposing the ambiguities and shadings of his characters' thoughts and feelings, he is left with only a crude extract of his habitual imaginative vision and the skeleton of his familiar practice.

Even more of a handicap in Mauriac's case was the elimination of the author in his traditional role as commentator on developing character and action. In his drama Greene had not only identified sympathetically with those who suffered, but had also given himself a voice in the person of Father Browne in *The Living Room*, and had acted to resolve the mystery in *The Potting Shed* and the comic dilemma in *The Complaisant Lover*. Faced with the same problem of whether or how to intervene in his dramas, Mauriac was much more guarded. One cannot locate him so closely in his plays. Although there is suffering enough, one can scarcely sense the presence of the author lovingly "struggling against his characters" as one can in the Catholic, or for that matter in all the early novels. The withdrawal of Grace was not just a subject for his plays; Mauriac himself withdrew from his fictional universe. More interesting still, the absence of the author is filled by the presence in each play of an authoritarian and grossly dominant character—Coutûre, Virelade, Bernard Lecêtre or Laure—who drives the other characters down the tragic slope of their destiny. Resistance to this strongly individualized fatality is feeble. Élizabeth's suffering is no match for Virelade's cruelty; the eleventh hour rescue of Émilie from Bernard is unprepared and unconvincing; Andrée is wooden and ineffectual as a rival for Laure. And even in *Asmodée*, the best balanced play, Marcelle's character is never fully developed; she is only a stalking horse for Coutûre. And finally, though these dominant characters are the most impressive feature of the plays, they are not, with the possible exception of Laure, treated as tragic heroes as similar types were in the novels. They are, rather, strong representations of a negative, destructive force. One might almost say that they are a parody of the omniscient author and the work of his deforming will over his characters.

In accepting the challenge of the dramatic form, in attempting to prove that his characters could exist in themselves, Mauriac set them too rigorous a test, and withdrew too completely into the wings himself. Theoretically, if Sartre's criticism were valid, this voluntary check on the habit of intervention should have improved Mauriac's art. In fact it was a denaturing of his own particular creative gifts. And it is for this reason that his plays are uneven, strained, and not wholly successful from an artistic standpoint. But the experience was not lost, and when he returned to fiction, his last novels were to bear the definite mark of this exercise in a stricter discipline.

It is an oversimplification, of course, to say that no redemptive force exists in the plays, and once again, deciphering it is all a question of perspective. Certainly, compared to Greene's challenging treatment of Grace, Mauriac gives only a glimmer of mercy in his plays. But if one adjusts the critical focus one can perceive it. "The essential thing, if one is not to succumb to despair or find my play marked by despair," Mauriac writes about Le Feu sur la Terre, "is to keep this truth constantly in mind: that however suffocating the prison in which passion locks a person, he nevertheless always possesses a key to open the door of his cell and escape, either to God's side, or to man's, which is another way of rejoining God. And the name of that key is charity."[64] There is little fundamental difference between this position and the gritty resistance of that wild hope, that irreducible core of faith, which keeps Greene's work in tension and prevents collapse into unregenerative despair. All one might say is that Greene, through provocation, encourages the audience to search for the key, while Mauriac leaves them to find their own encouragement. Yet in all fairness it must be noted that Mauriac makes these remarks ex *post facto*, and this other contemporary observation rings perhaps truer to the overall spirit of his drama: "One must not force one's talent. In my own life I am not at all given to despair. But it is true that, as an author, I show very little disposition for hope."[65]

One cannot claim that a change in outlook is dictated solely by an author's adoption of this or that form, but from the analysis of these two novelists' experiments in drama, choice of form does seem to complement their different developments. For Mauriac, however, other factors contributed to the general darkening of his artistic view. The main influence was the war. Until the mid-thirties Mauriac's interests had been absorbed wholly by literary matters. From the time of the Spanish civil war on, however, his attention turned increasingly outwards, away from the private universe of the creative artist and towards contemporary political affairs in the world at large. This change coincided with the growth of Mauriac's reputation. In the twenties he had won critical acclaim for his work; in the thirties came official recognition and its attendant responsibilities. In 1932 he was named president of the *Société des Gens de Lettres;* in 1933 he was elected to the Academy. On the one hand he was now called on more and more frequently to speak in a semi-official capacity on behalf of the literary and religious interests he represented. On the other, with the prestige that comes to the successful man of letters in France, he now felt it a public duty to declare himself on current political issues.

This new sense of obligation is reflected in his *Journal.* The first volume, which appeared in 1934, was made up of moral and philosophical reflections that had little bearing on world affairs. *Journal II* (1937) and *Journal III* (1940) continue the style of the private diary, but in them political preoccupations begin to declare themselves. After the war Mauriac became fully engaged in a brilliant second career as journalist for *Le Figaro,* and the fourth volume of his

Journal, Le Baillon dénoué (1945), is made up entirely of newspaper articles. There are now half a dozen other volumes of this type, among which must be mentioned *Le Cahier Noir*, a pamphlet published clandestinely during the occupation, and his most recent work in the field of journalism which is collected under the title of *Bloc-Notes* (1959, 1961). It is another instance of Mauriac's sense of public responsibility that after the award of the Nobel Prize in 1952 he should have emerged from what might well have been an honorable retirement at the age of sixty-seven to play a more active role than ever in public life. Today, at seventy-eight, he is a director of *Le Figaro*, director and founder of the review and publishing house *La Table Ronde*, writes a weekly article in the *bloc-notes* format for *Le Figaro Littéraire* and also reviews the week's television for that paper.

It is quite in keeping that, as Mauriac assumed a public role, his interest should turn to the drama which is, much more than the novel, a public art. And it is not surprising that his creative outlook should reflect the gloom and bitterness of the war and immediate postwar years to which he was now, as a journalist even more than as an individual, completely subjected. But there is one other important way that his new career as commentator on the drama of world events influenced his creative work in general. "I have taken journalism seriously," he writes. "It is, for me, the only genre which can acceptably be called *littérature engagée*. And in journalism the value of the commitment is as important to me as the literary value of the work: I do not separate the two."[66] This statement stands in marked contrast to Mauriac's refusal to accept the idea of commitment all through his creative career. Hitherto he had been as wary as Greene about the dangers of loyalty. But now, in his public life, he had become emphatically committed, and any work that he did in a creative vein, if it was to retain that necessary quality of compassionate objectivity, of sympathetic disloyalty, would run counter to an increasingly important part of his life. Here is another reason for the sense of strain in his dramas. A disassociation of interests, even of vocations had begun to set in, and Mauriac's plays were, in a real sense, written against the grain of his most pressing current interests.

But it is appropriate to follow up the opposition between "pure" literature and *littérature engagée* in examining the late novels, which is the task of the next chapter. And in closing this analysis of a novelist's experience in the theater one should let Mauriac have the last word in describing his return to the novel. "While I was writing *Le Feu sur la Terre*," says Mauriac,

I began to feel a nostalgia for my true metier and to imagine *The Loved and the Unloved* and *The Little Misery*. It was circumstance that turned me away from the novel rather than a deliberate act of will on my part. . . . When I had finished *A Woman of the Pharisees,* and all during those dark years that followed, not once did the temptation of the work of art touch me. After the liberation I was taken up by my job as a journalist. My solitude was invaded a little more every day. To write a novel one must have before one months of isolation and calm, and above all interior calm: one cannot be mixed up in the drama of public life. . . . Too much actuality is the enemy of the fiction writer; the real kills the imaginary.

Mauriac goes on to say that his work for the theater fit into this new pattern of life because he could get down the first draft of a play in a few weeks and rework the script in spare time. "A play," he explains, "does not demand such a total displacement of its author as a novel does, for the novelist must lose himself over a reach of years, in a variety of settings, and in a great many characters." And coming back to his satisfaction to have returned to the familiar form, he concludes: "From the author's point of view, one of the great superiorities of the novel over the theater is that in the novel we remain sole master of our work; we wholly assume its destiny."[67]

And though Greene's experience in the theater seems to have been richer from a creative point of view, he echoes Mauriac's thought, giving it a characteristic twist, when he speaks of returning with relief "to that one-man business where I bear full responsibility for failure."[68]

NOTES TO CHAPTER 9

1. Martin Turnell, *The Art of French Fiction* (London, 1959), p. 345.

2. "Préface," *Oeuvres Complètes*, IV, ii. (*Oeuvres Complètes* is hereafter cited as *O.C.*)

3. The first title for *The Frontenac Mystery* was *Le Nid de colombes*. See Robert J. North, p. 82.

4. "Préface," *O.C.*, V, i.

5. "Préface," *O.C.*, IV, i.

6. "Préface," *O.C.*, V, i.

7. *Ibid.*

8. "Préface," *O.C.*, III, iii.

9. "Préface," *O.C.*, IX, iv.

10. "The Art of Fiction," *The Paris Review*, No. 3 (Autumn, 1953), p. 35.

11. "Film Criticisms," *Garbo and the Nightwatchman*, ed. Alistair Cooke (London, 1937), p. 208.

12. *Ibid.*, p. 239.

13. "Subjects and Stories," *Footnotes to the Film*, ed. Charles Davy (London, 1937), p. 61.

14. *Ibid.*, p. 64.

15. *Ibid.*

16. *Garbo and the Nightwatchman*, p. 222.

17. *Footnotes to the Film*, p. 67.

18. *Ibid.*, p. 64.

19. *Ibid.*

20. *Ibid.*, pp. 67-8.

21. "Film Lunch," *The Lost Childhood*, pp. 181-2.

22. "The Art of Fiction," *The Paris Review*, No. 3 (Autumn, 1953), p. 40.

23. "A Stranger in the Theatre," *Picture Post* (April 18, 1953), p. 19.

24. J. D. Scott, "Polished Answer," *New Statesman and Nation*, XLII (September 8, 1951), 258.

25. "The Art of Fiction," *The Paris Review*, No. 3 (Autumn, 1953), p. 31.

26. "Books in General," *New Statesman and Nation*, XXXIX (January 28, 1950), 101.

27. "A Stranger in the Theatre," *Picture Post* (April 18, 1953), p. 19.

28. *The Third Man* (London, 1950), p. 4.

29. *Ibid.*, pp. 3-4.

30. "The Art of Fiction," *The Paris Review*, No. 3 (Autumn, 1953), pp. 29-30.

31. "Middle-brow Film," *Fortnightly Review*, CXXXIX (March, 1936), 304-5.

32. *British Dramatists* (London, 1942), p. 24.

33. *Ibid.*, p. 18.

34. *Ibid.*, p. 40.

35. "Introduction," Graham Greene, *The Living Room* (London, 1955), p. ix.

36. Evelyn Waugh, "The Point of Departure," *The Month*, CXCII (September, 1951), 174.

37. "Introduction," Graham Greene, *The Living Room*, p. x.

38. *British Dramatists*, pp. 18-19.

39. "Middle-brow Film," *Fortnightly Review*, CXXXIX (March, 1936), 304.

40. *British Dramatists*, p. 8.

41. *Ibid.*, p. 19.

42. "Fiction," *The Spectator*, CLI (November 17, 1933), 728.

43. "A Hoax on Mr. Fulton," *The Lost Childhood*, p. 160.

44. "The Job of the Writer," *The Observer* (September 15, 1957), p. 3.

45. *Why Do I Write?*, p. 47.

46. "The Cinema," *The Spectator*, CLVI (January 10, 1936), 50.

47. "Pawn's Move and Knight's Move," *Night and Day*, No. 8 (August 19, 1937), p. 30.

48. "Theatre," *The Spectator*, CLXVII (September 5, 1941), 225.

49. "The Austere Art," *ibid.*, CLXV (December 20, 1940), 682.

50. "Fiction," *ibid.*, CLII (June 1, 1934), 864.

51. "Journal III," *O.C.*, XI, 258.

52. *Ibid.*, p. 257.

53. "Le Romancier et ses personnages," *O.C.*, VIII, 301.

54. *Ibid.*, p. 302.

55. *Ibid.*

56. "Les Mal Aimés," *O.C.*, IX, 238.

57. "Journal III," *O.C.*, XI, 259.

58. *The Unknown Sea* (London, 1948), p. 206.

59. "Asmodée," *O.C.*, IX, 93; "Le Feu sur la Terre," *O.C.*, IX, 425.

60. "Préface," *O.C.*, IX, iv.

61. Philip Stratford, "One Meeting With Mauriac," *The Kenyon Review*, XXI (Autumn, 1959), 617.

62. "Préface," *O.C.*, IX, viii.

63. *Ibid.*, vi-vii.

64. In italics in the text. "Préface," *O.C.*, IX, xii.

65. *Ibid.*

66. "Préface," *O.C.*, XI, i.

67. "Préface," *O.C.*, IX, xiii-xiv.

68. Jenny Nicholson, "Graham Greene: A 'Third Man' in Real Life," *Picture Post* (August 14, 1954), p. 19.

10

THE NOVELIST AND COMMITMENT

Mauriac's last novel, *The Lamb* (1954), is an excellent illustration of the way his sense of commitment, expressed more and more vigorously in his journalism, made notable inroads on his work as a novelist. He describes it as "a novel designed especially to illustrate Catholic doctrine," and adds disparagingly, "I have become a preacher." This confession should be coupled with another made at the same interview, "I have lost faith in the novel."[1]

Despite this self-deprecation, *The Lamb* is not a bad novel. But quite apart from its artistic merit, it is particularly interesting because of the complete change in creative attitude that it represents. Without being in the least autobiographical, Mauriac takes as his central figure a young man whom he endows with all his own insights as a novelist. There is nothing unusual in his identification with the hero—he had entered fully into the passions and temptations of every major character—but he had never before made such a complete fictional transposition of his particular temptations and problems as a writer, and in so doing he allowed himself liberties which he had never taken before in his fiction. It is ironic that this novel which deals so intimately with the source of his creative sensitivity and drive should also be his fictional epitaph.

The hero, Xavier Dartigelongue, is not a writer by profession, but he is marked by all the traits of the novelist of Mauriac's breed. He is insatiably curious about other people and is gifted with the power of entering intuitively into the drama of their lives. He is haunted by this fascination which he calls "the temptation of others," by this "irresistible interest" which is aroused in him by people "who meant nothing to him, to whom he was united by no bond of flesh, of whom he knew nothing beyond what he could feel, beyond what, as he put it, he could 'scent.' " He is, in fact, drawn into the adventure of the novel because of the keen interest that stirs in him when he sees, from the window of his train, an unhappy couple saying good-bye on a station platform. And later, meeting another person for the first time, his reaction is recorded in these terms: "He knew who she was. Stranger to him though she might be, he could read her. It had all come to him in a flash, and now that his brain was working along the right lines, he no longer felt surprised."

Combined with his ardent curiosity and his gift of insight is an extreme sensibility. The way that his intuitive faculty operates is through the reconstruction of many sharply felt details in the life of the person who has captured his attention. As the train leaves the station, he follows the woman of the young couple in imagination:

His heart was melting with tenderness for these two strangers, for her, in particular, who must now be driving alone down one of the roads of Les Landes, or skirting that river all-in-a-blaze which led to some house buried in the depths of the country. . . . There she would find the shoes which the young man had taken off only a few hours before, the shooting-coat flung on the bed, and, on the table, the ashes of the last cigarette he had smoked.

284

By a supreme effort of will Xavier tore his mind from that vision. . . .

This imaginative power, described elsewhere in the novel as "that condition of mild excitement in which all thought becomes visual," is activated by an acute sensual awareness. Xavier is able to re-create the lives of others because he is as sensitive to the sounds, smells, touch and impression of things, landscapes, and climate, as he is to states of emotion and thought. And at the same time—another characteristic shared with his author—his sensuality is constantly accompanied by strong scruples of a religious nature.

Xavier is not a novelist, though he has so many of his creator's aptitudes. Instead he is a candidate for the priesthood. He is on his way to a seminary in Paris when he sees Jean de Mirbel and his wife Michèle on the station platform, and is persuaded to postpone his entry into the religious life and return with Jean to his country house in Les Landes to help save their marriage from foundering. But the fact that the hero of *The Lamb* is to become a priest, not a writer, does not seriously estrange him from his creator. On the contrary, at this point the parallels between Xavier and the novelist begin to multiply in a most interesting way.

For Xavier "the temptation of others" has deep religious significance. His spontaneous interest in everyone he meets is better called "love" than "curiosity" or even "creative insight." Late in the novel, another brief encounter, this time with four boys from a catechism class, sets up this train of thought:

Whence came this disproportionate, this ridiculous, feeling of love? He knew nothing about these boys, and would never see them again. Yet, he would have liked to call them all by their Christian names, to keep them there with him, to penetrate into the life of each, to protect them from dangers, to offer them the rampart of his strength. An extraordinary passion, a divine passion!—yes, that was it: the passion of a God for His creatures.

During the few seconds that he stood there with his feet among the nettles, Xavier thought that he could feel—what madness!—as the Uncreated Being feels for the least of His children.

While this passage defines the essence of Xavier's particular religious sensibility, the description of this "extraordinary passion" also fits exactly the compassionate interest of the novelist-God in his character-creatures. The urge to name, to individualize each of them, the desire to know the secrets of their hearts, to sympathetically become one with them, and finally the temptation to protect are, as we have seen, the peculiar characteristics of Mauriac's creative instinct.

The story of the novel tells how Xavier yields to this passion and becomes actively involved in the lives, not of these chance acquaintances, but of Jean and Michèle and the other occupants of the Mirbel house at Larjuzon—Brigitte Pian, Jean's mother-in-law; Dominique, her young secretary; Roland, a child whom the Mirbels are keeping on trial for adoption; and a parish priest who has lost his faith. Xavier surrenders to the call of distress which each of these in turn makes to him. "What a counterfeit Xavier was of the God he loved," says Jean, who is violently anti-Catholic, "convinced that he must give every scrap of himself to all and each: you first, then me, then all those others whom we found at Larjuzon when we turned up from the train. . . ." Xavier becomes their prisoner. "He could no more escape from this room, from this house, than a convict from his cell. . . ." "He was now the prisoner of this house, these trees, this sleeping man." But this voluntary imprisonment parallels his prospective servitude to the priesthood. In the train, Xavier quotes to Mirbel this passage from Rimbaud: " 'This priestly friend has assumed the priestly uniform . . . that he might have greater freedom.' "

" 'Who would voluntarily go to prison in order to get greater freedom?' " taunts Mirbel.

" 'Greater freedom to love,' " replies Xavier.

Xavier, of course, is not yet a priest and, in fact, never becomes one. He has been warned by his Director of conscience against his impulsiveness: "You no longer have any right to dispose of that heart which you are about to give freely, and without return, nor even of that faculty of attention to which every meeting with another person lays claim." But Xavier's fate is that he will, in extraordinary circumstances, in the space of a few crowded days, live out in an unorthodox fashion the whole of his future vocation as a priest. The household represents his parish; its various members all the problems and temptations that from youth to age he is likely to encounter in a life dedicated to their service. His whole destiny is dramatically heightened and foreshortened in this experience which, at the end of several days, leads to his death. It is also a highly individualized destiny which has nothing about it of the anonymity of the average priest's lifetime of devotion and suffering.

Through the hypersensitive character and career of his hero, Mauriac dramatizes, in a more forthright fashion than ever before in his fiction, what he understands by the vocation of the Christian. Xavier's feelings of tenderness and love are inextricably linked to suffering:

Anguish began once more to ooze up and fill his being, a suffering that had its source in nothing human, suffering which he must endure while he sat there at the table, eating and drinking in the company of these beings, hedged in by them as by a pack of hounds held in leash by somebody he could not see. . . .

He is bound to these others, to his own suffering, and to their suffering. "He belonged to this small creature," he thinks of the child Roland, "to whom he was united by a bond which, while life remained, would not be loosened, nor after life had gone." "He did not know whether he believed in the Communion of Saints but . . . he practiced it with such fervour that it had become for him a matter of evidence, a part of the living truth." Like other Mauriac heroes and victims—Alain Forcas is the nearest parallel, although there are many others—he feels that it is his inescapable responsibility to "carry all of them about with him—had he wished to do so, he could not have separated himself from them." "That too was part of his personal creed. He believed that the number of the elect was small, but that each of them had the power to enrol in his train all the souls, no matter how seemingly damned, who had ever turned to him." And although burdened by this cross, all he can do is accept his suffering and pray God that his own sacrifice may alleviate the suffering of others:

The sleeping creature there beneath his eyes, had made him once more conscious of God's presence in his heart. It had needed but a human body, a human soul, to set God there again, to bring God back to him. He could speak no word to the sleeping child, nor set his lips upon his forehead. He could do no more than speak to God of him in a passionate fervour of substitution. Always that—"take me in his stead," always the longing to assume the miseries of another's destiny.

Quoting these passages out of context does not do justice to the novel as a story. Although Mauriac had never before in fiction been so explicit in stating the articles of his own personal belief, Xavier is more than simply a spokesman for his faith. He has convincing moments of doubt and despair, and keenly experiences temptation and failure. The characters around him are vigorously portrayed and provide strong resistance to him. The events which occur as he passes from the interlocking distress of one character to that of another are vividly imagined. The atmosphere of the country house has seldom been better realized. But even in terms of plot this is no ordinary Mauriac novel. Here again he has risked explicitness and shows contours which are generally submerged in his novels. For while in one sense Xavier's story develops realistically from his suc-

cessive contacts with the various people he meets at Larjuzon, each representing different human problems, the
sub-structure of the novel is organized on another principle.
Step by step, Xavier retraces in his own experience the
stations of the cross. The novel is designed to reduplicate
in modern terms the passion and death of Christ. The cock
crows three times; Xavier prays, deserted in the garden
(the overgrown cemetery behind the church); his feet and
face are washed; he actually struggles and falls under the
weight of a heavy ladder in his own calvary, which makes
him realize what the real Calvary must have been like:

The Cross was not, as he had once believed, a love withdrawn,
an agonized bending of the spirit, an humiliation, an obstacle; it
was, quite simply, a crushing weight of timber, a bruised and
tortured shoulder, carried on feet flayed by stones and earth.
Stretching his muscles to the last bearable point, he still moved
forward, and thought, as he moved, that he could see before him
the thin back of a man. He could see the vertebrae quite clearly,
the ribs rising and falling under the thrust of painful breathing,
the purple weals of flagellation; the slave of all the ages, the
slave eternal.

This protracted parallel makes *The Lamb* quite distinc-
tive among Mauriac's novels, makes it more of a fable or
parable than any of his other fiction, makes it, in short,
something close to a novel of edification, the genre that
Mauriac had execrated and avoided all through his long
novelist's career. During his creative years Mauriac had
thought of himself, using Newman's distinction, as "a
Catholic who was a novelist, not a Catholic novelist." But
now he had become a committed public figure, "a
preacher," and could say, "It is because novels no longer
have any hold on me that I am given over more to history,
to history in the making."[2] Now that he had "lost faith in
the novel," he no longer felt any hesitation about using the
form to carry a message. "Now I am not afraid to write

Catholic novels,"[3] is the way he puts it, referring to *The Lamb.*

But this last novel, although it is different in type from all the others, is only different in that it makes a fuller and more open statement of his fundamental artistic and religious creed. It forces one to make the final identification of Xavier not with the novelist, nor with the average Christian or priest, but with Christ. At the center of Mauriac's creative attitude and faith has always been this special gift of vision—to see the image of Christ in every human being and in all human suffering. This is, transparently, the method he employed in tracing the history of Xavier Dartigelongue, and Xavier himself holds the same sense of vocation and the same belief:

> He was to be pushed along a road where it was past imagination that he could walk. This God of his had no face save that of those whom he had cherished all his life long, *those millions of Christs with tender, brooding eyes.* . . . He heard within himself the ardent words—"Inasmuch as ye have done it to the least of these my brethren, ye have done it unto me . . ." which meant that each of them was Christ, was one with Christ. There was a felt presence of Grace in human beings—felt only by himself. . . .

In his last novel Mauriac testified directly to that felt presence of Grace, but it is true to say that hidden, or partially obscured by passion or suffering, it had always been that same presence which had led him on in his own exploration of the souls of his characters.

The reappearance in *The Lamb* of several major characters from an earlier novel provides a useful gauge for measuring the change in Mauriac's artistic attitude. Jean de Mirbel, Michèle, and Brigitte Pian had been the central figures in Mauriac's last prewar novel, *A Woman of the Pharisees* (1941), probably his *chef d'oeuvre.* Mauriac claims that *The Lamb* is not a sequel and that there is no necessary continuity in character—only that the earlier novel may help to explain "all that is strange, perhaps even monstrous in the man of thirty who, in *The Lamb,* bears the name of Jean de Mirbel."⁴ Even without Mauriac's caution we are now familiar enough with his repetitive method not to look for accumulative effects, and the reappearance of the same cast of characters, all thirteen years older, serves mainly to emphasize the change in his approach to fiction over the thirteen years which separate the two novels.

The Lamb describes the positive results of Xavier's intervention through suffering in the lives of half a dozen people at Larjuzon. He gives in to "the temptation of others" just as Mauriac, in his role as author, gives in to the temptation of edification, the temptation to show Grace operating, not without subtlety but benevolently, in the lives of his characters, and through the agency of one of them in particular. *The Lamb* is Mauriac's nearest approach to the novel of sanctity. *A Woman of the Pharisees* belongs to his earlier genre. It describes not Grace, but that which resists Grace; it concentrates on malice, not benevolence; it is negative rather than positive; and it makes an example of the tyranny of intervention rather than indulging the urge to save others.

Brigitte Pian is the negative counterpart of Xavier Dartigelongue but she is not simply black to Xavier's white; she is far more reprehensible than that. She is a religious hypocrite so she is no stranger to the Christian code. What she represents is perversion, not hostility. This is her attitude, for example towards "the temptation of others":

"One is always punished when one attaches too much importance to other people," murmured Brigitte Pian on a note of bitterness. "I sometimes wonder, dear child, whether I don't give too much of myself when I work for the salvation of my neighbours. Oh, I know that the least among them is of infinite worth. I would give my life that one might be saved. But there are moments when I am frightened to think how much time I have wasted (at least, it *seems* wasted, but of that God alone is judge) over insignificant, nay, evil persons. It is the cross laid upon the great-hearted that they shall exhaust themselves in darkness and uncertainty on behalf of the spiritually mean and inferior. . . ."

This is almost a perfect parody of Xavier's code and behavior in *The Lamb*. What Mauriac finds so dangerous in Brigitte's character is, in general, her monumental self-complacency—"The only thing I hate in the world and can scarcely tolerate in a human being."[5] But it is profitable to analyze her particular kind of selfishness more closely, keeping in mind the parallels we have established between the attitude of the novelist in creating character and the Christian attitude towards others as exemplified by Xavier in *The Lamb*. Brigitte Pian is never in doubt, never vacillates. Although extremely scrupulous, she never hesitates to apply what to her are the obvious remedies for every situation. "She was a logically minded woman who kept to a straight road marked out by clearly labelled principles. She never took a step that she could not immediately justify." This formidable self-assurance is exercised on others rather more than on herself. "Always, in every circumstance of life, and in all her relations with other people, she knew precisely what her words, what her attitude, ought to be." Her cold certitude makes her a frighteningly mechanical figure, an inhuman Fury in the service of an inflexible Destiny.

It also allows her to intervene without compunction in the lives of others. Not that she does so in a spirit of ill will: "In every circumstance of her life Brigitte Pian was sincerely anxious to do good. Or that, at least, was what she believed." But she arrogates to herself the right to dictate to others what is for their certain good. She feels that "her true vocation" is "to make clear to others what God had planned for them from the beginning of time." She wishes "to act as the mouthpiece of Divine Will," and is frequently satisfied that she is "tasting the pleasure that belongs, of right, to God alone: the pleasure of knowing to the full the destiny of someone . . . of feeling that it was in her power to mold that destiny as she willed." She shares, one might say, Xavier's passionate curiosity about the souls of others, but acts on this passion in an entirely un-Christlike way.

In Brigitte Pian, Mauriac embodies not only qualities which he personally finds insufferable in a human being, but also ones which he totally rejects as a novelist, as a creator of character. As if his implicit denunciation of Brigitte Pian's interpretation of Godhead were not clear enough, he occasionally breaks out, in the character of the first-person narrator, in an open accusation: "Thus it was that Brigitte Pian attributed to our Father in Heaven the complexities and perversities of her own nature." Her error, of course, is a basic one: she attempts to imitate God in His justice, not in His mercy. She has "a gift of judgment and condemnation," but no aptitude for compassion. Since she practices the letter of her Christian faith, however, she is aware of her shortcoming: "Madame Brigitte did her utmost to encourage thoughts of mercy in herself, for mercy is a virtue that must not be neglected," but she administers pity from the icy heights of self-righteousness: "Whenever my stepmother cast a fellow human creature into the depths of affliction," the narrator writes ironically, "it gave her pleasure to raise the victim by a spontaneous act of mercy." And her compassion is so distant, so judicious, so far from causing her any pain, so calculated to win her merit, that it does not deserve the name of mercy. One is put in mind again of the distinction between compassion and pity, although in this case indulgence might be a better word, for Madame Brigitte's pity is really self-indulgence.

In sounding the character of *la pharisienne*, Mauriac had two things constantly in mind. First, the danger to his art of exercising Brigitte Pian's kind of god-like judgment over the destinies and characters of his creation; and second, the danger to belief of giving way to the same propensity for judgment in spiritual matters. "The abuse of human logic in divine matters is the long and the short of Jansenism,"[6] Mauriac wrote in *Bonheur du chrétien.* It was a temptation that he knew well in himself, which accounts for the accuracy of his analysis of Jansenistic tendencies in the character of Brigitte Pian.

But so far we have only examined one aspect of this novel, which is far from being simply a negative object lesson, however much it may seem to parallel *The Lamb.* "*A Woman of the Pharisees* in my eyes," Mauriac writes in the preface to his *Oeuvres Complètes,* "is the story of a saintly priest and a tormented adolescent before it is that of a proud, hard woman."[7] Brigitte Pian's proneness to judge and to dominate is counter-balanced throughout the novel by the attitude and conduct of the Abbé Calou. Rather than act in the certainty of a few fixed principles, "he had always had an eye for the unforeseeable repercussions, the mysterious consequences, of our actions when we intervene in the destinies of others, for no matter what good reasons." Due to this wisdom and humility, he does not try to enforce his will on Jean de Mirbel who, as a recalcitrant youth, has been left in his charge in the hope of a brutal uncle that he may be broken and brought to heel. But, "it's no use trying to force one's way into other people's lives, if they don't want one there," the Abbé Calou tells Jean. "Never push open the door of another person's life, for it can be known only to God." He tells Jean that his attitude towards others must be one of pity, "not a corrupt and furtive pity, but the pity of Christ, the pity of a man and of a God who knows well from what imperfect clay He has made His creatures." This is the attitude the Abbé tries to assume towards Jean, and despite the fact that most of the time his love is rejected, he finds in this strayed sheep a reason for his vocation:

This predilection for "bad lots" was doubtless due to a strain of romanticism which still remained in him. . . . But it responded, too, to some deeper more secret yearning, to a desire to help young creatures who might be threatened, who might already have been hurt by life, who did not care whether they were saved or not, who needed a sponsor at the Father's throne. It was not a matter of virtue so much as of preference and inclination.

This is another instance of what Mauriac called in *The Lamb* "the passionate fervour of substitution." It is a form of intervention but totally different from Madame Brigitte's sad reflection on the great-hearted exhausting themselves on behalf of the spiritually mean and inferior. Whereas she counts the cost to herself and adds the equivalent merit to the balance sheet of her salvation, for him the calculation of conduct is much simpler, "I can suffer: I know that. One can always suffer for others. . . ."

To abstract the principles of these two characters' behavior from the concrete facts of their action in the story must give an imperfect picture of the novel. The book is beautifully designed to give both Brigitte Pian and the Abbé Calou opportunity to test their opposing codes in realistic situations. Nor do they operate in isolation but meet and clash in decisions governing their respective wards, for the novel tells of the strong young love that grows up between Michèle, Brigitte's stepdaughter, and Jean de Mirbel. Their common problem, then, is how to treat rebellious love, and each meets it in characteristic fashion, she by imposing disciplinary strictures for the good of Michèle, he by trying to see sympathetically into the turbulence of Jean's passionate nature and gently to coax the good in him into fulfillment. Both fail, and the Abbé Calou, now identifying himself with Brigitte, makes this charitable analysis of their failure:

She would probably be quite genuinely surprised if I told her that my mistake and hers are at bottom identical. They pursue different roads, only to reach the same end. Both of us, she ruled by her reason, I by my feelings, have been inclined to believe that it is our duty to interfere in the destinies of those around us. I do not deny that it is the first duty of the sacred office conferred by priesthood—as, indeed, it is part of the duty of every Christian—to preach the Gospel: but that does not mean that we should try to turn our neighbour into a replica of ourselves, nor force him to see with our eyes. Of ourselves we can do nothing. Our concern should be limited to walking before the Divine Grace as the dog goes in front of the invisible hunter. . . . But when it comes to measuring the havoc that accumulates about what we conceive to be our mission, we must give full weight to all those unadmitted interests, all those secret desires the existence of which in our hearts we scarcely realize. That is why we should allow full play to the spirit of compassion.

The complexity of the novel does not end with the opposition of pride and humility. As Graham Greene writes:

La Pharisienne herself under her layer of destructive egotism and false pity is disclosed sympathetically to the religious core. She learns through hypocrisy. The hypocrite cannot live insulated forever against the beliefs she professes.[8]

At the end of the novel it is the Abbé Calou who is the agent of her conversion. Under his influence this woman "strong in her assurance of Grace, convinced of her right to interfere in the lives of those over whom she had authority," learns to "rid herself . . . of her old tendency to dominate." It is no easy conversion. As the Abbé predicts: "If ever that gift of judgment and condemnation which she now exercises at the expense of others is turned against herself, she's in for a bad time," and this painful act of lucid introspection, which reveals to her "a countenance till then undreamed of and beyond words horrible," provides the continuity in character which makes the conversion credible. Suffering opens her eyes, not only to her own iniquities but to another's way of seeing things. Given a final opportunity to intervene in the lives of Michèle and Jean, she remembers these words of the Abbé Calou:

Each of us, he had said, has his own peculiar destiny, and it is, perhaps, one of the secrets of that compassionate Justice which watches over us, that there is no universally valid law by which human beings are to be assessed.

And instead of interfering, she gives them her blessing. No longer self-righteously pleased at the suffering of others, she becomes "passionately concerned." She understands at last "that it is not our deserts that matter but our love."

As it has been presented, *A Woman of the Pharisees* seems, perhaps, to be nothing but a more ample and more complex exploitation of themes which are treated again in *The Lamb,* and it is true that it must be classed among Mauriac's Catholic novels, that it is, as Mauriac himself says, "one of those books in which religious experience has best served the novelist in me."[9] But it is not, in the same sense as *The Lamb,* a novel of edification. The "message" of the novel is diffused through the narrative texture much more than it has been possible to suggest in this analysis. The complicated background and events of the story itself, and the method of its telling (it is a retrospective novel recounted in the first person by Louis, Michèle's brother, a character who is not entirely objective but who plays his own part in the drama), put it outside the range of moralizing *littérature engagée.* On this very question one might quote Louis in the novel who this time speaks for Mauriac when he says: "An author is neither moral nor immoral in himself. It is our own attitude of mind that decides what his influence on us is to be."

But more important still, is the presence in the novel of an amoral character who neither accepts nor rejects Mauriac's philosophy as represented positively in the Abbé Calou, and negatively in Brigitte Pian. He is, of course, the tormented adolescent Jean de Mirbel who revolts against discipline and revolts against love. He is the intractable, passionate character who stubbornly defies the best efforts of others, whether benign or malicious, to dominate him, to make him serve their will. He is the prodigal son, and the lost sheep. "You are not virtuous, I know," says the Abbé Calou. "You're not of that kind. . . . You are one of those whom Christ came into the world to save." He is indeed the embodiment of the human mystery of free will which has as its divine counterpart the mystery of God's mercy. And in the artistic sense he is the guarantee that the novelist will not overindulge his desire to dominate and save, but will leave to his characters that mysterious but essential right to their own independence.

In *The Lamb* the character called Jean de Mirbel has not become docile, but he has hardened into a savage and stereotyped version of the earlier Jean. He has lost his independent vitality as, indeed, have the others—Michèle is a vague symbol of a woman, and Brigitte Pian nothing but an ominous shadow of her earlier incarnation. No other character in *The Lamb* is of sufficient stature to take the role of the recalcitrant lost sheep (the boy Roland is the most likely candidate but remains embryonic). There is nothing to be done with Jean but to play him off as a foil for Xavier throughout most of the novel and, finally (Mauriac having lost the qualms he felt about the end of Thérèse), to bring him to an inconsistently sudden conversion.

In the last pages of *A Woman of the Pharisees*, the narrator, obviously speaking again for Mauriac, promises at a later date to pursue the adventures of his characters, to "tell the story of the sainted Abbé Calou's road to Calvary," the story of his own years in Paris with Jean de Mirbel, and twice speaks of telling of "the interminable succession of storms and stresses," which made up the married life of Jean and Michèle. *The Lamb* can be considered as one chapter in "the constant eddy of strife and reconciliation which made up their existence." But before *The Lamb* Mauriac wrote two other short novels, *nouvelles* more properly speaking, which are in no sense sequels and which belie the tone of fatigue and resignation to diminished powers that such hinting at future fictions betrays. *The Little Misery* (1951) and *The Loved and the Unloved* (1952) are sharp, bitter little masterpieces which show a gain in precision and objectivity due to Mauriac's experience in the theater. They are almost completely dark, like his plays, and in no way reflect his growing sense of commitment. They are, in short, his last true works of fiction.

The first of these, *The Little Misery*, might have been prefaced by this quotation from *A Woman of the Pharisees*: "No man can bear a child's cross. It is something beyond the comprehension of the fully grown." In this novel Mauriac tries to penetrate the suffering of a backward, twelve-year-old boy, Guillou de Cernès. The story deals with adult anxieties too, particularly through the characterization of Guillou's mother, Paula. She has made a loveless marriage out of her own class to the half-wit Galéas de Cernès which is described as "the pit into which she had fallen of her own free will, knowing there was no escape." She is alone in "this hell in which she lived," considered "the enemy" by son, husband, her mother-in-law la Baronne, and Fräulein, the family's old Austrian cook. She meets no sympathy outside the circle of the family, her one contact, in the past, with a young priest, having been a source of scandal—"But all that had ever happened had been the meeting, in their persons, of two solitary sufferers whose loneliness had never mingled." She exerts a "baleful influence on those with whom she had to live," felt all the more keenly because they realize, in varying degrees, that they are her "torturers."

But this familiar development of a woman's suffering serves only as a background to the child's torment in *The Little Misery*. Childhood had long remained a last stronghold of purity for Mauriac. Writing of the adolescents Jean and Michèle in *A Woman of the Pharisees* he says: "The poor human insects had to trace backwards the stages of their metamorphosis before each could see once more in the other the child whom he or she had loved," and in the plays, particularly in *Les Mal Aimés,* adult unhappiness at least reposed on a foundation of childhood happiness and innocence. In this late novel, however, Mauriac traces the genesis of despair back to childhood itself through the character of the helpless, abused Guillou who has no other defense in the quarreling, fearsome adult world than "to learn to be numb and sottish," to play dead when danger threatens, and who, at last, leads his unhappy father to the edge of a mill pond where both drown.

In the age of the child, in the constitution of his family, and in many details of his surroundings and experience, there are close parallels with Mauriac's early autobiographical novel *The Stuff of Youth. The Little Misery* is, in a sense, a cruel travesty of that tender, happy, nostalgic fiction based on his Bordeaux childhood. *Questions of Precedence* (1920) had been Mauriac's satirical postwar reaction to the sentimentality of such a book and had announced his coming of age as a novelist. Now, at his career's end, thirty years later and after another war, he turned again to the subject of childhood and treated it not satirically, but tragically. Nowhere does Mauriac give a harsher description of his "poor human insects." Not one of the characters, from the masculine Paula with "her bilious cheeks with their thick growth of down," to Galéas with his "drooling, open mouth and thick tongue," to the snuffling child Guillou, "his legs . . . like two twigs ending in enormous boots," his "chicken-neck" sticking out above his cape—not one is spared the relentless cruelty of Mauriac's description. There is no sympathetic Xavier or understanding Abbé Calou to love these ugly creatures. A schoolmaster is briefly moved to help the child, but a mixture of pride, indifference, selfishness, and fear leads him "to throw him out like a stray puppy which he had warmed a moment at his fire." Nor does Mauriac, as narrator, dwell pityingly on the child's predicament. Leaving the mystery of Guillou's suffering intact, what comment he does make shows in the child only a partial awareness, and the instinctive behavior of a frightened animal:

. . . for other people he felt neither hate nor love. His grandmother, his father, Fräulein provided that climate of security which he found so necessary, from which his mother fought tooth and nail to drive him, like a ferret attacking a rabbit deep in his warren. At no matter what cost, he had got to come out, and, dazed, bewildered, submit to her furious rages. When that happened he just rolled himself in a ball and waited for the storm to pass.

Guillou is almost less than human: "In that suffering body a human spirit had laid unawakened," says Mauriac, and, restraining the urge to intervene, he leaves it so. The story is a tragedy, not a moral fable. Its message is not a doctrine but an appeal. And all one can say in point of edification is that from this desolate childhood a cry goes up, which, in the novel, is left unanswered.

The chapel at Cernès had been left unconsecrated, and although there is a cathedral in the "little half-dead town" of Dorthe in the second of these short novels, *The Loved and the Unloved* (1952), Mauriac describes the religious observances there with calculated malice:

The faithful barked the responses with a sort of gluttonous haste, and the vaulted roof echoed back the subdued growl which, rather surprisingly, was produced by the thin scattering of female worshippers.

Six rows of little girls were bombarding the altar at point-blank range with their "Priez pour nous." Their fire was being directed by two aged nuns. . . . The great organ . . . emitted a series of intermittent grunts, wheezing asthmatically, like a broken-down lion in a cluttered forest of stone.

The Cathedral looked like some enormous Ark left stranded by an ebbing flood—something given over to the predatory rats of a rotting countryside.

The story principally concerns the misery of a sex-starved governess, Madame Agathe, whose dilemma is summed up in these questions:

What use was there in praying? All the praying in the world would not make her less repulsive-looking, nor less flat-chested. How could so dead a soul, somebody so miserably equipped in the matter of physical charms, have any inkling of Eternal Love?

Nor has she any luck in the matter of earthly love though she strains to practice her own advice: "The most important thing in life, my dear, is to know how to use your brain, even in matters of the heart," an attitude which earns her the nickname of "Galigaï." Her scheming temporarily traps a soft-hearted victim, Nicolas Plassac, who yields to the temptation "to bring to life a being who is dying of love." But in the end his revulsion gets the better of him, "nausea is something that one cannot control,"[10] and he escapes, telling her, "we should have been, you and I, each other's executioner."

As in The Little Misery Mauriac's description of these characters is of an unprecedented brutality. In different places Galigaï is likened to a cat, a snake, a bitch, a bat, a bird, a fish, an ant, a fly, a spider, a corpse. When she fails to capture Nicolas she takes as second prize her widowed employer who, in the engagement scene, is described as a toad. Social prejudices and taboos and material motives play an increasingly important part as a background to warped passions in these late stories. Passion itself is reduced to the level of sex. Playing opposite Nicolas and Galigaï is a pair of handsome and happy lovers, Gilles, Nicolas' friend, and Marie, the governess' charge. But it is never suggested that their love is anything more than an impermanent physical hunger, a coursing of the blood in two healthy animals, a twitching of the nerves. And even Nicolas, the most sympathetic character, the victim, has little to redeem him. The only one whose actions are prompted by conscience in this drama, his motives are obscured by his infatuation with Gilles. He is "good" to Galigaï but cannot bring himself to sympathize with her: "I am moved to pity for others," he says, "except only for the woman who loves me. The passion I have inspired in this poor creature, and do not share, alone leaves me unmoved. It actually irritates me so much, that it drives me into a perfect frenzy. . . ." For Gilles's sake he accepts her advances: " 'How good you are,' she sighed." But Mauriac comments, "Yes, to her undoing, he was good." Though loved but unloving, he is sensitive and not willingly cruel, but his sacrifice is scornfully described in these words: "Well, then, immolated he must be, poor, stupid victim."

This bleak fiction ends after the storm of Galigaï's passion has blown over and Gilles is safely bedded with Marie, with the intimation that Nicolas is now free to seek out God.

He saw the black bulk of the stranded Cathedral caught among the roofs. The human insects had, at least, reared high that ship, and built it to the measure of the love which had some of them by the throat. He started to walk again and reached the place where the road crossed the Leyrot. He sat upon the parapet, a stranger to himself, detached from all his fellows. It was as though he had agreed with Somebody to meet him there.

This conclusion might be taken as an indicator of the development Mauriac's fiction would take in The Lamb. But rather than accentuate the change, this is a good place to insist on the consistency of Mauriac's vision, even in that moral fable. For all its difference in emphasis and intent, The Lamb, it must now be said, remains deeply marked by the bitterness and despair that characterized the two preceding novels. The child Roland is a snotty-nosed, sulky

brat, a second little misery. "Childhood is essentially a period of ingratitude," says Xavier. "To be ungrateful is the
very law of its being, and, with ingratitude goes jealousy."
Brigitte Pian at seventy-eight, although "a human look had
come into the large, lined face," is still a monster. Her
mouth "empty of teeth," "the yellowish-white coils of hair
that sprouted from her skull" supported by a pad, she sits
"motionless in her armchair, her eyes concealed by the
black glasses, like an enormous night-owl perched on a
dead branch." If he had been concerned to trace the stages
of her conversion in the latter part of *A Woman of the
Pharisees,* here Mauriac illustrates the antithesis, that
"people do not change."[11] Her old enmity with Jean flares
up again in *The Lamb,* and all that can be said for her gain
in prudence is that she leaves Larjuzon in anger instead of
staying to do battle. Jean himself remains wild, cruel, deformed by hatred, and though he is deeply afflicted by
Xavier's death, and is moved by it to what has been called
a conversion, his statement of faith, far from being a triumphant assertion is painful acknowledgment of the coexistence of peace and suffering: " 'What Xavier believed,
you believe, too?' " Michèle asks him.

"He did not deny it. 'Yes, Michèle, I know now that love
does exist in this world. But it is crucified in the world and
we with it.' "

In a "Postscript" at the end of *The Loved and the Unloved* Mauriac takes an objective look at the harsh story
he has just written and, since at the time he is correcting
proof for the collected edition of his works, by the same
token passes in review the whole of his fictional creation.
"The picture I have painted is indeed black," he writes. "It
shows mankind as warped, as showing to the world a mask
fixed in a hard and hateful grimace. It shows humanity untouched by Grace. In favour of whom, or of what, can such
a portrait bear witness?" "How can I reconcile so distorted

a view of the human animal," he asks further, "with the faith I claim to have in his vocation to sanctity?" And he feels obliged to admit, in a detailed examination of the limitations of his art, that his novel serves no useful purpose.

For the creative writer to pretend that he helps us to an understanding of mankind by painting a picture in dark and extravagant colours, is sheer hypocrisy. Living persons are never like the characters of fiction. The people presented in novels or on the stage are a race apart. They in no way instruct us about ourselves, or, at least, not usefully; in the first place because these invented creatures are conditioned and circumstanced by the author; in the second, because, no matter how complex they may be, they inevitably express some tendency, some passion, or some vice, and are, to that extent detached from the human context. . . . And even when an artist goes out of his way to avoid the introduction of "types" and "characters," the colourless and insubstantial world into which he introduces us has little in common with our own. . . . There is no such thing as a novel which genuinely portrays the *indetermination* of human life as we know it.[12]

This is not all of Mauriac's apologia but it is the confessional part, and it expresses sincerely the doubts which, at this time, were leading him to lose faith in the novel. In his postwar fiction, novels and plays, he had set himself the difficult goal of increased objectivity while, simultaneously, he was becoming more and more *un écrivain engagé* in political and religious matters as a journalist. In the novels that he wrote during this period, to check his inclination towards commitment, he forced himself to withdraw from his fictional universe and to coldly contemplate the surface of his creation. But the duality between the demands of art and religion on which tension of all his creative work had depended now became too contradictory. He was no longer able to sustain the ambiguity between the dispassionate and the passionate which we have defined as the compassionate mean. With the dissipation of this creative stress Mauriac leaves the world of fiction behind. In just such a way, at the end of *The Loved and the Unloved*, Nicolas is freed from his love of Gilles Salone and from Galigaï's love for him. "It was necessary," Mauriac writes, "that Nicolas should be detached from appearances. . . . Galigaï makes him realize that the lusts of the flesh are productive of intense unhappiness, that he is no less capable of cruelty than other men, and that he has never really loved anyone but God. The world I have described is the world as it appears to Nicolas when the scales fall from his eyes."[13] But the novelist cannot be detached from appearances. He must be able to describe the world with, as well as without, the scales on his eyes. It is significant, in the same metaphorical sense, that Xavier, hero of *The Lamb* and the last representative of Mauriac's own type as a novelist, should, at the end of the novel, be suspected of committing suicide. It is through this character that Mauriac signals the end to his own creative career.

Greene encountered the same problems of commitment at about the same time. While Mauriac was writing *The Lamb*, he was working (from March, 1952, to June, 1955) on his first novel since *The End of the Affair*. He had announced that *The Quiet American* would "not deal explicitly with Catholic themes at all."[14] Giving due weight to that ambiguous "explicitly," and to the fact that he had temporarily transferred his treatment of Catholic themes from the novel to the drama, his prediction was true. In the new novel, as in the two entertainments of the fifties, *Loser Takes All* (1955) and *Our Man in Havana* (1958), he buried his religious obsessions, and when Catholics appeared in his fiction (for example, the hero's daughter, Milly, in *Our Man in Havana*), he treated them lightly, not critically or tragically.

This movement away from the Catholic novel was

prompted by the same desire for renewal which led Mauriac to expand the scope of his novels in the late thirties and which led both novelists to experiment in the theater. Stated in even stronger terms, it was the horror of being snugly classified as "Catholic novelists" which drove them both to assert their artistic independence in works which did "not deal explicitly with Catholic themes at all."

In many ways Greene had reached the limit of religious commitment in *The End of the Affair*. With its miracles, and its saint, and non-believer Bendrix forced to reluctantly accept the existence of God, it came closer than any of Greene's novels to an out-and-out demonstration of faith. Of course he had created dramatic tension in choosing a skeptic as narrator for this story of belief. And he was not concerned to retail any standard orthodoxy, for Sarah is no conventional saint, and the relationship which Greene establishes between her two love affairs, the one with Bendrix and the other with God, scarcely falls within the scope of common Catholic piety.

These were Greene's personal safeguards against edification, but they do not alter the fact that he had become more directly an exponent of his faith in this novel than in any other. It is John Atkins' contention that the two years following *The End of the Affair* "constituted the peak period of Greene's religious enthusiasm."[15] He draws attention to the several essays which Greene wrote on Catholic matters about this time, and concludes that *The Living Room* is little more than a religious exercise, "a penance," he calls it, in which Greene forced himself to uphold a strictly doctrinal position. Without going to such extremes, it is generally true to say that in the early fifties Greene came closer than he had before, or has since, to what passes for an acceptable Catholic norm. Evelyn Waugh, who had referred to *The Heart of the Matter* as "mad blasphemy,"[16] welcomed in *The End of the Affair* "a defiant assertion of the supernatural," and wrote:

His earlier books tended to show Catholics to themselves and set them puzzling. *The End of the Affair* is addressed to the Gentiles. It shows the Church as something in their midst, mysterious and triumphant and working for their good. One might say that in places it is too emphatically sectarian.[17]

Perhaps the best evidence that the problem of commitment deeply concerned Greene at this time, and certainly the best commentary on the question, was provided in the new novel that Greene was working on. Commitment to religious belief was not in question in *The Quiet American*, but the problem had simply been translated to the sphere of politics as can be seen in the following analysis. The first person narrator and central character is an English journalist called Fowler. He makes a fetish of his professional objectivity:

"I'm not involved. Not involved," I repeated. It had been an article of my creed. The human condition being what it was, let them fight, let them love, let them murder, I would not be involved. My fellow journalists called themselves correspondents; I preferred the title of reporter. I wrote what I saw: I took no action —even an opinion is a kind of action.

This jaded attitude, dictated by "age and despair," invades every corner of Fowler's life. He stands aloof from the political issues of the Indo-China war he is covering for his London paper: "I don't know what I'm talking politics for. They don't interest me and I'm a reporter. I'm not engagé. . . . I don't take sides. I'll still be reporting, whoever wins." His cynicism sours his belief in human beings and in God:

'Wouldn't we all do better not trying to understand?' he asks, accepting the fact that no human being will ever understand another, not a wife a husband, a lover a mistress, nor a parent a child? Perhaps that's why men have invented a God—a being capable of understanding. Perhaps if I wanted to be understood or understand I would bamboozle myself into belief, but I am a reporter; God exists only for leader-writers.

Detachment reaches into his personal habits. He smokes opium because "it calms the nerves and stills the emotions," and lives with an Indo-Chinese girl, Phuong, who provides him the same kind of passive Eastern pleasure: "she was the hiss of steam, the clink of a cup, she was a certain hour of the night and the promise of rest."

Into his quietistic life comes one of the opposite extreme, a naïve Harvard graduate on an Economic Aid Mission to Vietnam, called Pyle. He is a professional do-gooder, "absorbed . . . in the dilemmas of Democracy and the responsibilities of the West." A textbook politician, he takes motive for action from the works of a certain York Harding, described by Fowler as "a superior sort of journalist—they call them diplomatic correspondents. He gets hold of an idea and then alters every situation to fit the idea." Beside Harding's *The Rôle of the West* on Pyle's bookshelves is a paper-backed book called *The Physiology of Marriage.* "Perhaps he was studying sex," Fowler comments sneeringly, "as he had studied the East, on paper. And the keyword was marriage. Pyle believed in being involved."

In these two characters, positions are drawn up for dramatic antagonism—between youth and age, innocence and experience, romanticism and realism, between Pyle's naïve faith and Fowler's tired skepticism, between the energetic meddling of the one, and the impotent non-intervention of the other. But this basic opposition is nothing but the premise of the novel which describes not only the clash of character, but the interpenetration of the two points of view, particularly the effects of Pyle's behavior on Fowler. He disrupts Fowler's peace. He saves his life, steals Phuong with a promise of marriage, rouses Fowler's latent political conscience, makes him take sides, makes him, in fact, become an accomplice in murder, in Pyle's murder. All this would remain on the level of melodrama if Pyle's death meant no more to Fowler than being rid of a rival. But he is shaken out of his weary complacency by it, and reconstructs the story (which is told in retrospect) out of a sense of guilt. On any level of interpretation but the most superficial, *The Quiet American* must be seen as the story of how Fowler is forced out of his initial position of non-commitment, and in this sense the novel closely parallels Bendrix's story in *The End of the Affair,* though the terms of narrative are political and not "explicitly" religious.

This being the case, it is important to trace the steps which lead Fowler to an inescapable sense of involvement and to carefully define what that involvement implies. The first time that the nerveless surface of his objectivity is ruffled is when his life is endangered in a Vietminh attack on a Vietnamese watchtower on the road to Saigon. Fear opens his imagination and makes him see himself as "a frightened fool who could not recognize his own trembling, and I had believed I was tough and unimaginative, all that a truthful observer and reporter should be." In the same engagement the pain of one of the wounded Vietnamese guards breaks through his indifference and not only gives him a sense of personal involvement, but gives it a familiar orientation.

I was responsible for that voice crying in the dark: I had prided myself on detachment, on not belonging to this war, but those wounds had been inflicted by me just as though I had used the sten, as Pyle had wanted to do.
I made an effort to get over the bank into the road. I wanted to join him. It was the only thing I could do, to share his pain.

Certain other scenes of suffering in the war stir his latent sympathy. A Vietnamese mother and child shot in a crossfire; a sampan strafed by a French bomber. These are accidents of war but they affect him deeply; he cannot get them out of his head. "Unfortunately," he thinks, "the innocent are always involved in any conflict. Always, everywhere, there is some voice crying from a tower." The French pilot whose own attitude as a professional soldier varies between coldness and pain, answers his "I won't be involved" with: "It's not a matter of reason or justice. We all get involved in a moment of emotion and then we cannot get out. War and Love—they have always been compared." In his stress, and threatened by Pyle's interest in Phuong, Fowler sees that he has been inventing a character for her and begins to see her as she is, an innocent involved in their rivalry over her. Finally, stung by Pyle's success with Phuong, but more by Pyle's responsibility in a bomb blast which kills and mutilates a number of innocent Vietnamese, Fowler himself becomes actively involved. Goaded on by pressure from a Chinese communist, who tells him "sooner or later . . . one has to take sides. If one is to remain human," he provides the information and collaboration which lead to Pyle's murder.

The transfer has taken place—Fowler has become "as engagé as Pyle," but the cycle is not quite complete. The success of his involvement gives him no satisfaction. He is left feeling that "no decision would ever be simple again." He is forced to wonder, "Was I so different from Pyle? . . . Must I too have my foot thrust in the mess of life before I saw the pain?" He admits, "I've been blind to a lot of things . . ." and cannot shake the sense of guilt: "Everything had gone right with me since he died, but how I wished there existed someone to whom I could say that I was sorry."

In view of the indignation that The Quiet American aroused in the United States and its smug reception in England, it is necessary to doubly underline a few facts about the novel as novel. Greene's use of national and political symbols to carry his story stirred popular emotion much more than any of his Catholic novels, and this has obscured both the artistic value of the work and its real meaning. American readers were incensed, perhaps not so much because of the biased portrait of obtuse and destructive American innocence and idealism in Pyle (that portrait had been painted many times before), but because in this case it was drawn with such acid pleasure by a middle-class English snob like Fowler whom they were all too ready to identify with Greene himself. English readers who vicariously enjoyed Fowler's spleen, though they could attribute its excess to Greene, were just as short-sighted, and hypocritical into the bargain. The point is that Greene is not Fowler any more than he is Andrews or Farrant, Bendrix or Querry, or any of his other unpleasant characters. Fowler is a fictional creation made out of his author's experience and imagination, but neither a self-portrait nor a mouthpiece. It is fair to expect the total novel to carry Greene's viewpoint, but fatal to equate Fowler and Greene, the narrator and the author. That is why, in interpreting the novel, one must avoid quick judgment and use great care and latitude in establishing Greene's central position as creator.

In the dramatized debate between Fowler and Pyle it is clear that Greene condones neither the selfishness of one nor the other. Fowler's inert non-commitment is no more compatible to him than Pyle's high-principled meddling. As author, he is not in the position of "diplomatic correspondent"—altering every situation to fit his thesis—but he is not a detached "reporter" either. He is a novelist, and his approach to truth through fiction is a paradoxical composite of these two attitudes. As reporter he must record what he sees with dispassionate accuracy. Greene had twice quoted Chekov on this need for objectivity: "Fiction is called artistic because it draws life as it actually is,"[18] and later: "The best artists are realistic and paint life as it is." But the second quotation continues to incorporate the idea that "one has to take sides if one is to remain human."

"But because every line is permeated, as with a juice, by awareness of a purpose," Chekov goes on, "you feel, besides life as it is, also life as it ought to be."[19] The idea of this dual function remained with Greene. He had used it as a standard for criticism of books and films; he wrote that as a description of an artist's theme it had never been bettered;[20] and introducing additional terms he wrote: "The mood of the author . . . should be one of Justice and Mercy, and while Justice sees and draws the world as it is, the mood of Mercy is aware of what it might be—if the author himself as well as all the world, were different."[21]

The essential contradiction in this dual duty is similar to what Mauriac calls, in theology, "the eternal contradiction between man's liberty and divine prescience," between God's foreknowledge and the human necessity of choice. This contradiction has special significance for the novelist who is at once a God over his creation and, through his characters, a creature in it. It is a contradiction which cannot be resolved, though it can be assumed in the novelist's paradoxically ambivalent attitude. One cannot expect from him either extreme of commitment or non-commitment, and the nearest one can come to an analogy for his equivocal position is in the figure of an incarnate God.

Not less than in the Catholic novels, though not so explicitly stated, the central attitude in *The Quiet American* is a Christian one. It is not embodied in Pyle or Fowler but does briefly appear in two minor characters in the novel, in Captain Trouin, the French pilot, and in Vigot, the French officer at the Sureté. Although Trouin is the man who tells Fowler, "we all get involved in a moment of emotion," his involvement is not characterized by a shallow sense of justice or partisan idealism. "The first time I dropped napalm," he tells Fowler,

I thought, this is the village where I was born. That is where M. Dubois, my father's old friend, lives. The baker—I was very fond of the baker when I was a child—is running away down there in the flames I've thrown. The men of Vichy did not bomb their own country. I felt worse than them.

He said with anger against a whole world that didn't understand, "I'm not fighting a colonial war. Do you think I'd do these things for the planters of Terre Rouge? I'd rather be court-martialled. We are fighting all of your wars but you leave us the guilt."

Trouin's humanity is a composite of his clear-sightedness— the cool objectivity with which he views the facts of fighting a losing war—and the obligation he feels not to hide behind the shield of professionalism and wash his hands of responsibility, but to assume the guilt of the crimes to which he is professionally committed. He envies Fowler his escape through opium. For him there is no escape. He is a prisoner of conscience. In this sense of involvement, the phrase "one has to take sides if one is to remain human" takes on not a judicial but a Christian connotation. It is an admission of human limitation rather than a plea on behalf of humanity.

Vigot, the sad police officer who keeps a copy of Pascal on his desk, is another man who holds the difficult balance between justice and compassion. His job is to find the facts, but his purpose is not to total them up into a sentence. Fowler sees in him a man with a vocation. "You would have made a good priest, Vigot," he says. "What is it about you that would make it so easy to confess—if there were anything to confess. . . . Is it because like a priest it's your job not to be shocked, but to be sympathetic?" Vigot's methods resemble those of a priest: he does not accuse but listens. He is "silence sitting in a chair." "I had the feeling of some force immobile and profound. For all I knew, he might have been praying." He shows the same kind of humility as another minor character, Fowler's Indian assistant, Dominguez, of whom Fowler says:

. . . where other men carry their pride like a skin-disease on the surface, sensitive to the least touch, his pride was deeply hidden

314

and reduced to the smallest proportion possible, I think, for any human being. All that you encountered in daily contact with him was gentleness and humility and an absolute love of truth. Perhaps truth and humility go together, so many lies come from our pride.

Fowler lies to Vigot about his implication in Pyle's murder and Vigot is obliged to close his file uncompleted. As he goes, he turns and looks at Fowler "with compassion, as he might have looked at some prisoner for whose capture he was responsible undergoing his sentence for life." And he does, of course, leave Fowler sentenced by his own sense of guilt. The whole novel is, in fact, a confession, an answer to Vigot's silent and sympathetic appeal, and it is made with all the humility and concern for truth that Fowler can muster.

Greene's position as novelist is obviously at one remove from this, for he must be true to Fowler's character as well as to the facts that Fowler describes. Hence the falsity of a facile identification between Greene and his hero. His position as novelist is more truly indicated by the painful ambivalence of Captain Trouin or the sadly sympathetic attitude of Vigot or by the humility of Dominguez. Or, if it is necessary to identify him with Fowler—and we have said that his creative act depends on his compassionate identification with his characters—one must allow that his identification is not with one side, the non-committal reporter's side of his character, but with this and with the total complexity of the man. He is also, and finally, the Fowler who hesitates—"I don't know. I don't know"—before agreeing to Pyle's death. He is the Fowler who sees his own error in judging in terms of quantity and says, "Suffering is not increased by numbers: one body can contain all the suffering the world can feel." Without leaving his character, Greene shares Fowler's hatred and Fowler's guilt. His one aim as a novelist has been to achieve something of that God-like understanding which at the beginning of the novel Fowler feels is so far beyond his reach, but which at the end he feels so badly in need of. In this sense, and in the highest sense of the word, Greene has done Fowler justice.

It must be admitted that, comparatively, Greene does Pyle less than justice in *The Quiet American*. But the title is misleading, for this is really the story of Fowler, not of Alden Pyle. Also, of course, we are bound by the convention of the narrative to see Pyle, not in terms of Greene's personal prejudices, but dramatically through Fowler's eyes. Furthermore, any serious consideration of this novel must take into account two facts. First, there are the many instances in the novel where Pyle's and Fowler's characters are shown to overlap (the whole story is one of the transfer of Pyle's traits to Fowler and to some extent vice versa). Second, when one considers Pyle in the context of all Greene's fiction, one sees him not so much as an isolated caricature of the American, but as a familiar Greene type. In one respect he is very like Greene's pious Catholics who live by the letter and the law of an impenetrable idealism, although he is treated more sympathetically than many of these, than, for example, Louise Scobie, or the aunts in *The Living Room,* or Rycker in *A Burnt-Out Case*. In another way he resembles Greene's earlier adolescent heroes—Andrews, and Oliver Chant, and the young Arthur Rowe, "the Happy Man" of *The Ministry of Fear.* They too were caught up in the excitement of commitment and melodramatically simple rules until experience thrust their feet into the mess of life. It is a standard theme in Greene's fiction and one of those conflicts which as an artist he has left unsolved. It is just unfortunate for the self-conscious that this time Greene happened to give this stock figure American nationality.

An interesting contrast between Greene and Mauriac, and a good commentary on the different stages they had reached in their careers in the early fifties, is provided by their two ways of handling of this common problem of commitment. Mauriac's solution is radical. Making a sharp distinction between public and artistic responsibilities, he writes two severely objective novels in which he voluntarily curtails his own artistic freedom to intervene, while at the same time he is becoming more and more outspoken on religious and political issues as a journalist. When the duality becomes intolerable, he writes one last propaganda novel, *The Lamb,* then abandons fiction.

Greene's reaction to the problem represents an earlier stage in development. Faced with the same conflict he transmutes it into fiction, dramatizes the duality and finds in it a source of creative vitality. The fact that he was working on the novel did not prevent Greene from writing a dozen journalists' reports on the situation in Indo-China from 1952 to 1955. Certain of the battle scenes described in these articles were incorporated almost word for word in the novel. These passages are relatively objective, but he did not always maintain the same reporters' standard. Like his accounts of religious persecution in Mexico (collected in *The Lawless Roads*) he gave a strongly personal interpretation to events and had the courage (as he has had in all his journalism, as for that matter has Mauriac), to hold non-conformist and unpopular opinions. For the occasion he was involved, though not in a conventional capacity. "If anyone has anything direct to say about society or politics," Greene told Philip Toynbee in an interview for *The Observer,* "let him say it as journalism." In 1953 he had written a series of articles for *The Sunday Times* on the Mau Mau, sympathizing with the blacks, but if he had written a story on the subject, he went on to say, "the hero and the villain of such non-fictional writing might well turn out to have their roles reversed in a novel. . . . It's in this way that one's function as a novelist seems to differ so much from one's function as a reporter of events."[22] Unlike Mauriac, Greene did not feel the same pressing need for total engagement. He was able to separate his responsibilities without feeling a disassociation of interests, and continued to enjoy that freedom of the ambivalent attitude which allows one to remain a novelist.

As we observed in the last chapter, Greene's experience in drama was a rewarding one. It was not terminal, as for Mauriac, but opened a new creative vein of comic potential. This genre is richly exploited in Greene's next novel, *Our Man in Havana* (1958). The underlying theme is again the problem of commitment, and Greene handles it with as much sensitivity and penetration as in *The Quiet American*. But the humorous aspects of the problem are now those which engage his attention, which testifies to that broadening of attitude and increased tolerance which we noted in *The Complaisant Lover*. Wormold, the hero of *Our Man in Havana,* combines elements of both Pyle and Fowler. Like Fowler, he is weary and middle-aged, lives separated from his wife, is happy in a country no longer foreign, and wishes nothing better than to live out his life there, quietly doing a routine job. But also, like Pyle, he is an innocent who "gets mixed up" in a political affair which gets out of hand and ends in violence and murder. Since this is a comic, not a tragic treatment of the theme, the extremes of Pyle's and Fowler's attitudes cancel out in Wormold. For one thing, he does not become involved for any high-principled motive but simply to make money to try to satisfy the extravagant tastes of his whimsical daughter, Milly. For another, the espionage in which he becomes involved is a marvelously wild travesty of the operations of the British secret service; it has nothing of the ominous purpose of Pyle's "special duties." From the romantically-minded, one-eyed Chief in his subterranean London office to the Boy's-Own-Paper, Caribbean head-agent Hawthorne, the whole service is treated as an incredible farce. It is really as much not to disappoint the cloak and dagger idealism of Hawthorne and the London office as for any other reason that Wormold, who has absolutely no information, begins to invent secret military installations (out-of-scale drawings of vacuum cleaner parts) and to recruit fictitious sub-agents. This obliging duplicity puts Wormold in the position of practical joker before an invitingly gullible victim. Another distinction of capital importance between Wormold and Pyle is that Pyle, who even misses the point of Fowler's bitter sarcasms, has no sense of humor. This is Wormold's saving grace and accounts for the undeniable charm of his character. It is a sad and whimsical sense of humor rather than a boisterous one, but it allows him to view Hawthorne and the fantastic adventures into which he is thrust with a detached quizzical gravity. Also, since we have equated a sense of humor with a sense of humility, it lets him see himself and his own actions in the same comic light.

This gentle, bemused, but not unsubtle attitude is very well captured in Wormold's relations with his daughter, Milly. According to his wife's wishes she is being brought up a Catholic. She condescendingly considers her father a "good pagan" and with seventeen-year-old innocent guile is maddeningly pious when it suits her purpose. She is a juvenile version of Greene's "natural" heroine who wears in her face, like Cary, heroine of the previous entertainment, *Loser Takes All* (1955), "the sign of Original Innocence." She is one of those who blandly expect the impossible like Anne Callifer or Mary Rhodes. Wormold's patience with her, his concern to protect her belief though he is constantly puzzled by the eccentricities of her observance, and, not least, his deep love for Milly—one could almost say his deep amusement in her—beautifully convey his character.

Wormold represents an attitude towards reality which neither Pyle nor Fowler reach, though they begin to learn it. His values are simple though they are not oversimplifications. He loves Milly because, not in spite of the fact that she is an erratic, unpredictable individual. He is faithful to his old friend Dr. Hasselbacher, even when he is discov-

ered to be on the enemy's side, because he respects him as
a human being and knows and appreciates his faults, temptations and idiosyncrasies. He falls in love with Beatrice,
the girl sent out by the London bureau to be his secretary,
because she is not just a stereotyped cog in the organization
but is capable of the surprising and personal act and word.
The only reality that matters for Wormold, as for Greene,
here and in *The Quiet American,* is that which corresponds
to basic, simple, and individual human values. Wormold
realizes these values in his love for Milly:

He couldn't afford the time not to love . . . that evening hour was
real, but not Hawthorne, mysterious and absurd, not the cruel-
ties of police-stations and governments, the scientists who tested
the new H-bomb on Christmas Island, Khrushchev who wrote
notes: these seemed less real to him than the inefficient tortures
of a school dormitory.

Beatrice too rebels against anything that disregards the importance of the individual.

"I don't care a damn about men who are loyal to the people who
pay them, to organizations . . . I don't even think my country
means all that much. There are many countries in our blood,
aren't there, but only one person. Would the world be in the
mess it is if we're loyal to love and not to countries?"

But of course the unreal, grotesque world of Hawthorne
and police-stations and Khrushchev does exist, and Wormold is paid to know it. He becomes involved, innocently
and innocuously at first, sending out his faked reports, em-
ploying an imaginary chain of sub-agents and feathering
his bank account. But he is too good at fraud and under-
estimates the credulousness of Hawthorne and the London
office. Real agents, Beatrice and a radio operator, are sent
out to help him. Word of his increased activities leaks to
the equally credulous enemy. The forces of cruelty and
nightmare gather and there is an accidental death. Then
his own life is threatened. Then Dr. Hasselbacher is shot.

Wormold had been able to face the unreal reality of the world of espionage and state secrets and global strategy by remaining uncommitted, by playing a double game, by masquerading as agent 59200 stroke 5 in the spirit of a practical joke, by seeing himself as a clown.

The cruel come and go like cities and thrones and powers, leaving their ruins behind him, he thought. They had no permanence. But the clown whom he had seen last year with Milly at the circus—that clown was permanent, for his act never changed. That was the way to live; the clown was unaffected by the vagaries of public man and the enormous discoveries of the great.

He had played the clown in his detached double attitude to the whole espionage farce that he had helped to set afoot. But now, with Hasselbacher's death he becomes committed.

He stood on the frontier of violence, a strange land he had never visited before; he had his passport in his hand. "Profession: Spy." "Characteristic Features: Friendlessness." "Purpose of Visit: Murder." No visa was required. His papers were in order.

It is interesting to note that his position at this moment is the exact reverse of Raven's in *A Gun for Sale* who stood, in like fashion, on the frontier of sympathy and affection. The whole of this scene is nicely counterpointed, for as Wormold sits on his bed making up his mind to vengeance, he hears in the next room the voices of Milly and Beatrice "talking in the language he knew" of simple things, of a kind of perfume, and marriage, and love. For the time he shuns that reality, but it is characteristic that even when he is playing the melodramatic secret service world's game in deadly earnest, he is true to his own principles:

Wormold said to himself, At least if I could kill him, I would kill for a clean reason. I would kill to show that you can't kill without being killed in your turn. I wouldn't kill for my country. I wouldn't kill for capitalism or Communism or social democracy or the welfare state—whose welfare? I would kill Carter because he killed Hasselbacher. A family-feud had been a better reason for murder than patriotism or preference for one economic system over another. If I love or hate, let me love or hate as an individual. I will not be 59200/5 in anyone's global war.

Wormold does kill Carter but only in self-defense and only after having abandoned the idea, after having "proved conclusively to himself that he wasn't one of the judges; he had no vocation for violence." After this he exposes his hoax and goes to London to be cashiered where, with great embarrassment, the authorities discover that the only thing they can do is sheepishly retire him with an O.B.E. Beatrice stands triumphantly by him denouncing impersonal institutions and organizations and stating "I can't believe in anything bigger than a home or anything vaguer than a human being." And Milly excuses their love for one another and their decision to marry with: "Oh, pagans can do anything, and you are pagans. Lucky you." Of course, Milly may be right when she tells her father with convent correctness that he is "invincibly ignorant" in matters of theology, but the values that he and Beatrice represent in this wistful farce are the same as those that Greene described ten years earlier in *Why Do I Write?* in these words:

The writer, just as much as the Christian Church, is the defender of the individual. The soldier, the loyal man, stands for the mass interment, the anonymous grave, but the writer stands for the uneconomic, probably unhealthy, overcrowded little graveyard, with the stone crosses preserving innumerable names.[23]

One does not like to overload a story like this with interpretation, for the great merit of *Our Man in Havana* is that it remains an entertainment in the richest sense, and moves deftly and swiftly along, full of delightful incident and humor, the continuous play of surface making one careless of possible depths. But this is a good occasion to question again that artful distinction between "novel" and "entertainment," for although Greene's aim is to please, and he achieves it brilliantly, his mature point of view works as surely and effectively beneath the surface of this story as it does in books more portentously called "novels." One last commentary on *Our Man in Havana,* then, will not sink it.

In a serious sense this is a fiction about fiction-making. Wormold not only bears the characteristics of Christian and writer in his championship of the individual and in his refusal to sit with the judges, but also, in a more practical sense, in creating characters for his own secret service farce. Through his invention of sub-agents we get a last glimpse of some of the phenomena of the creative process. Writing of *The Loved and the Unloved* Mauriac admits that when he started the book he was not sure of his final intention . . . "the artist stresses this or that characteristic almost unconsciously, and in obedience to his creative instinct."[24] Wormold is caught up in his creation in the same fashion. The hoax develops its own momentum; almost involuntarily his string of sub-agents and informers increases. He even enlists Captain Segura of the Cuban police, without his knowledge of course, as a counter-agent. Seeing a blind beggar in front of the Cathedral, "the creative instinct stirred in Wormold." He tells Beatrice:

"You know, he's not really blind. He sees everything that goes on."
"He must be a good actor. I've been watching him all the time you were with Segura."
"And he's been watching you. As a matter of fact he's one of my best informers!" . . . He said slowly as the story grew of itself, "The beggar's name is Miguel. He really does all this for love. You see I saved his life once. . . ."

It astonished Wormold how quickly he could reply to any questions about his characters; they seemed to live on the threshold of consciousness—he had only to turn on a light and there they were, frozen in some characteristic action. . . . Sometimes he was scared at the way these people grew in the dark without his knowledge.

The secret of Wormold's creative instinct is his tolerance, his somewhat amazed interest in other people, and his own humility—"I don't think I love myself enough to satisfy them," he says when the question comes up of what retaliatory measures the enemy may take against him. These qualities of his are the ones which condemn to failure his own plans for vengeance. He tries to dismiss them: "A murderer should be a machine, and I too have to become a machine, Wormold thought." But Carter, his victim, refuses to remain that inert abstraction, "the enemy," which Wormold might easily eliminate. He talks to Wormold of his fears and shortcomings; he comes alive as an individual. "I have to do it, Wormold thought, before he confesses any more to me. With every second the man was becoming human, a creature like oneself whom one might pity or console, not kill."

So Wormold, like the creative writer, is condemned to sympathy. He cannot fool himself into thinking that he is an instrument of justice or an agent of this or that cause. He is obliged to see the other's point of view and say: "There, and may God forgive me, goes myself." He is condemned to inaction, except through sympathy and love. Or, like the clown, he is obliged to ridicule himself in ridiculing human nature.

This, then, is Greene's position as novelist. To take sides is to blind oneself to the total complexity of the human situation; is to limit understanding; is to restrict one's freedom. He himself finds this necessary freedom in the world of fiction, and the characters that he has created embody his impractical, unworldly belief that one must remain free to hold the double view, that of the guilty as well as that

of the innocent, to take reality into account, but also to believe that "anything is possible." The double agent is the
perfect representative of this saving ambiguity. So are the
clown and the practical-joker, both caught in Wormold's
character. By extension in a different mood, Greene's earlier
tragic heroes—his outcasts, criminals, prodigals, adulterous
lovers and sinners—share the same characteristics. They
are untrustworthy in the world's eye, paradoxical and free.

In his most recent fiction, a collection of four stories entitled *A Sense of Reality* (1963), Greene has invented a new
species in this category. In "Under the Garden," the longest
story and a dream fantasy, dedicated to illustrate the principle that "what seems is," the grotesque central character,
Javitt, calls himself "a rogue," in the sense of rogue-weed or
rogue-elephant. "Be disloyal," is his advice.

It's your duty to the human race. The human race needs to survive and it's the loyal man who dies first from anxiety or a bullet
or overwork. If you have to earn a living, boy, and the price they
make you pay is loyalty, be a double agent—and never let either
of the two sides know your real name. The same applies to wom-
en and God. They both respect a man they don't own, and they'll
go on raising the price they are willing to offer. Didn't Christ say
that very thing? Was the prodigal son loyal or the lost shilling or
the strayed sheep?

This is the same appeal and act of faith which Greene, a
rogue-writer himself, has made all through his career: an
appeal for freedom for the individual, not the partisan freedom of being free to belong to a certain party, sect, country,
class, or race, but the more challenging freedom to prefer
the independent, the prodigal, and the onerous duty of free
choice; to prefer compassion to commitment, and charity to
justice; to prefer the Christian characteristics of "the divided mind, the uneasy conscience and the sense of personal failure" to any facile creed.

One final word on the question of commitment. It does

not fall within the scope of this study to comment on the exact color and shading of the political or the religio-political views to which Greene and Mauriac have both committed themselves in their journalism. The focus of our attention has been the reason why a novelist should abandon his creative work in favor of *littérature engagée* whatever the character of the engagement. In the preface to *Bloc-Notes* Mauriac explains that the simplest reason for his journalistic endeavor was to give expression to the reaction of an individual, with all his particular ideas, tastes and idiosyncracies, to the facts of history as they shaped themselves week by week under his regard. *Bloc-Notes,* he writes, "is the confrontation of the individual with the universal."[25] In this sense, even in his journalism, Mauriac remains true to his novelist's training and vocation, and commitment does not mean for him narrow conformity to any set position, religious or political, but still implies the shifting, individualistic approach. The change is, after all, not so much a change in attitude as a change in the object of observation. It is this fact which permits Mauriac to call "the doctrine of commitment" basically false. "I feel no more committed now," he writes,

than I did in the old days. All that has happened is that I can no longer interpose a fiction between myself and reality. . . . Old men are irremediably forced back on what is happening now. . . . They can find no refuge in the future, because for them there is no future, and because that void so suited for the proliferations of the novelist, which constituted the natural field of their activity, has become the unalterable past.

The characters of fiction no longer find in us sufficient room to give them freedom of movement. They are caught between the hardened, solidified mass of our past which nothing, from now on, will ever penetrate again, and the death, more or less imminent which will, for such time as remains, be our constant companion.

If there existed anywhere a world of fiction which took account of eternity, I would still have recourse to it . . . Bernanos? Graham Greene? But all fiction, even when it does admit the active presence in this world of Grace, merely has the effect of cheapening a truth which is not the product of invention, and is beyond the power of words to communicate.[26]

In keeping with this final, disillusioned view of the validity of the novelist's vocation, one must ask one last difficult question with regard to the creative analogy which has been central to this whole study. If it is true that many of the aims and problems of the novelist can be clarified by drawing an analogy to his God-like and even Christ-like function in the creative act, one must also ask, if the novelist is like the incarnate Christian God, what, finally, does his own work make incarnate?

In most of my analyses of Greene's and Mauriac's novels I have concentrated on those qualities to which their characters aspire, or which they love, or against which they are forced to measure their own failure. In short, I have written about the faith of their characters and about their own novelists' faith. But there is another side to the picture, and both Mauriac and Greene have been honest in showing it. Mauriac's self-examination at the end of The Loved and the Unloved and his bitter conclusions about the limitations of the novel, and the uselessness and inefficacy of his own novel in particular, are typical of this sincerity.

The most that can be concluded is that the novel, though it does not throw any revealing light on persons living in the actual world, does give us some information about the novelist himself. . . But that is no very great achievement and [one] would be perfectly within [one's] rights in judging that the interest to be derived from absorbing a certain amount of information about François Mauriac as a result of reading his novels, is insufficient compensation for the total uselessness of his works, to say nothing of their possible harmfulness to those among whom he is called upon to labour.[27]

In characteristic fashion Greene does not comment so openly on this problem but treats it in fictional form, for *A Burnt-Out Case*, among other things, is an admission of the uselessness of the work of art and the ugliness of the artist. We have already examined the element of faith in that novel, now let us realistically state what it says about failure.

We can safely take Querry as our guide for he is a man who "always saw himself in the hardest possible light." Having reached the end of his career, his faith, his love, he is still left with clear-sightedness: "I won't pretend. All I have left now is a certain regard for truth. It was the best side of the small talent I had." We can trust, then, what he tells us about the artist's vocation. He tells us that one comes to the end of it: "Possibly sex and a vocation are born and die together." He tells us: "Self-expression is a hard and selfish thing. It eats everything, even the self. At the end you find you haven't even got a self to express." We learn that: "It needs a very strong man to survive an introspective and solitary vocation." Querry says, "A writer doesn't write for his readers, does he?" and carrying on in terms of architecture, "I wasn't concerned with the people who occupied my space—only with the space. . . . My interest was in space, light, proportion. New materials interested me only in the effect they might have on those three. . . . Materials are the architect's plot. They are not his motive for work." And in the fable of the jeweler that he tells to Marie Rycker he speaks of the curse of facility and fame. "He was finished with his profession—he had come to an end of it. Nothing could ever be so ingenious as what he had done already, or more useless. . . ." Here and elsewhere he shows that one can create without feeling, without suffering, without love.

This is the place to give due credit to these statements, for in *A Burnt-Out Case* Greene thoroughly exposes the Ryckers, Parkinsons and Father Thomases who refuse to accept such facts and idolize Querry out of all recognition. And there can be no doubt that Greene had his own critics in mind in his satire of these differently motivated but all selfish, partisan and erroneous interpretations of an artist's life, faith, and work.

But one is not obliged to take Querry's harsh self-evaluation as the total picture either, or to leap to the easy conclusion that Greene is the burnt-out case that he describes. The enigmatic Querry is surrounded by half a dozen figures who provide as many interpretations of his character. One need not see him with Marie Rycker's romantic naïvete or her husband's preposterous snobbery, Parkinson's cynical sensationalism or Father Thomas's impenetrable piety. Nor is he completely described from the viewpoint of Doctor Colin's broad humanism, Father Joseph's practical kindliness, or the cheroot-smoking Superior's quiet charity. "You are my looking-glass," Querry told Parkinson. "I can talk to a looking-glass, but one can be a little afraid of it too. It returns such a straight image." In fact, each of these characters is a different glass which returns an image that contains part of the truth, and Querry is a composite of all of them. If the hero of *A Burnt-Out Case* is a self-portrait, it is of this many-faceted kind, for why should Greene be any less complex than one of his own characters.

The most that can be conceded says Mauriac, is that the novel, useless as a tool for the schoolmaster or moralist, does give us some information about the novelist himself.

It follows, then, that the Christian who happens also to be a novelist must resign himself to pleading no better an excuse than that of "vocation." He writes novels because he has some reason to think that he was born into the world to write, seeing that from childhood on he has struggled endlessly to do so.[28]

This note of humility has been carried into Mauriac's public life where, at the end of his creative vocation, he has accepted himself, so to speak, as a character, and in his journalism has granted himself the freedom to speak out in his own voice. Querry too reaches a level of self-acceptance far removed from the callous self-criticism that characterizes his feeling of sterility and disgust at the opening of the novel. For *A Burnt-Out Case* is the story of a cure, not just of a case. Querry learns companionship, interest in others, learns to forget his anguish at the loss of vocation as an architect and is satisfied to say, "I have become a builder." He learns to smile, and the symbol of his final humility and self-acceptance is that he dies laughing at himself.

What finally, inevitably, the writer makes incarnate in his work is no abstract principle of truth but his own contradictory, fallible and complex personality. "Almost all the works die while the men remain," writes Mauriac. "The rarest thing in literature, and the only success, is when the author disappears and his work remains." But Greene and Mauriac are not Shakespeare and Racine, the writers whom Mauriac chooses to exemplify this kind of literary success. Neither is, or will be, "lost in the radiance of his creation."[29] They are both too inextricably and forcefully present in everything they have written. And it is fitting to admit, to close this comparison, that as writers they remain very different individuals, as different, perhaps, after all, as chalk and cheese.

Yet however much they are imprisoned by what they are —and the parallel passages that I am about to quote reemphasize their singularity—they have both aspired to testify to an extrapersonal truth, and that, too, is part of their personality. With typical understatement Greene says of his motive to write:

What it all really adds up to is that I write novels about what interests me and I can't write about anything else. And one of the things which interests me most is discovering the humanity in the apparently inhuman character.[30]

And Mauriac's final word on his vocation as a novelist is this:

I am only too well aware how rash it is to conclude that what seems, on all evidence, to be our determined destiny, must be the expression of God's will. . . . Still, it may be that I was created and set down in one tiny segment of the Universe . . . for the sole purpose of bearing witness to man's guilt judged by the infinite innocence of God.[31]

To what degree the works of these two novelists artistically attain these complementary goals may remain an open subject for critical debate. But their case should not be closed without recording one last expression of a Christian novelist's faith. "Today I know," says Mauriac, "that God pays no attention to what we write; He uses it."[32] "La Grace se sert aussi d'un romancier comme moi."[33]

NOTES TO CHAPTER 10

1. Philip Stratford, "One Meeting with Mauriac," The Kenyon Review, XXI (Autumn, 1959), 614, 616.

2. "François Mauriac," Writers at Work (New York, 1959), p. 45.

3. Stratford, op. cit., p. 616.

4. "Preface," The Lamb (London, 1955).

5. "Le Romancier et ses personnages," Oeuvres Complètes, VIII, 300. (Oeuvres Complètes is hereafter cited as O.C.)

6. "Bonheur du chrétien," O.C., VII, 252.

7. "Préface," O.C., V, iii.

8. "François Mauriac," The Lost Childhood, p. 72.

9. "Préface," O.C., V, iii.

10. The Little Misery (London, 1952), p. 108.

11. A Woman of the Pharisees (London, 1946), p. 190.

12. "Postscript," The Loved and the Unloved (London, 1952), pp. 140-41.

13. Ibid., p. 136.

14. "The Art of Fiction," The Paris Review, No. 3 (Autumn, 1953), p. 31.

15. John Atkins, Graham Greene (London, 1957), p. 204.

16. Evelyn Waugh, "Felix Culpa?" Commonweal, XLVII (July 16, 1948), 323.

17. Waugh, "The End of the Affair," *The Month*, CXCII (September, 1951), 176.

18. "Fiction," *The Spectator*, CLI (September 22, 1933), 380.

19. "Subjects and Stories," *Footnotes to the Films*, ed. Charles Davy (London, 1937), p. 57.

20. *Ibid.*

21. "Books in General," *New Statesman and Nation*, XXXIV (October 11, 1947), 292.

22. "The Job of the Writer," *The Observer* (September 15, 1957), p. 3.

23. *Why Do I Write?*, p. 48.

24. "Postscript," *The Loved and the Unloved*, p. 136.

25. *Bloc-Notes* (Paris, 1958), p. 3.

26. *Mémoires Intérieurs*, pp. 68-9.

27. "Postscript," *The Loved and the Unloved*, p. 141.

28. *Ibid.*, pp. 141-2.

29. "François Mauriac," *Writers at Work*, p. 48.

30. "The Job of the Writer," *The Observer* (September 15, 1957), p. 3.

31. "Postscript," *The Loved and the Unloved*, p. 142.

32. "François Mauriac," *Writers at Work*, p. 49.

33. "Ma vie et mes personnages," Interviews with Jean Amrouche, R.D.F., 1952.

BIBLIOGRAPHICAL NOTES

Since this is an interpretive study, not a definitive one, since none of my source material is recondite, and since extensive bibliographies are available for both these authors, I will let my chapter notes stand in lieu of a bibliography of works consulted and confine myself to a few additional remarks here.

1. *Bibliographies*

GREENE

A definitive bibliography of all Greene's published work compiled by A. R. Redway and Neil F. Brennan is scheduled to appear this spring at Rupert Hart-Davis. The most complete published bibliography to date has been prepared by Phylis Hargreaves: "Graham Greene: A Selected Bibliography," *Modern Fiction Studies*, III (Autumn, 1957), 269-80. A useful short bibliography is included in Francis Wyndham, *Graham Greene*, London, 1955.

MAURIAC

The most complete bibliography of Mauriac's works is contained in the standard reference, Talvart and Place, *Bibliographie des auteurs modernes de langue française*, Paris (1928-   ), which, since it just reached Mauriac in

1956, is quite up to date. A full, but not definitive bibliography (complete to 1947) is appended to Nelly Cormeau's *L'Art de François Mauriac*, Paris, 1951. And the best concise bibliography is contained in Pierre-Henri Simon, *Mauriac par lui-même*, Paris, 1953.

2. *Major Works of Fiction*

For the reader's convenience I include a check list of novels and plays dealt with in this study, with their dates of publication.

GREENE

The Man Within	1929	*The Heart of the*	
The Name of Action	1930	*Matter*	1948
Rumour at Nightfall	1931	*The Third Man*	1950
Stamboul Train	1932	*The End of the Affair*	1951
It's a Battlefield	1934	*The Living Room*	1953
England Made Me	1935	*Loser Takes All*	1955
A Gun for Sale	1936	*The Quiet American*	1955
Brighton Rock	1938	*The Potting Shed*	1957
The Confidential		*Our Man in Havana*	1958
Agent	1939	*The Complaisant*	
The Power and		*Lover*	1959
the Glory	1940	*A Burnt-Out Case*	1961
The Ministry of Fear	1943	*A Sense of Reality*	1963

MAURIAC

Titles are given in English where translations exist, but dates are of first French publication.

Young Man in Chains	1913	*A Kiss for the Leper*	1922
The Stuff of Youth	1914	*The River of Fire*	1923
Flesh and Blood	1920	*Genetrix*	1923
Questions of		*The Enemy*	1924
Precedence	1921	*The Desert of Love*	1925

Thérèse	1927	The Unknown Sea	1939
Lines of Life	1928	A Woman of the	
That Which Was		Pharisees	1941
Lost	1930	Les Mal Aimés	1945
The Knot of Vipers	1932	Passage du Malin	1948
The Frontenac		The Little Misery	1951
Mystery	1933	Le Feu sur la Terre	1951
The End of the Night	1935	The Loved and the	
The Dark Angels	1936	Unloved	1952
Asmodée	1938	The Lamb	1954

3. *Selected Criticism: Books*

GREENE

The first two major studies of Greene's work were French: Madaule's book mainly descriptive, Rostenne's far more interesting. Kenneth and Miriam Allott's *The Art of Graham Greene*, which has just been reissued (Russell and Russell, 1963), remains the best study of Greene's work. Victor de Pange's essay is a good introduction, and Ronald Matthews' book, a record of conversations with Greene, contains some interesting personal revelations.

Allott, Kenneth and Miriam. *The Art of Graham Greene.* London, 1951, 1963.

Atkins, John. *Graham Greene.* London, 1957.

Kunkel, Francis L. *The Labyrinthine Ways of Graham Greene.* New York, 1959.

Madaule, Jacques. *Graham Greene.* Paris, 1949.

Matthews, Ronald. *Mon Ami Graham Greene.* Paris, 1957.

Mesnet, Marie Beatrice. *Graham Greene and the Heart of the Matter.* London, 1954.

de Pange, Victor. *Graham Greene.* Paris, 1953.

Pryce-Jones, David. *Graham Greene.* London, 1963.

Rischik, Joseph. *Graham Greene und sein Werk*. Bern, 1951.

Rostenne, Paul. *Graham Greene témoin des temps tragiques*. Paris, 1949.

Wyndham, Francis. *Graham Greene*. London, 1955.

MAURIAC

The first critical study of Mauriac's work is de Sacy's essay which dates from 1927, just after Mauriac had been awarded *Le Grand Prix du Roman*. His election to the *Académie* prompted several new books, the best among them Charles Du Bos's. Since the war new critical works have appeared almost every year. These often tend to argue the pros (Rideau) and cons (Vier) of Mauriac's orthodoxy; the most scholarly examination of Mauriac's Catholicism is Robert J. North's. The best general work is Nelly Cormeau's *L'Art de François Mauriac,* and the best short study is Pierre-Henri Simon's *Mauriac par lui-même*. The most recent criticisms (Grall, Vandromme) are devoted to Mauriac's journalism.

de Catalogne, Gérard. *François Mauriac ou le goût du péché*. Paris, 1928.

Cormeau, Nelly. *L'Art de François Mauriac*. Paris, 1951.

Du Bos, Charles. *François Mauriac et le problème du romancier catholique*. Paris, 1933.

Fillon, Amélie. *François Mauriac*. Paris, 1936.

Grall, Xavier. *Mauriac Journaliste*. Paris, 1960.

Hourdin, Georges. *Mauriac, romancier chrétien*. Paris, 1945.

Jarrett-Kerr, Martin. *François Mauriac*. London, 1954.

Landry, Sister Anne Gertrude. *Represented Discourse in the Novels of François Mauriac*. Washington, 1953.

Majault, Joseph. *Mauriac et l'art du roman*. Paris, 1946.

Moloney, Michael F. *François Mauriac: A Critical Study*. Denver, 1958.

North, Robert J. *Le Catholicisme dans l'oeuvre de François Mauriac.* Paris, 1950.

Palante, Alain. *Mauriac, le roman et la vie.* Paris, 1946.

Pell, Elsie E. *François Mauriac in Search of the Infinite.* New York, 1947.

Rideau, E. *Comment lire François Mauriac.* Paris, 1945.

Robichon, Jacques. *François Mauriac.* Paris, 1953.

de Sacy, S. S. *L'Oeuvre de François Mauriac.* Paris, 1927.

Simon, Pierre-Henri. *François Mauriac par lui-même.* Paris, 1953.

Vandromme, Pol. *La Politique littéraire de François Mauriac.* Paris, 1957.

Vier, J. *François Mauriac, romancier catholique?* Paris, 1935.

4. *Selected Criticism: Articles*

GREENE

The most complete bibliography of articles on Greene's work is by Maurice Beebe, "Criticism of Graham Greene: A Selected Checklist with an Index to Studies of Separate Works," *Modern Fiction Studies*, III (Autumn, 1957), 281-8. A useful descriptive bibliography of Greene criticism by William Birmingham, "Graham Greene Criticism: A Bibliographical Study," appeared in *Thought*, XXVII (Spring, 1952), 71-100. A selected bibliography of criticism will also appear in a forthcoming volume of *The Cambridge Bibliography of English Literature.*

Among the hundreds of articles and reviews devoted to Greene's work, I have selected, with a few exceptions, the most recent studies. During the thirties Greene's novels received review article attention only. The first retrospective study is by Arthur Calder-Marshall in 1940. Of the many criticisms that have followed I have found particularly stimulating those by R.-M. Alberès, Ian Gregor, R. W. B. Lewis, David Lodge, Conor

Cruise O'Brien (Donat O'Donnell), and Elizabeth Sewell. The Autumn, 1957, number of *Modern Fiction Studies* was devoted to articles on Greene, as was the Autumn, 1959, number of *Renascence*.

Alberès, R.-M. *Les Hommes Traqués*. Paris, 1953.

Barnes, Robert J. "Two Modes of Fiction: Hemingway and Greene," *Renascence*, XIV (Summer, 1962), 193-8.

Calder-Marshall, Arthur. "The Works of Graham Greene," *Horizon*, I (May, 1940), 367-75.

Consolo, Dominick P. "Music as Motif: The Unity of *Brighton Rock*," *Renascence*, XV (Autumn, 1962), 12-20.

De Vitis, A. A. "The Entertaining Mr. Greene," *Renascence*, XIV (Autumn, 1961), 8-24.

Dooley, D. J. "*A Burnt-Out Case* reconsidered," *Wiseman Review*, CCXXXVII (Summer, 1963), 168-78.

Duffy, Joseph M. "The Lost World of Graham Greene," *Thought*, XXXIII (Summer, 1958), 229-47.

Glicksberg, Charles I. "Graham Greene: Catholicism in Fiction," *Criticism*, I (Autumn, 1959), 339-53.

Gregor, Ian. "The Greene Baize Door," *Blackfriars*, XXXVI (September, 1955), 327-33.

Gregor, Ian and Brian Nicholas. *The Moral and the Story*. London, 1962.

Hess, M. Whitcomb. "Graham Greene's Travesty on *The Ring and the Book*," *Catholic World*, CXCIV (October, 1961), 37-42.

Kermode, Frank. "Mr. Greene's Eggs and Crosses," *Encounter*, XVI (April, 1961), 69-75.

———. "The House of Fiction: Interviews with seven English novelists," *Partisan Review*, XXX (Spring, 1963), 65-8.

Lewis, R. W. B. *The Picaresque Saint*. New York, 1959.

Liebling, A. J. "A Talkative Something-or-Other," *New Yorker*, XXXII (April 7, 1956), 136-42.

Lodge, David. "The Use of Key-words in the novels of

Graham Greene," *Blackfriars*, XLII (November, 1961), 468-74.

Mauriac, François. "Mes Grands Hommes," *O.C.*, VIII, 429-32.

———. "Préface," V. de Pange, *Graham Greene*, Paris, 1953.

Mueller, William R. *The Prophetic Voice in Modern Fiction*. New York, 1959.

Noxon, James. "Kierkegaard's Stages and *A Burnt-Out Case*," *Review of English Literature*, III (January, 1962), 90-101.

O'Brien, Conor Cruise. *Maria Cross*. London, 1963.

O'Faolain, Sean. *The Vanishing Hero*. London, 1956.

Rolo, Charles J. "Graham Greene: The Man and the Message," *Atlantic Monthly*, CCVII (May, 1961), 60-5.

Sackville-West, Edward. "The Electric Hare: Some Aspects of Graham Greene," *The Month*, CXCII (September, 1951), 141-7.

Sewell, Elizabeth. "Graham Greene: A Discussion of his Work," *Dublin Review*, CCXXVIII (Spring, 1954), 12-21.

Smith, A. J. M. "Graham Greene's Theological Thrillers," *Queen's Quarterly*, LXVIII (Spring, 1961), 15-33.

Stratford, Philip. "Graham Greene: Master of Melodrama," *Tamarack Review*, No. 19 (Spring, 1961), 67-86.

———. "The Uncomplacent Dramatist: Some Aspects of Graham Greene's Theatre," *Wisconsin Studies in Contemporary Literature*, II, No. 3 (Fall, 1961), 5-19.

———. "Greene's Hall of Mirrors," *Kenyon Review*, XXIII (Summer, 1961), 527-31.

———. "Unlocking the Potting Shed," *Kenyon Review*, XXIV (Winter, 1962), 129-43.

———. "Chalk and Cheese: A Comparative Study of *A Kiss for the Leper* and *A Burnt-Out Case*," *University of Toronto Quarterly*, XXXIII (January, 1964), 200-18.

Voorhees, R. J. "Recent Greene," *South Atlantic Quarterly*, LXII (Spring, 1963), 244-55.

Wassmer, Thomas A. "Faith and Reason in Graham Greene," *Studies*, XLVIII (Summer, 1959), 163-7.

————. "The Sinners of Graham Greene," *Dalhousie Review*, XXXIX (Autumn, 1959), 326-32.

MAURIAC

The most extensive bibliography of articles on Mauriac is in Talvart and Place. Fernand Vial has published an interesting descriptive bibliography, "François Mauriac Criticism: A Bibliographical Study," in *Thought*, XXVII (Summer, 1952), 235-60. Nelly Cormeau's *L'Art de François Mauriac* contains a large bibliography of articles on his work. Since the early thirties Mauriac has received treatment from every major critic of modern French fiction. I note only those articles which were most personally challenging to him (by Maritain, Gide and Sartre), and two longer studies (Fernandez, Jaloux). Otherwise I concentrate mainly on recent studies, among which I have found most interesting those by Rayner Heppenstall, Claude-Edmonde Magny, Françoise Mallet-Joris, Conor Cruise O'Brien and Martin Turnell. Special numbers of *La Revue du Siècle* (July-August, 1933), *La Table Ronde* (January, 1953) and *La Parisienne* (May, 1956) were devoted to essays on Mauriac.

de Boisdeffre, Pierre. *Métamorphose de la littérature*. Paris, 1950.

Davies, R. T. "Reservations about François Mauriac," *Essays in Criticism*, IX (January, 1959), 22-36.

Dillistone, Frederick W. *The Novelist and the Passion Story*. New York, 1960.

Fernandez, Ramon. "François Mauriac et le roman moderne," preface to François Mauriac, *Dieu et Mammon*, Paris, 1929.

Fowlie, Wallace, "Mauriac's Dark Hero," *The Novelist As Thinker.* Ed. B. Rajan. London, 1947.

Gagnepain, Jean. "Le Monde de François Mauriac," *Bulletin de l'Association Guillaume Budé.* No. 1 (Paris, 1956), 133-58.

Gide, A. "Lettre à Mauriac." See François Mauriac, "Dieu et Mammon," *Oeuvres Complétès,* VII, 330-1.

Greene, Graham. *The Lost Childhood.* London, 1951.

Gregor, Ian and Brian Nicholas. *The Moral and the Story.* London, 1962.

Heppenstall, Rayner. *The Double Image: Mutations of Christian mythology in the work of five French Catholic writers of to-day and yesterday.* London, 1947.

Hérisson, Charles-D. "Mauriac: Essai de mise au point," *Revue de l'Université de Laval,* XV (October, 1960), 121-30.

Hopkins, Gerard. "François Mauriac et les Anglais," *Mercure de France,* CCCII (April, 1948), 590-5.

Jaloux, Edmond. "François Mauriac romancier," preface to François Mauriac, *Le Romancier et ses personnages,* Paris, 1933.

Le Hir, Yves. "Temps et durée dans *Le Noeud de Vipères* de Mauriac," *Lettres Romanes,* XIV (February, 1960), 3-13.

Liebling, A. J. "M. Mauriac's Automobile," *New Yorker,* XXXIV (June 21, 1958), 39-61.

Magny, Claude-Edmonde. *Histoire du roman français depuis 1918.* Paris, 1950.

Mallet-Joris, Françoise. "Les personnages féminins dans l'oeuvre de François Mauriac," preface to François Mauriac, *Le Désert de l'amour,* Paris, 1959.

Maritain, Jacques. "Dialogues," *Chroniques,* Le Roseau d'or, No. 30. Paris, 1928.

Mary Humiliata, Sister. "The Theme of Isolation in Mauriac's *The Desert of Love,*" *Twentieth Century Literature,* VII (October, 1961), 107-13.

O'Brien, Conor Cruise. (Donat O'Donnell) "Mauriac and Gide: Great Adversaries," *Commonweal*, LXXI (October, 1959), 161-2.

———. *Maria Cross*. London, 1963.

Robichon, Jacques. "Mauriac et le travail du romancier," *Mercure de France*, CCCXXXII (January, 1958), 21-42.

Sartre, Jean-Paul. "M. François Mauriac et la liberté," *La Nouvelle Revue Française*, LII (February, 1939), 212-32.

Stratford, Philip. "François Mauriac and His Critics," *Tamarack Review*, No. 3 (Spring, 1957), 64-77.

———. "One Meeting With Mauriac," *Kenyon Review*, XXI (Autumn, 1959), 611-22.

Turnell, Martin. *The Art of French Fiction*. London, 1959.

West, Anthony. *Principles and Persuasions: The Literary essays of Anthony West*. New York, 1957.

INDEX OF NAMES CITED
AND WORKS EXAMINED

A

Aiken, Conrad, x, 126, 127
Alain-Fournier, 141
Allott, Kenneth, 103, 104, 180, 182
Asmodée, 270-7

B

Balzac, 12, 69, 84, 158, 203
Ballantyne, R. M., 88
Barrès, 68-9, 74
Bates, H. E., 117
Baudelaire, 28, 67, 69, 76, 78, 82
Belloc, 17
Bernanos, Georges, 221-2, 261, 327
Bloy, 165
Bossuet, 28, 149, 164
Bost, Pierre, 251
Bourdet, Edouard, 245
Bourget, Paul, 12, 84, 144, 203
Bowen, Marjorie, 15, 88-9, 113, 118, 176
Brereton, Captain, 88
Brighton Rock, 32, 163, 166, 167, 168, 170, 180, 188, 192-3, 194, 195, 196, 197, 217-8, 229, 236, 247, 248, 251
Browne, Sir Thomas, 91
Browning, 253

Buchan, John, 15
Bunyan, 22, 24
Burnt-Out Case, 1-30, 194, 316, 328-9, 330

C

Caillard, C.-F., 74
Calder-Marshall, Arthur, 136
Camus, 3
Carlyle, 103
Chaplin, 266
Chapman, 131
Chateaubriand, 69, 142, 154
Chekov, 124, 266, 274, 312-3
Chesterton, G. K., 15, 17
Claudel, 69
Clouard, Henri, 211-2
Colette, 141
Complaisant Lover, 255-8, 263-7, 275, 318
Confidential Agent, 232-3, 235, 248, 249
Conrad, 14-15, 22, 103, 104-105, 116, 118, 124, 160
Constant, 12
Corneille, 13
Coward, Noel, 248
Crane, Stephen, 118
Curé d'Ars, 117

D

Daiches, David, 95
Damien, Father, 28-9, 218, 219
Dante, 22
Dark Angels, 163, 195, 196, 197,
   198, 245, 288
Dean, Basil, 251
de la Mare, Walter, 57, 95, 128,
   131
Demange, Charles, 78
Desert of Love, 38, 80, 146-7, 148,
   150-3, 159, 160, 184, 186, 269
Dickens, 48, 60, 213
Dostoevski, 203-204
Dryden, 256
Dugas, 265
Duhamel, 125, 245
Du Maurier, 117
Du Parc, 80

E

Edel, Leon, 251
Einstein, 225
Eliot, T. S., x, 15, 126, 127, 132, 166,
   167, 168, 228, 253
Enemy, 160, 173, 182, 184
End of the Affair, 163, 196, 197-8,
   205-206, 229, 230, 249, 251, 252,
   306, 307-308, 310
End of the Night, 159, 223-6, 232,
   236, 237
England Made Me, 122, 132-7,
   188, 192, 229

F

Fenby, Charles, 104
Feu sur la Terre, 269, 270, 272-7,
   279
Flaubert, 12
Flesh and Blood, 71, 72, 78, 79,
   80-81, 83, 141, 143, 146, 173
Fleuriot, Zenaïde, 66
Ford, Ford Madox, x, 27, 116-7,
   118, 120, 125, 127, 257

Ford, John, 16, 127, 128
Forster, E. M., 2
Freud, 20, 143, 145, 151, 183
Fromentin, 12
Frontenac Mystery, 33, 34, 244-5

G

Gauguin, 35, 77
Genetrix, 35, 84, 148, 149, 157, 159,
   160, 187, 245, 268, 269
Gide, 69, 143, 144, 153-4, 164-5,
   183, 202
Gilson, Captain, 88
Glenville, Peter, 253, 254
Green, Julian, 117
de Guérin, Maurice, 12, 68, 75,
   141
Gun for Sale, 188-92, 214-6, 235,
   248, 321

H

Haggard, Rider, 15, 88
Hardy, G. H., 266-7
Hardy, Thomas, 131
Heart of the Matter, ix, 7, 11, 24,
   163, 180, 194, 195, 229, 232, 234-7,
   249, 251, 252, 259, 307, 316
Hermant, Abel, 12
Hitchcock, Alfred, 130
Hope, Anthony, 15, 88
Huysmans, 69
Hyde, Rev. Dr., 29, 218

I

It's a Battlefield, 120-22, 132, 133,
   188, 189, 192, 229

J

James, Henry, x, 16, 98, 116, 118,
   119, 120, 124, 126, 127, 131, 132,
   168, 217, 219, 251, 267
Jammes, Francis, 12, 67-8, 69, 75,
   78

Jarrett-Kerr, Martin, 158
Joyce, 127, 136

K

Kingslake, 124
Kipling, 60
Kiss for the Leper, 1-30, 140, 143, 145, 146, 149, 157, 158, 159, 160, 161, 182, 212
Knot of Vipers, 40, 81, 163, 193, 194, 195, 197-8, 208, 212, 243, 244, 268
von Kühnelt-Leddihn, Eric, 124

L

Lacordaire, 69
Lafon, André, 68, 141, 142
LaFontaine, 69
Laforgue, 69
Lamartine, 67
Lamb, 283-90, 291, 292, 297, 298, 303-304, 306, 317
Lines of Life, 46, 79, 145, 147, 148, 149, 153, 159, 160, 163, 184, 211
Little Misery, 243, 279, 299-301
Living Room, 194, 252-62, 264, 266, 275, 307, 316
Loser Takes All, 306, 319
Loved and the Unloved, 153, 243, 279, 299, 301-303, 304, 306, 323, 327
Lubbock, Percy, 116

M

Maeterlinck, 69
Magny, Claude-Edmonde, 42, 223-5
Majault, Joseph, 158
Mal Aimés, 270, 272-7, 300
Mallet-Joris, Françoise, 42, 43, 45, 149
Mann, Thomas, 248
Mansfield, Katherine, 223
Man Within, 91-8, 100, 101, 102, 103, 105, 108, 113, 115, 116, 170, 171, 174, 178, 179-81, 189, 316

Maritain, Jacques, 169
Marsh, William, 123
Masefield, 95
Matthews, Ronald, 178, 229, 237
Ministry of Fear, 106-109, 232, 233-4, 235, 249, 316
Montalembert, 69
Morell, Lady Ottoline, 124
Munro, H. H., 60
Murry, John Middleton, 124
Musset, 67

N

Name of Action, 98-102, 103, 104, 105, 108, 133, 134, 170, 171, 178, 179, 316
Narayan, R. K., 130
Newman, 289
Nietzsche, 193

O

Ohnet, Georges, 12
Our Man in Havana, 3, 306, 318-25

P

Pascal, 2, 66, 68, 69, 149, 182, 186, 314
Passage du Malin, 268-9, 271-7
Péguy, 24, 142, 177, 180, 195
Perreyve, Henri, 69
Potting Shed, 254-8, 260-62, 275
Power and the Glory, 7, 29, 163, 167, 194, 195, 197, 218-9, 236, 249, 251
Priestley, J. B., 248
Proust, 20, 143, 144-5, 157, 183
Psichari, 142, 169

Q

Questions of Precedence, 40, 71, 79-80, 81-2, 83, 85, 111, 145, 146, 147, 149, 159, 185, 269, 300
Quiet American, 4, 56, 251, 306, 308-16, 317, 318, 319, 320

R

Rachilde, 140
Racine, 12-13, 25, 66-7, 82, 164, 245, 274, 330
Read, Carol, 252
Read, Herbert, 61, 127
Reitlinger, G., 123
Rimbaud, 35, 67, 71, 77, 79, 286
River of Fire, 80, 143, 145-6, 148, 149, 153, 159, 160, 184, 185, 197, 269
Rivière, Jacques, 142, 202
Rogers & Hammerstein, 251
Rolfe, Frederick, 168
Rolland, Romain, 69
Rousseau, 73, 154
Rumour at Nightfall, 102, 103-106, 108, 111, 115, 118, 119, 120, 133, 135, 140, 170, 171-3, 179, 188
Russell, John, 60

S

Saint-Beuve, 47
St. Thérèse, 202
St. John of the Cross, 3
Sangnier, Marc, 73
Sartre, J.-P., 3, 223, 224, 225-7
Sense of Reality, ix, 325
Shakespeare, 253, 255, 266, 330
Shaw, 256
Simenon, 245
Soloveytchik, George, 123
Souday, Paul, 140
Stamboul Train, 4, 21, 111-6, 119, 120, 122, 123, 130, 133, 136, 140, 188, 190, 192, 247
Stevenson, R. L., 15, 22, 28-9, 58, 90-91, 95, 98, 104, 118, 219
Stuff of Youth, 33, 34, 35-9, 40, 41, 71, 72, 74, 77, 78, 79, 80, 82, 83, 141, 300
Swinnerton, Frank, 105, 116

T

Taine, 203
Tennyson, 248
That Which Was Lost, 159, 163, 165, 193, 195
Thérèse, 28, 32, 80, 152, 154-7, 159, 160, 184, 185, 186, 212, 216-7, 231, 245
Third Man, 247, 252, 253
Tourneur, 16, 127, 128
Turnell, Martin, 243

U

Unknown Sea, 159, 245, 272

V

Van Gogh, 76
Verlaine, 69
de la Ville de Mirmont, Jean, 68, 141
Vigny, 67

W

Walpole, Hugh, 222, 223, 248
Waugh, Evelyn, ix, 15, 123, 254, 307
Webster John, x, 16, 127, 128, 131, 132, 248, 249, 253
Westerman, Percy, 15, 88
Weyman, Stanley, 88
Whitaker, Mrs., 223
Woman of the Pharisees, 9, 38, 40, 81, 84, 212, 213, 226, 243, 245, 279, 290-98, 299, 304
Woolf, Virginia, 2, 213
Wordsworth, 32

Y

Young Man in Chains, 69-71, 73, 74, 77, 80, 82, 94, 97, 111, 140, 153, 174, 179, 182

Z

Zola, 12